MW01621001

THE PORTRAITS OF MADAME DE POMPADOUR

ABOUT THE DISCOVERY SERIES

Innovative and generously illustrated,
books in the Discovery Series focus on a single
important work of art, artist, or theme in the history of art.
Each is distinctive for the richness of detail and
insight it conveys in a concise format, and
each is written in prose that appeals to
both specialists and general readers.

I.
The Devil at Isenheim: Reflections of Popular Belief in Grünewald's Altarpiece,
by Ruth Mellinkoff,
1988

II.
The Forgotten Hermitage of Skellig Michael,
by Walter Horn, Jenny White Marshall, and Grellan D. Rourke,
1990

III.
The Arnolfini Betrothal: Medieval Marriage
and the Enigma of Van Eyck's Double Portrait,
by Edwin Hall,
1994

IV.
Made in God's Image? Eve and Adam in the Genesis Mosaics at San Marco,
by Penny Howell Jolly,
1997

V.
Michelangelo's Last Judgment: The Renaissance Response,
by Bernadine Barnes,
1998

VI.
The French Revolution as Blasphemy:
Johan Zoffany's Paintings of the Massacre at Paris, August 10, 1792,
by William L. Pressly
1999

VII.
The Portraits of Madame de Pompadour: Celebrating the Femme Savante,
by Elise Goodman
2000

VIII.
My Laocoön, or Yours, or Theirs: Alternative Claims in the Interpretation of Artworks,
by Richard Brilliant,
2000

IX.
Behind Closed Doors: The Art of Hans Bellmer's Dolls in the Context of Nazi Germany,
by Therese Lichtenstein
2001

The Publisher gratefully acknowledges the contribution provided by the Art Book Fund of the Associates of the University of California Press, which is supported by a major gift from the Ahmanson Foundation.

THE PORTRAITS OF MADAME DE POMPADOUR

Celebrating the Femme Savante

ELISE GOODMAN

UNIVERSITY OF CALIFORNIA PRESS BERKELEY LOS ANGELES LONDON

University of California Press
Berkeley and Los Angeles, California

University of California Press, Ltd.
London, England

Library of Congress Cataloging-in-Publication Data

Goodman, Elise.
The portraits of Madame de Pompadour : celebrating the femme savante / Elise Goodman.
p. cm. (Discovery series)
Includes bibliographical references and index.
ISBN 0-520-21794-2 (cloth : alk. paper)
1. Pompadour, Jeanne Antoinette Poisson, marquise de, 1721–1764—Portraits. 2. Art, French. 3. Art, Modern—18th century—France. I. Title.
N7639.P66 G66 2000
757'.4'094409033 21—dc21 99-041133

Manufactured in the United States of America

08 07 06 05 04 03 02 01 00 99
10 9 8 7 6 5 4 3 2 1

The paper used in this publication meets the minimum requirements of ANSI/NISO Z39.48-1992 (R 1997) (*Permanence of Paper*). ♾

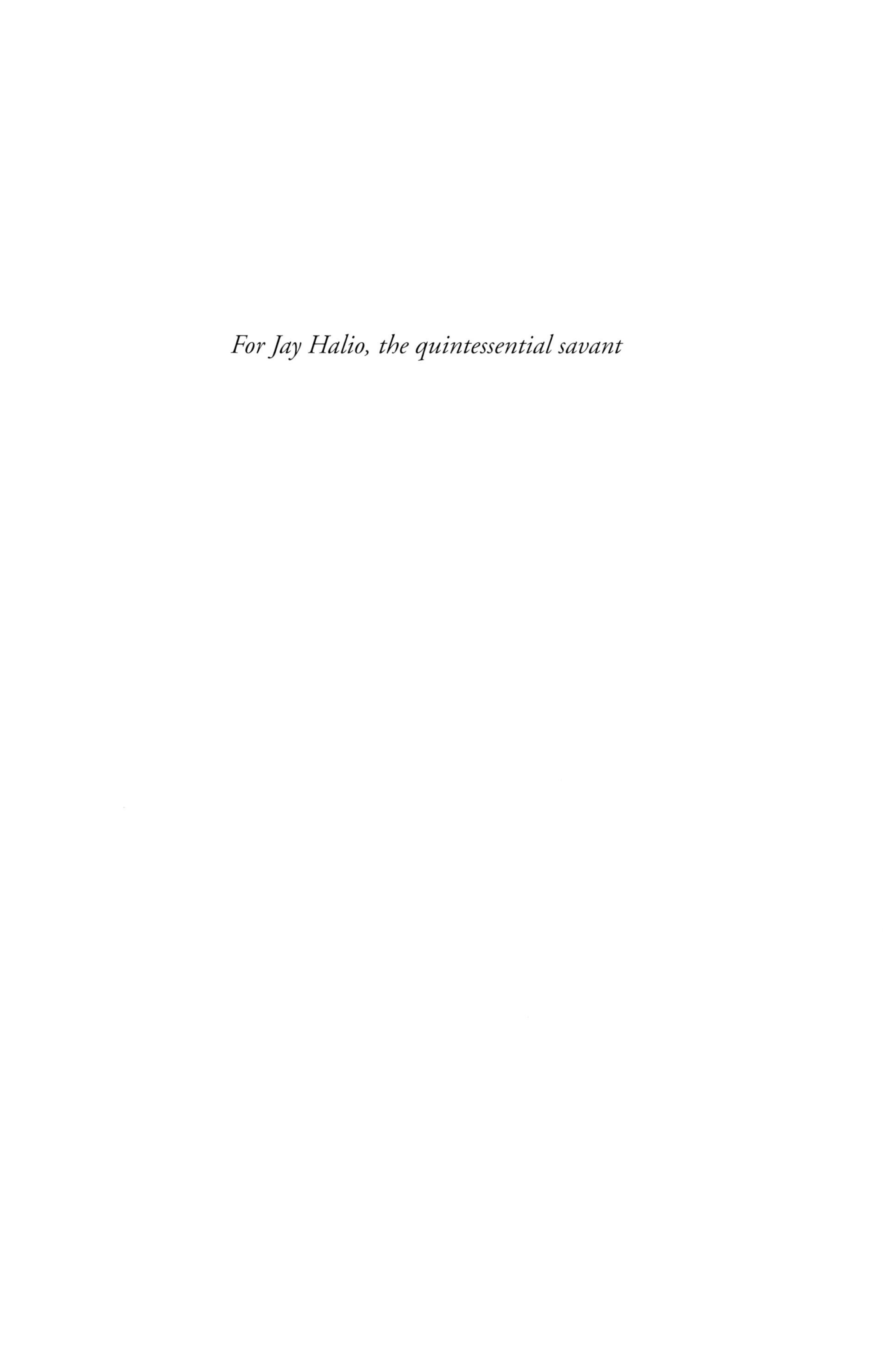

For Jay Halio, the quintessential savant

CONTENTS

ILLUSTRATIONS

Photographic sources and location are the same except where indicated.

PLATES
(*following page 44*)

FIGURES

EDITORIAL NOTE AND ACKNOWLEDGMENTS

To evoke the highly saturated intellectual atmosphere of the French Enlightenment in which Mme de Pompadour's savante portraits are embedded, I have referred to and quoted mostly period sources. I have followed the principle of using as much as possible the best scholarly texts, eighteenth-century or recent, and I have left the orthography as I found it. The exceptions, of course, are my own translations; but for these I have taken the slight liberty of regularizing the capitalization of French titles, but not the spelling, to facilitate their recognition by the reader. Except where indicated, all translations are my own.

My book has benefited from the largesse of both institutions and individuals. The National Endowment for the Humanities generously sponsored most of the research and writing of my study with a Summer Stipend in 1994 and a Fellowship for College Teachers in 1996. The Research Council of the University of Cincinnati contributed a sizable grant in 1994, and Dean Barbara Bardes of the University of Cincinnati, Raymond Walters College, very kindly funded my travel in 1996. During the course of this study, I have enjoyed the stimulating and congenial environments of the Bibliothèque Nationale, the Folger Shakespeare Library, the Library of Congress, and the Library of the National Gallery of Art, whose staffs have helped me immeasurably.

Parts of this book were delivered as lectures at the CUNY Graduate Center; Syracuse University; Trinity College, Washington, D.C.; the University of Cincinnati; and the University of Maryland. Abbreviated versions of chapters 3 and 5, respectively, were presented at the 1999 meetings of the American Society for Eighteenth-Century Studies and the College Art Association.

I welcome the opportunity to thank many colleagues and friends who have enriched this book with their good counsel and encouragement. At the outset, the late Rolf Soellner helped me to formulate my ideas on Pompadour. Along the way, I have been fortunate to have had four eminent scholars as readers of the manuscript:

two literary critics, Dympna Callaghan and Jay Halio, and two art historians, Donald Posner and Janis Tomlinson. I am also grateful to Electa Arenal, Joseph Baillio, George Basalla, Peter Bender, John Burke, Sarah Cohen, Judith Colton, Patricia Crown, Laurinda Dixon, Charles Ebner, Martin Elsky, Suzanne Ferguson, Wayne Franits, Danielle Gallet, Barbara Haeger, June Hargrove, Stephena Harmony, Richard Hutton, Eda Levitine, Walter Liedtke, Franklin Ludden, Debra Oswald, William Parsons, Maxime Préaud, William Pressly, Orest and Patricia Ranum, Aileen Ribeiro, David Riede, Jonathan Riess, Dianne Sod, Perrin Stein, James Grantham Turner, Natalie Tyler, and John Wilson for their help. The proficient typists Lois Moore and Eileen Rehring have given willingly and cheerfully of their time and expertise. Finally, I take pleasure in acknowledging the expertise of the staff at the University of California Press, particularly that of Kimberly Darwin and Stephanie Fay, as well as the consummate professionalism of Deborah Kirshman, Fine Arts Editor, who believed in and shepherded this book from its inception to its completion.

INTRODUCTION

> If I were king . . . I would redress an abuse that cuts back, as it were, one half of human kind. I would have women participate in all human rights, especially those of the mind. . . . The new education would greatly benefit the human race. Women would be worth more and men would gain something new to emulate.
>
> *The marquise du Châtelet*

Mme de Pompadour, the beautiful, influential, and cultivated companion of Louis XV from 1745 until her death in 1764, commissioned portraits representing her as a femme savante, an educated woman accomplished in letters and the arts. These works, admired as the most glamorous, celebrated likenesses of a woman created during the French Enlightenment,[1] were fashioned in the 1750s and 1760s by three of the greatest artists of the eighteenth century: François Boucher, who invented and perpetuated the femme savante Pompadour portrait type through three images; Maurice-Quentin de La Tour, who made a majestic pastel; and François-Hubert Drouais, who poignantly re-created Pompadour's features at the end of her life.

Although Pompadour's portraits are among the most famous likenesses of an eighteenth-century woman, they have evoked surprisingly little scholarly attention. French eighteenth-century painting in general has been neglected until recently, as has rococo portraiture—one of the most popular and distinguished genres of the period. Only a few articles have focused on the portraits of Pompadour; some of them have been merely descriptive, others have focused on Boucher's great portrait in Munich.[2] None considers the portraits' multiple visual, literary, cultural, and intellectual significations. This is the first book that does so.

The most important of the extant studies, Donald Posner's "Mme. de Pompadour as a Patron of the Visual Arts,"[3] warrants special attention here. In a meticulously researched and documented essay, Posner concludes that Pompadour was an "exquisitely tasteful and wondrously lavish" (76), though not a particularly imaginative or insightful, patron of the arts. This may be true, but she was an important one. At times, however, Posner underestimates Pompadour's refined sensibility and her interest in architecture independent of Louis XV.[4] He believes, as I do, that Pompadour's decision to commission Boucher to paint portraits of her was "decidedly original . . . and positively inspired" (98) and that "through art she portrayed herself to the public as a cultivated woman of enlightened, wide-ranging tastes and knowledge" (77). But when Posner casts Pompadour as a mere "public relations" expert rather than a woman of learning and intellectual substance, his argument contradicts the testimony of contemporaries and modern evaluations. In this book, using the memoirs of Pompadour's contemporaries, I show that she was an exceptionally well educated woman, who amassed her library because of her great love of learning in many fields of interest.

This book rides the current of recent scholarship on portraiture, viewing Pompadour's femme savante portraits as products of visual culture,[5] re-creating the multifaceted visual, intellectual, and sociocultural terrain in which her portraits are embedded by evoking a wide array of primary and secondary sources in paintings, prints, literature, philosophy, science, and music. It is grounded in iconographic analysis. The portraits are thoughtfully wrought iconographic works—collections of signs[6]—meant to convey Pompadour's persona as a learned woman. I examine the roles Pompadour herself adopted and lived out both in the real world and in art,[7] her self-fashioning and social masking.[8] The portraits manifest the system of gender in which a woman's commission was rooted.[9] In their deliberate idealization, they are sites for the reconstruction of selfhood and identity.[10]

Pompadour's portraits quietly participate in the Enlightenment's penchant for picturing genius.[11] They foreshadow by about twenty years the more overt and expressive representations of enthusiasm.[12] In Pompadour's portraits, as in those of her fellow intellectuals, inspiration and self-conscious superiority are encoded in philosophical reflection: her gaze is directed toward an exalting force outside her fictive realm.[13]

This book does not engage with many other literary, philosophical, and critical-theoretical issues that have been foregrounded in the past twenty years. I deliberately avoid esoteric language and methodology so that my text will be accessible not only to scholars and students of art history, French cultural history, and women's studies but also to general readers interested in these subjects. I am concerned with gender issues and re-create the progressive feminist matrix of Pompadour's own time, but without the overlay of much current gender theory. Although I embrace social history, I do not critique the ruling classes to which Mme de Pompadour belonged. Moreover, because this is an iconographic and cultural study of eighteenth-century French portraiture, it does not address issues of attribution and dating; for these it relies on the solid monographs and catalogues raisonnés of earlier scholars.

Mme de Pompadour's portraits celebrate a quintessential femme savante, a woman of beauty, intelligence, learning, and sophistication. This study ranges more widely, however; it is also the first treatment of the educated woman in eighteenth-century French portraiture and culture. Along with related portraits of other femmes savantes, the images of Pompadour are imbued with eighteenth-century ideas on women's intellectuality and education. While influenced by visual and literary conventions for depictions of ideal women, the portraits reflect the progressive values of the Enlightenment.

I begin in chapter 1 with a biographical "portrait" of Pompadour, followed by stylistic and iconographic analyses of her femme savante portraits, a discussion of possible reasons for the commissioning of each one, their reception by salon critics, and the contemporaneous ideas about beauty they reflect. Chapter 2 addresses Pompadour's education and her accomplishments as singer, musician, and actress; it then discusses the relevance of the literary, sociocultural debate called the "Women's Quarrel," in which liberal writers campaigned for equity in women's education. Chapter 3 demonstrates that the concept of the learned woman informing Pompadour's portraits was foreshadowed by fashion plates of cultivated figures dating back to the reign of Louis XIV; particularly persuasive are the prototypes imaging Mme de Montespan and Mme de Maintenon, on whom Pompadour fashioned herself as royal mistress in the 1750s. Another strain of engravings privileging France's greatest learned women also contextualizes Pompadour's pictorial role as femme savante.

Chapter 4 shows the iconographic affinities between Pompadour's portraits and the "intellectual portraits" produced by major French painters from about 1740 to about 1760. The efflorescence of women readers, scientists, and musicians occasioned the Enlightenment's ardent interest in picturing its accomplished women. The final chapter introduces the Parisian salon as the primary arena in which intellectual women educated themselves and contributed to Enlightenment culture. It then provides a comprehensive iconographic analysis of La Tour's 1755 pastel, which highlights Pompadour's personae as *salonnière* (that is, the female arbiter of an intellectual coterie) and as Enlightenment philosophe. The Appendix lists only the painted and drawn portraits of Mme de Pompadour generally accepted as authentic likenesses, with solid attributions.[14]

Eighteenth-century lexicons nowhere define "femme savante." This silence bespeaks the rarity of learned women in Enlightenment culture. Rather, in Furetière's *Dictionnaire universel* (4th ed., 1727), an educated woman appears under the rubric of "Femme Auteur": "One says, this *woman* is an Author, is a Poet, is a Philosophe, is a Physician, is a painter,"[15] implying the recognition that such accomplished women existed.

For "sçavant" or "savant," an adjective that of course could be feminized, we find the expected definition "learned": "one who has read and studied much; who has great learning, and erudition," as well as a "person who is well educated, well informed about something."[16] Only in Furetière's examples do we discover that the term "femme savante" had pejorative connotations: "This groom has discovered his wife more *sçavante* than he had wished"; and, in a reverberation of Molière's learned ladies who are only pseudo-intellectuals: "Women who affect the title of *sçavantes* are not in good standing in the world."[17]

The *Encyclopédie*, which Pompadour promoted, is even more oblique. Under the rubric "Femme," an author expostulates, in the tradition of the Women's Quarrel, that the education of women has been so egregiously neglected in civilized societies that it is surprising to find any who have distinguished themselves by their erudition and their works.[18] Under another category of "Femme" in this volume, the author Desmahis inveighs against the inadequate education of women, praising their peculiar biological qualities that dispose them to study: delicate organs, which encourage a lively imagination; an attentive mind; and a quickness to learn that outstrips the relatively sluggish apprehension of men.[19]

For an early definition of "femme savante," we must look to the seventeenth century, to the writings of the celebrated novelist Madeleine de Scudéry, who mused in 1656:

> I would like it said of a person of my sex that she knows a hundred things of which she makes no boast, that her mind is extremely enlightened, that she has an exquisite knowledge of beautiful literature, that she speaks well, writes properly, and that she has savoir-faire, but I wouldn't want it said of her that she's a learned lady.[20]

In other words, a really enlightened "lady" should never parade her learning. In the late seventeenth and eighteenth centuries, this characterization was amplified to include the woman who occupied herself with philosophy and the sciences.[21]

Except for a few erudite women, whom I discuss in chapter 3, the definition of a femme savante must follow the circumscribed and relative definition of Scudéry. A savante was by no means equivalent to the widely and deeply learned savant or philosophe of the Enlightenment, the male intellectual Pompadour admired and sponsored, or to the erudite female academic of our time. Pompadour's portraits represent this qualified notion of a woman of learning and accomplishment.

Virtually every specialist who has discussed the portraits of Pompadour assumes that she commissioned a host of images to fashion multifarious identities or to proclaim her cultural or sociopolitical agendas to the world, thereby consolidating her position and enhancing her status at court.[22] I agree with them. Some of these scholars, either directly or by implication, also believe that, like other intelligent patrons of the period, male or female, she collaborated with her portraitists in orchestrating her own iconographic programs,[23] though no documentation of such a contribution exists. What we know about Pompadour—her quality of mind, her eloquence, her accomplishments in the fine arts and the theater, her role as adviser to the king in cultural matters, her sponsorship of Enlightenment intellectuals, even her position as the king's virtual "prime minister"—would eminently qualify her to do so. Further, some of the portraits picture personal attitudes and situations—for example, the reflective attitude she described in private letters and her love of reading and of solitude—that only she would have known about and deemed important enough to record in paint. Finally, who else would so effectively have concocted her iconography and "carried" it from portraitist to portraitist? This book shows how she capably took charge of her own images.

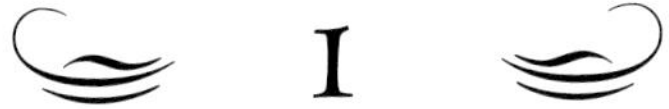

I

POMPADOUR AND HER PORTRAITS

Jeanne-Antoinette Poisson was born into the world of upper-middle-class finance in Paris on December 29, 1721.[1] Her father, François Poisson, a steward to the Pâris brothers who financed the economy of France, was exiled during a large part of her childhood; thus Jeanne-Antoinette owed much of her upbringing and education to her socially ambitious mother, Louise-Madeleine de La Motte; to her godfather, Jean-Pâris de Montmartel, Secretary to the King's Household and the court's most important banker; and to her mother's lover, Charles-François Paul Lenormant de Tournehem (who is now generally recognized as her biological father), an immensely wealthy and ennobled tax farmer—a collector of taxes for the crown—who wielded much power in the financial world.

From 1727 to 1730, Jeanne-Antoinette received an elementary education at the Ursuline convent at Poissy, after which she returned to Paris to finish her education in music, acting, and singing with the finest tutors in the city. In her teens she was introduced to the sophisticated society of Paris. In this world of the intellectual salons frequented by the greatest thinkers of the day, including Montesquieu and Voltaire, Mlle Poisson was extolled for her beauty, talents, and charm; she enthralled high society with her singing, harpsichord playing, and dancing.

From her childhood onward, then, Jeanne-Antoinette Poisson was pampered, praised, and encouraged by her family and friends to ascend to the summit of French society. Her sobriquet, Reinette (Little Queen), bespeaks her ambition and self-confidence. Self-assurance was the hallmark of her personality, and it sustained her through fragile health and chronic illnesses and during her years as the king's bourgeois mistress and companion.

Jeanne-Antoinette and her younger brother, Abel-François, were the privileged children of an increasingly powerful and visible moneyed middle class, which in the eighteenth century had sufficient economic and social clout to rise into the ranks of the French aristocracy and influence the financial state of the nation. Later, as

Louis XV's companion and mistress, Mme de Pompadour became the very personification of the newly arrived middle class.

This industrious, ambitious, and affluent middle class also appreciated and cultivated art, which came to signify its eminence in society. During her childhood and her teens, Jeanne-Antoinette was exposed to the opulent architecture, decoration, and paintings of her Parisian relatives and friends. This early exposure to art most likely contributed to her mature interest in and cultivation of the arts and letters during her tenure as marquise de Pompadour. Portraiture in particular, which burgeoned in eighteenth-century France, in part because of patronage by the successful middle class, signified its cultivation and status; Pompadour's femme savante portraits grew out of the French bourgeoisie's penchant for self-aggrandizement.

Jeanne-Antoinette's charmed life culminated in a suitable marriage. In 1741, Lenormant de Tournehem arranged a marriage between the twenty-year-old Mlle Poisson and his nephew, Charles-Guillaume Lenormant d'Etioles. Through their union, Mme d'Etioles inherited a vast fortune and an estate, where she played host to intellectuals of the Enlightenment. She also performed for them and members of Parisian high society in an opulent theater that rivaled the grandeur and splendor of the Paris Opéra. The abbé de Bernis, who became her close friend and confidant, wrote in 1745: "Mme d'Étioles had all the graces, all the freshness, and all the gaiety of youth: she danced, sang, and played comedy marvelously well; no agreeable talent was lacking in her. She loved letters and the arts."[2]

In 1745 Mme d'Etioles met and fell in love with Louis XV, the king of France, to whom she would be devoted until her death. From the first, Mme d'Etoiles had designs upon the king. Therefore, she arranged to be present, splendidly decked out in her open carriage, while Louis was hunting in the Forest of Sénart near her château. She deliberately interposed herself so that Louis could not help taking notice of her. Then Le Bel, her mother's former lover and valet to the king, praised her to Louis, who invited her to the Yew Tree Ball, held at Versailles on February 25, 1745, where they met and fell in love. After this encounter, they met again three days later at a masked ball at the Paris Opéra. Louis XV, who, at least at first, was as smitten with her as she with him, made her his official, acknowledged mistress—a rank and title that had arisen with the custom of arranged marriages among the French aristocracy. She, in turn, separated legally from her husband. By the eighteenth century, the office of royal mistress was the rule rather than the exception for the king's personal female companion.[3]

To be presented formally to the king and queen at court, Mme d'Etioles needed a title, an estate, and an aristocratic coat of arms. Therefore, on June 24, 1745, with the financial assistance of her protector and family friend, Pâris de Montmartel, Louis XV purchased the marquisate of Pompadour for her, the title and estate in the Limousin region of central France having fallen into disuse for lack of heirs. The

Pompadour coat of arms, three towers embossed on an azure oval shield, appears in abbreviated form in her femme savante portraits. This purchase, orchestrated by the king and the financier Pâris de Montmartel, newly ennobled, attests to the fluidity of class lines in the mid–eighteenth century.

From the moment she appeared at court, Pompadour exhibited her charm, effervescence, wit, politeness, grace, and diplomacy. She was a stimulating and witty conversationalist, and her speech was also disarmingly forthright, her candor contrasting notably with the restrained circumlocutions of court parlance. Above all, as Bernis put it, "Her heart [was] naturally kind and feeling."[4] This sensitivity manifested itself chiefly in her relations with Queen Marie Leczinska, her lover's wife, whom she treated with deference and kindness throughout her tenure as royal mistress. In letters of 1746 and 1748 to the duchesse de Luynes, she wrote: "I would give my life for her, whose kindnesses are every day more precious to me. . . . All that I desire is to pay my addresses and to indicate to her my profound respect."[5]

As official mistress, Pompadour had to be continually on duty, fulfilling court duties, traveling with the king, serving as his hostess, and receiving courtiers. To these requirements she sacrificed her health, well-being, and love of quietude, instead amusing the king and maintaining her position at court. And she was very successful. The duc de Croÿ noted that she fulfilled her role as if she had been born to it and that she had a great influence on Louis XV.[6] She secured the powerful post of director of royal works for Lenormant de Tournehem and later for her brother, who was made marquis de Vandières, then marquis de Marigny. While her influence on the king enabled her to advance a few of her relatives and friends, she always did so with good sense and respect for merit. Thus when her father asked her to intervene for the advancement of a distant relative, she replied in a letter of November 5, 1752:

> I am very sorry that you ask for Vincennes for M. de Malvoisin. I cannot understand what has come over you to want to put there a man of twenty-five, who has only six years of service (however intelligent he may be). . . . Certainly I am not going to lend myself to such an injustice.[7]

And on May 19, 1750, she advised her brother: "I hope that you will think as I do, and that you will not place an inordinate amount of value on fugitive honors that one gives to the office rather than the person."[8]

In her role as the king's favorite and companion, Pompadour lavishly patronized the arts and architecture and promoted many advanced writers and thinkers. In her theaters at Versailles and Bellevue she proved herself to be the consummate woman of the Enlightenment, organizing, producing, directing, and starring in a comprehensive repertoire of seventeenth- and eighteenth-century operas and plays. She saw herself and was seen as an accomplished singer, dancer, and actress. If these talents and achievements were not enough to endear her to the crown and thus help to cement her fragile position at court, she also made herself, tutored by Boucher, into an able amateur engraver.[9] She was the most intelligent, talented, and influential royal companion in France's history. And she knew it. The political philosopher Montesquieu knew it too: "In the eyes of posterity, the representatives of the eighteenth century will be Voltaire and Mme de Pompadour."

Montesquieu was not being obsequious. Granted, out of necessity, Pompadour was politically astute, but she also was a woman of character: the duc de Croÿ noted her "irreproachable integrity," and Voltaire asserted that she was "born with good sense, and [was] kind-hearted." Pompadour was confident of her good character, too. In her letter to the duchesse de Luynes, she wrote: "I hope, Madame, that the friendship that you have for me, and still more your knowledge of my character, will be guarantees of that which I write."[10]

There is ample evidence in her will, moreover, that she was generous. She gave large sums to the needy; generous gifts to religious institutions, including her convent at Poissy; and sizable pensions to the men of letters she protected. She was not mercenary. True, she spent large sums from the Royal Treasury to finance her patronage of art and architecture, but she also drew on her own meager allowance and even sold her jewelry to pay for her houses and the expenses connected with them, as letters to her intimates attest. She confessed to her father on January 12, 1753:

> I am far poorer than I was in Paris. Never have I asked for what has been given to me, but the expenditures on my houses have vexed me greatly; but all of this amuses the master, so no more to be said. If I ever wanted to be rich, the money that has gone on all those things would have brought me a considerable income; but I never wanted it.[11]

Concerned about the delayed payment to the workers on the Ecole Militaire, the grand military school for boys she helped to found and assiduously sponsored, she wrote to her friend Joseph Pâris-Duverney, brother of Jean Pâris de Montmartel and powerful director of military provisions, who financed the construction of the school, on August 15, 1755:

> My income for the year has not come in yet. I will use it all to pay the workmen every two weeks. I do not know whether I can find sureties to have the money lent me, but I know that I will gladly risk 100,000 livres to make those poor boys happy.[12]

Earlier, in her personal life, although her sexual relations with Louis XV began to wane because of her fragile health, ceasing altogether around 1750—a change referred to in the works she commissioned and attested to by her contemporaries at court—Pompadour retained the position of official mistress. During this period, however, she was forced to tolerate her consort's numerous but inconsequential escapades with younger, more ardent mistresses. They were not as well endowed intellectually as she and thus never really threatened her position. Pompadour became, oxymoronic as it may sound, an asexual mistress. But rather than allowing her liaison with Louis XV to expire, she renegotiated it from physical passion to unshakable friendship; in short, she managed her precarious situation with delicacy and finesse. Bernis aptly characterized their relationship in 1757 and 1758:

> The king knew that the marquise was only his friend. . . . She was the depository of the secrets of his soul; she knew intimately all his affairs; she was the centre of his ministers; she was not a mistress to be sent away; she was a friend, whom no one could replace. . . . Mme de Pompadour was, in point of fact, the king's prime-minister, without the title.[13]

Louis XV recognized Pompadour's indispensability—as adviser, confidante, and companion. On October 12, 1752, he elevated her to duchess and, in 1756, to the most exalted rank possible for a woman at court, supernumerary lady-in-waiting to the queen. This position made her situation at court impregnable.

As lady-in-waiting, Pompadour wielded much power and influence. She mediated advancements, favors, and dismissals; played an active role in domestic and foreign politics; and became effectively the king's minister of culture, presiding over the arts and sciences, patronizing the arts and the artists who fashioned them, and protecting Enlightenment thinkers.

During this period when, according to Bernis, she was seated "upon the throne," she comported herself publicly with "supreme grandeur and omnipotence."[14] She became infatuated with her power and the superiority of her mind. Although she was vain and imperious—"I would have preferred the grand niche, and I am displeased to have to settle for the small one; it does not at all suit my humor"[15]—she retained what Bernis characterized as her "lofty, sensitive, and generous spirit."[16]

De Meinières, president of the Paris Parliament and a foe of Mme de Pompadour and Louis XV, gives us an incisive portrait of the marquise at the height of her power in 1757:

> She looked me up and down with a haughtiness I shall remember all my life, her head leaning on her shoulder, without a curtsy and sizing me up in a very

imposing fashion. . . . I must admit that I was as struck by her easy speech as by the perfection of her style . . . and I looked at her with pleasure and admiration while she spoke so well.[17]

This unflappable self-assurance—"I am like Cicero, who had no need of others to be esteemed"[18]—buttressed Mme de Pompadour from the time of her elevation to marquise in 1745 until her death on April 15, 1764. It supported her when members of the royal family snubbed her, when venomous machinators plotted her downfall, and when she lost her looks with age, fatigue, and infirmity. She was rightly proud of her advancement, knowing that she owed it to her intelligence and dedication.

But her life at court took its toll. She confessed that she despised "this monstrous place." Why, then, did she bear it? For the sake of ambition and glory, of course, but even more, she endured her arduous and draining life at court for love, as we learn from her letter to Vandières of May 19, 1750: "And except for the happiness of being loved by one whom one loves . . . I would much prefer a solitary and less brilliant life."[19]

The femme savante portraits by Boucher, La Tour, and Drouais are the most famous images of Pompadour, but they are not the only likenesses fashioned during her lifetime. Pompadour assumed many identities and played several roles in her portraits, though a few had no pretext but the hymning of her beauty and her attractions within the prescribed gender roles for women.[20] Jean-Baptiste Pigalle's elegant bust (New York, Metropolitan Museum of Art, 1749–51; Fig. 1), as Donald Posner has shown, is an intensely intimate evocation of the young Pompadour's physical allure. She is draped in a fashionable shawl that provocatively reveals her smooth shoulders, long neck, and naked breast. Posner suggests that the bust may have been a delicious surrogate for the marquise herself, stimulating Louis XV's longings when she was not with him.[21]

The equally intimate but searingly candid portrait Carle Van Loo completed of Pompadour only four years before her death (Versailles, Musée National du Château, ca. 1760; Fig. 2) styles the marquise not simply as the beloved but as a sagaciously mature yet still attractive shepherdess, whose inveterate love of gardens is indicated by the profusion of flowers in her basket.[22] The portrait also evokes the pastoral roles Pompadour enacted on stage.

But Pigalle's and Van Loo's uncomplicated likenesses are the exceptions to the rule in the repertoire of Pompadour's portraits. Most of them, like her learned-woman images, are surely imbued with a programmatic content concocted to clarify and solidify her political and social position at court and to reinforce her status as royal mistress.

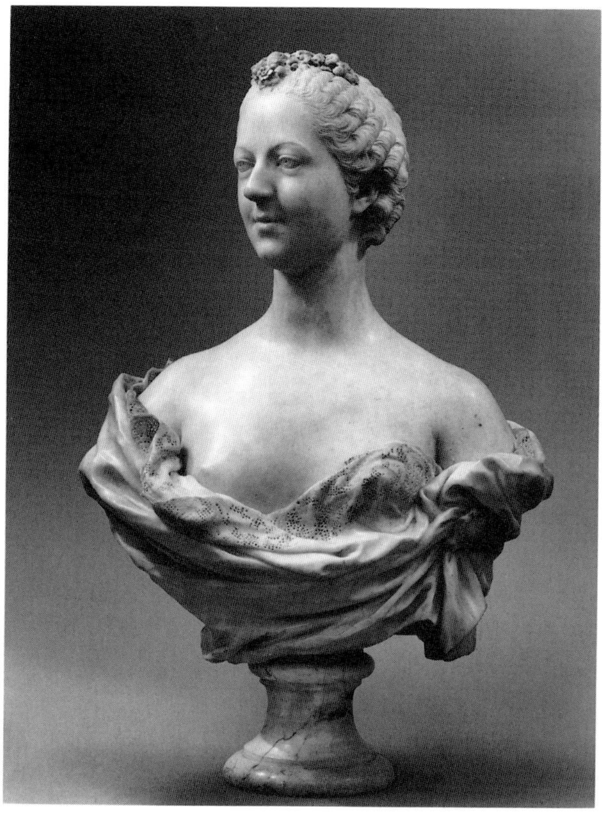

FIGURE 1.
Jean-Baptiste Pigalle, *Bust of Mme de Pompadour*, 1749–51. New York, Metropolitan Museum of Art, Jules S. Bache Collection, 1949.

The earliest of these programmed likenesses is Jean-Marc Nattier's exquisite evocation of the young marquise in the guise of Diana, goddess of the hunt (Versailles, Musée National du Château, ca. 1748; Fig. 3). Painted when she was still mistress of the king, in both title and deed, the portrait hung in Louis XV's hunting château at Fontainebleau, perhaps recalling the beautiful "Diana" who in 1745 attracted the king's attention when she followed him in her carriage while he was on the chase in the Forest of Sénart. Defying those who at first vigorously opposed their liaison, as Posner has demonstrated, the portrait declared to the couple's guests at Fontainebleau that Diana was there to stay.[23] But the image has another dimension: Pompadour,

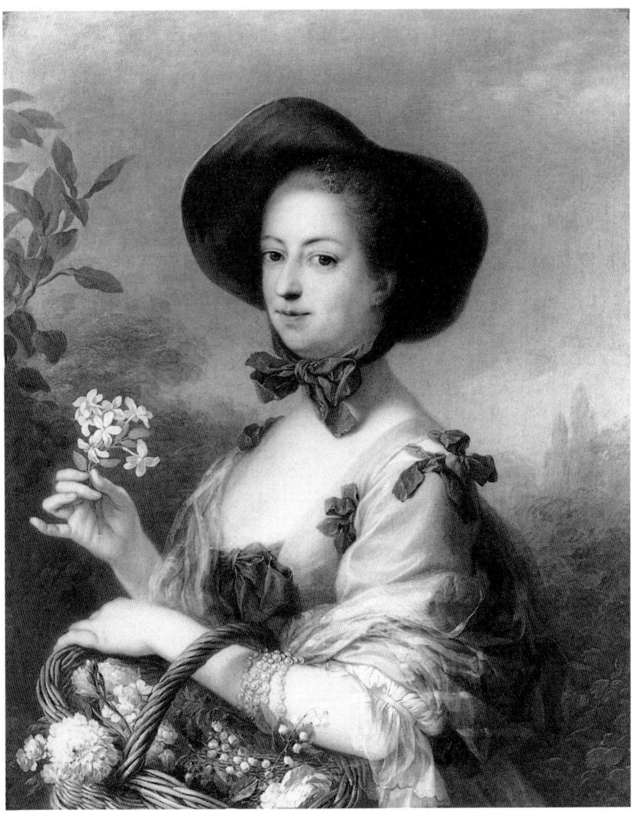

FIGURE 2.
Carle Van Loo, *Portrait of Mme de Pompadour*, ca. 1760. Versailles, Musée National du Château (photo: RMN).

a serious student of French history and art, situated herself squarely in a long lineage of royal mistresses disguised as Diana. Diane de Poitiers, in her portrait by Lucca Penni, a painter of the school of Fontainebleau (Musée du Louvre, ca. 1550), streaks through the forest, armed with bow and arrows, in pursuit of her royal prey, Henri II. In Pierre Mignard's portrait of Mme de Montespan, Louis XIV's mistress and Pompadour's model in cultural and intellectual pursuits, the ravishing consort reclines languorously before a landscape, her quiver and arrows resting at her side, the hunt ended, Louis captured (Geneva, Cailleux Collection, ca. 1670–78).[24] Portraits of royal companions as Diana proclaimed that the sitters' youth and beauty made them worthy of the king's attentions.

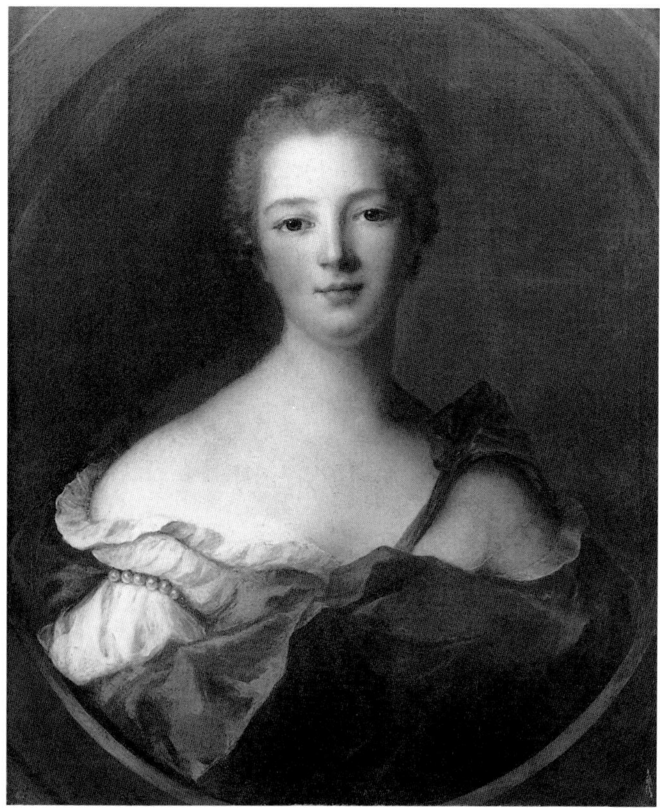

FIGURE 3.
Jean-Marc Nattier, *Portrait of Mme de Pompadour as Diana*, ca. 1748. Versailles, Musée National du Château (photo: RMN).

Later, in 1758, her youth and comeliness spent, plagued by a host of ailments—migraines, fevers, choking seizures, and palpitations of the heart among them—Pompadour called upon Boucher to rejuvenate her. Recasting his early *Portrait of the Marquise Standing at Her Dressing Table*, in which Pompadour, hat in hand, prepares to go out for a walk (private collection, 1750),[25] Boucher, in the *Portrait of Mme de Pompadour at Her Toilette* (Cambridge, Fogg Art Museum; Plate 1), styles her as the ideal mistress applying makeup at her dressing table. In this role Pompadour becomes a member of another distinctive family of French royal mistresses, similarly depicted. Giving a new twist to the theme of the lady, the lover, and the looking glass, Boucher presents Pompadour wearing on her arm a prominent cameo image of Louis XV, thus paying tribute to her position as mistress to the king, for whom she beautifies herself. The Fogg portrait is an aesthetic dream as well as an instrument of politics. It celebrates her past glory and further consolidates her position at court.[26]

The politics of buttressing her position at court took on an exotic cast in Carle Van Loo's *Portrait of Mme de Pompadour as Sultana Taking Coffee* (Saint Petersburg, Hermitage Museum, ca. 1750–54; Fig. 4), created for the Turkish room at her château de Bellevue. As Perrin Stein has shown, Pompadour likened her continuing powerful role at court to that of a sultana. Even when her sultan sought out the younger concubines of his harem, she would still hold sway, retaining her power and title, over the royal seraglio at Versailles.[27]

During these years, Pompadour disseminated a more direct iconography to advertise her changed relationship with Louis XV. Around 1750, she commissioned the sculptor Pigalle to fashion two allegorical portraits reflecting the metamorphosis of the relationship from love to friendship. In one of these she is Friendship offering her heart to an unseen Louis XV, and in the other Amitié embracing Cupid to illustrate the maxim "Love owes its existence to Friendship." But it was Boucher who gave the theme its most lyrical twist. His *Portrait of Mme de Pompadour* (London, Wallace Collection, signed and dated 1759; Fig. 5) pictures the sickly and infirm marquise as the paragon of eternal youth and beauty, sporting her modish dress *à la françoise* and standing insouciantly alone in front of Pigalle's sculpture *Amour et Amitié*, her faithful spaniel, Inès, at her side.[28]

But that was in 1759, when Pompadour was firmly entrenched at Versailles. Around 1750, when she realized she could no longer please the king physically and would have to please him chiefly with the beauty of her mind, her femme savante portraits were born. She began to refashion herself into the king's intelligent adviser and companion and to establish her image as a learned woman and an intellectual in her own right. Consequently, her portraits expanded to privilege a new intellectual persona that escaped the constructs of conventional womanhood. In this regard, Pompadour forged a new identity above and beyond that of "beautiful woman."[29]

Pompadour also may have commissioned the femme savante portraits to rebut the scurrilous satirical verses and songs known as "Les Poissonnades," a title that puns insultingly on Pompadour's maiden name, Poisson (Fish). (The suffix "-nades" has a slightly pejorative connotation.) Surfacing for the first time in 1745 and reappearing intermittently until her death, the "Poissonnades" assailed her middle-class origins, her allegedly ignoble character, and her physical appearance. Most likely instigated by her aristocratic nemesis at court, the comte de Maurepas, the "Poissonnades" alleged that Pompadour's overweening arriviste ambition and illicit power upset the established order and debased the monarchy.[30]

It is not fortuitous, I believe, that Boucher fashioned his first savante portrait of

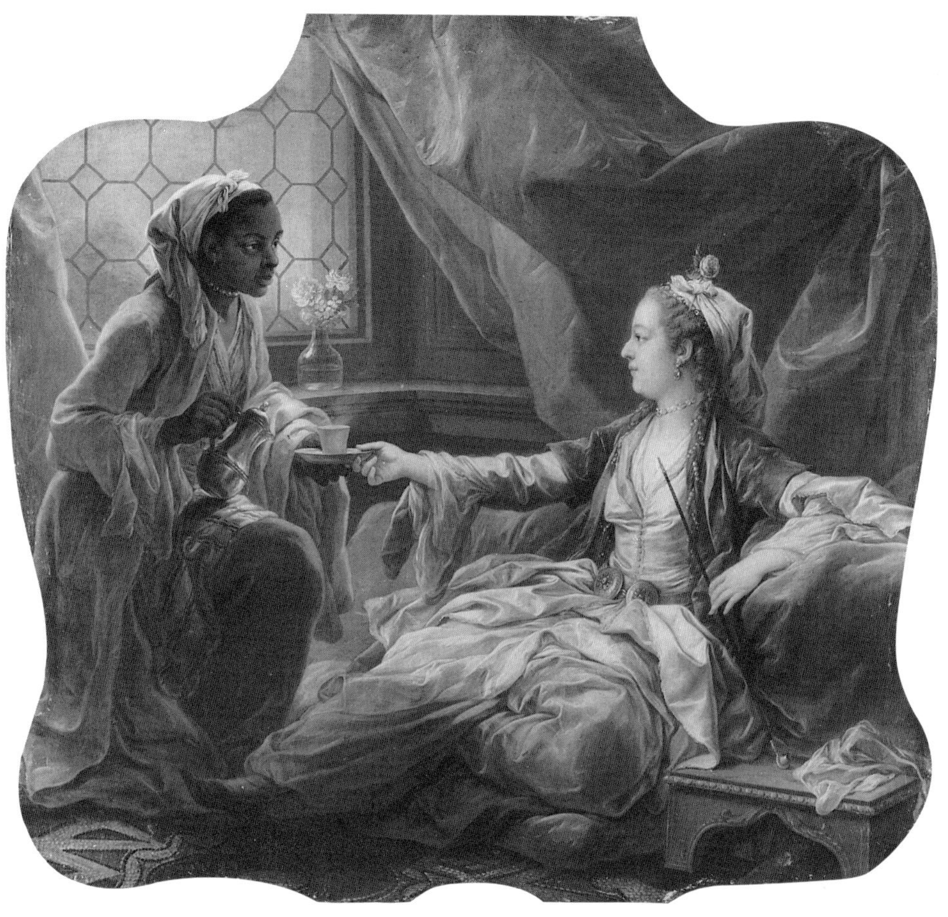

FIGURE 4.
Carle Van Loo, *Portrait of Mme de Pompadour as Sultana Taking Coffee*, ca. 1750–54. Saint Petersburg, Hermitage Museum.

Pompadour shortly after the "Poissonnade" that, in 1749, vilified her intelligence, talents, and appearance. The eleven-stanza poem opens with a ferocious attack on Pompadour and her bourgeois relatives for enriching themselves with the royal purse and usurping the power of the aristocracy. The author then launches an invective against her appearance—her alleged stale countenance, yellow wrinkled skin, insipid

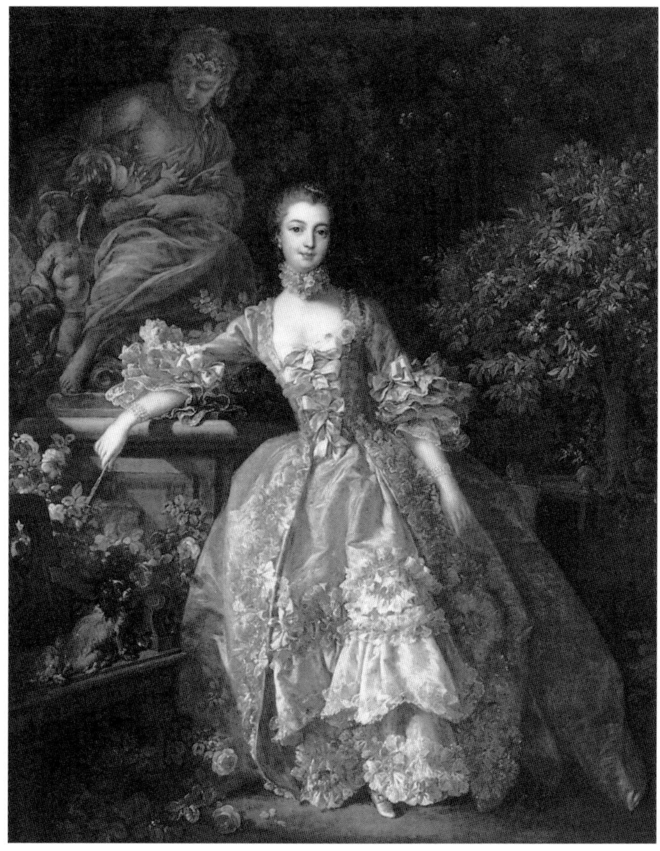

FIGURE 5.
François Boucher, *Portrait of Mme de Pompadour*, 1759. London, The Wallace Collection (reproduced by permission of the Trustees).

eyes, stained teeth, emaciated figure, and ugly throat. These foul disfigurements were matched only by her "lack of intellect and character" and "the indecent folly" of her operatic performances, in which she showcased her "quivering voice, frenzied acting, and feeble talents."[31] Deeply wounded, Pompadour refuted her slanderers in likenesses that depict her as an ideal beauty and assert, not her acquired nobility as a marquise, but her rank as a learned woman.

To affirm her new status and proclaim her cultural agenda to the world, Pompadour again relied on the power of art. Her portraitists utilized the accouterments of the "domestic court" portrait and the "intellectual" portrait, genres popular in eighteenth-century France. The "domestic court" portrait confirms the subject's rank in its monumental scale, elaborate setting, and luxurious clothing, while depicting that subject pursuing the activities of daily life. The "intellectual" portrait, which flourished concurrently with the "domestic court" likenesses, focuses on a man or a woman of the arts, letters, or science in the privacy of his or her study, cabinet, or boudoir engaged in scholarly activities and surrounded by emblems of these pursuits.[32]

Pompadour called upon Boucher to inaugurate her femme savante portraits. She enjoyed a long professional friendship with this artist, who was her trusted decorator, her tutor in engraving, probably her artistic counselor, and her favorite painter, from whom she commissioned several works. We may infer their mutual esteem from Pompadour's having witnessed the marriage contracts of Boucher's two daughters. Their relationship notwithstanding, Boucher was perhaps a surprising choice as Pompadour's primary portraitist, for he was not known for his ability to capture a likeness. Pompadour herself commented in two letters of 1750 to her brother, the marquis de Vandières, that, while Boucher's Louvre sketch was "charming" and "quite pleasing," it did not resemble her.[33] Led by his penchant for idealization and by the literary and cultural ideals of eighteenth-century womanhood, he perfected Pompadour as a timelessly youthful, flawless beauty. His seminal Louvre portrait (1750, 60 × 45.5 cm; Plate 2), as Alastair Laing has shown, was most likely a sketch for a full-length court portrait. Along with Carle Van Loo's state portrait of the king (Versailles, Musée National du Château; Fig. 6), the Louvre image was sent in 1750 to the marquis de Vandières, traveling in Italy to complete his artistic education in preparation for his post as director of royal works, to which he was appointed after his return in 1751. The two portraits reinforced Vandières's status abroad: the one of Louis XV signified his sovereign's favor; the other, of Pompadour, portrayed the king's éminence grise.[34] When Pompadour's portrait returned to France around 1751, it probably hung in Versailles or another château, where members of her circle—both enemies and friends—could study her learned-woman persona.

In the Louvre sketch the twenty-eight-year-old Pompadour is a harpsichordist and a bibliophile, a woman of culture, breeding, and talent, accompanied by her signature iconography of learning: a globe, a rolled-up architectural plan, drawing and engraving tools, musical instruments with scores, and a bookcase and books, at least one of which is embossed with a truncated version of her coat of arms. The portrait also crystallizes her youthful effervescence and charm.

At roughly the same time that she commissioned Boucher's portrait, Pompadour commissioned Maurice-Quentin de La Tour, the portraitist of the intelligentsia,[35] to shape another image of her (Musée du Louvre; Plate 3). Notoriously eccentric

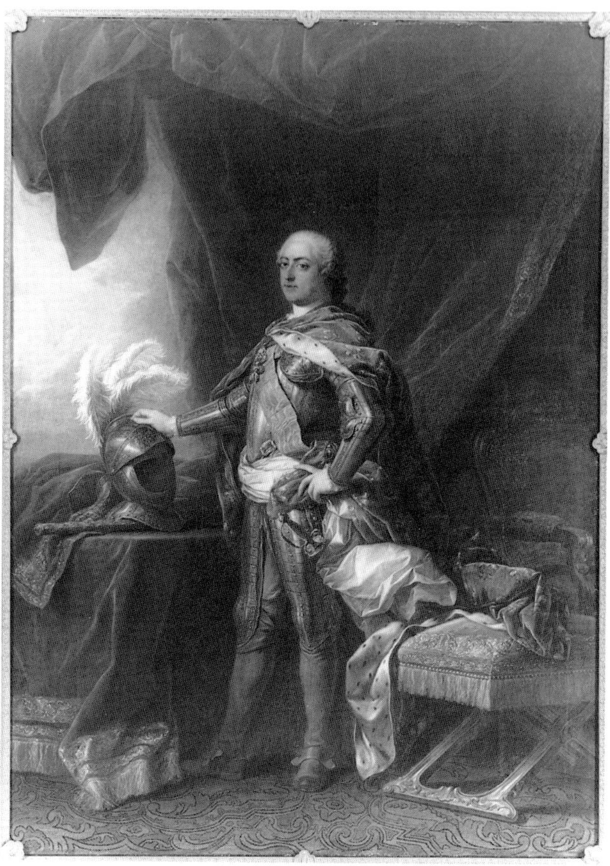

FIGURE 6.
Carle Van Loo, *Portrait of Louis XV in Armor and Red Cloak*, 1750. Versailles, Musée National du Château (photo: RMN).

and recalcitrant, he delayed completing her portrait. "There is absolutely nothing to be done with de Latour; his madness increases by the hour," the exasperated patroness complained to her brother in a letter of 1750. She had to wait about five years to receive his monumental pastel, for which La Tour had the temerity to charge an astronomical sum—forty-eight thousand livres—half of which she paid.[36]

La Tour's eccentricity and impudence notwithstanding, Pompadour evidently liked his work. He came highly recommended by members of the royal family, whose portraits he had fashioned. His pastel of Pompadour was exhibited at the Salon of 1755, and the marquise probably kept it in her possession until her death.

In fact, patron and pastelist were kindred spirits and undoubtedly had much to talk about during the marquise's sittings. Both were ardent devotees of the theater, music, literature, and science; they attended the philosophical salon of Mme Geoffrin in Paris (Mme Geoffrin was one of Pompadour's mentors; see chapter 5) and supported the advanced ideas of the day as well as the intellectuals who promulgated them. For instance, La Tour's close friends—Diderot, Duclos, Alexis Piron, and Voltaire—were protected by Pompadour, and she knew and sponsored many of the philosophes La Tour drew. Both supported the reforms of the *Encyclopédie,* the great compendium of knowledge of the Age of Reason.[37] We can surmise their collaboration in the 1755 pastel, which itself is a banner of the latest philosophical ideas.

La Tour's full-length portrait of the thirty-four-year-old Mme de Pompadour is a masterpiece of the pastel medium. It is a tour de force for its life-sized format (177.5 x 131 cm) and its virtuosic evocation of textures: Pompadour's silk dress, the gilt wood of the furniture, the leather-bound books, the floral upholstery of her chair and *canapé* (couch).

The composition is masterful. The solid pyramidal shape of the upright marquise enhances the dignity of her pose. This shape in turn is counterpointed by the diagonal of the plummy velvet drapery at the left and by the curves of the meandering floral designs on her dress, her musical score, the furniture, and the frame of the inset landscape on the wall. Pompadour turns leftward to face a stream of daylight, which vigorously models her form, picks out the textures of nearby objects, and creates a sense of space around her. The light is also symbolic: it strikes her high forehead, the sign of an intellectual in eighteenth-century France, encoding her mental activity as she gazes out from her fictive space, presumably toward an unseen source of inspiration.[38] The coloration is felicitous; La Tour composes a polyphony of blues, whites, rose, and gold, all of which coalesce into a pleasing harmony of color and shape.

La Tour fashions Pompadour as a veritable "philosophe," to repeat the characterization of a critic of the Salon of 1755. In having La Tour portray her as a philosophe[39] and a *salonnière,* Pompadour proclaimed herself to the Salon-going public as the embodiment of the Enlightenment as well as its Maecenas, identifications made by the embossed portfolio of engravings, guitar, musical scores, and volumes of Montesquieu, Voltaire, and the *Encyclopédie* on her console table. In La Tour's detailed pastel we can read the titles of Pompadour's books, making it anomalous among Pompadour's portraits. Although we also would like to know what musical score she holds in her hands and what engravings or drawings poke out of her portfolio on the floor at the right, these, like all the books and scores in Boucher's and Drouais's portraits, were not meant to be known. We must be content to read the evidence of Pompadour's learning more generally.

Boucher's splendid portrait in Munich (Alte Pinakothek, 1756; Salon of 1757; Plate 4), as Laing has shown, was commissioned to consecrate the thirty-four-year-old Pompadour as supernumerary lady-in-waiting to the queen. Her elevation, first to marquise, in 1745, and then to duchess, in 1752, had already made her less of a bourgeois interloper in the eyes of the public. Her new rank made her position at court unassailable, and to let the public know this, she had her portrait prominently exhibited on its own dais at the Salon of 1757 (Fig. 7).[40]

Boucher's life-sized portrait (201 × 157 cm) is a ravishing essay on high rococo luxury and ornament and shimmering color and light. As opposed to La Tour's upright pyramidal structure, Boucher's portrait depicts a diagonal, Pompadour's full-length figure echoed by the slanting rosewood writing table at the right, which is pictured from above, thus defying the rules of perspective. In her relaxation, she personifies aristocratic nonchalance and composure. This diagonal is played off against the verticals of the gilded mirror frames that flank her; the soaring pilaster reflected in the mirror behind her, a sign of her exalted status; and the bulk of the rectangular bookcase that is also reflected in the mirror. Pompadour's elongated, attenuated figure is placed ambiguously on a daybed, and she is clad in a dress of extraordinary richness. As Georges Brunel put it, the gown "is superbly spread out like a fan." While the mirror extends the space of the shallow library-boudoir, it also reflects inaccurately—but to advantage—the lovely nape of the anachronistically youthful and beautiful marquise.[41]

In Boucher's Munich portrait, Pompadour, in the opulent dress she may have worn during her first week's service to the queen,[42] poses with supreme confidence and authority not only as the devotee of reading, correspondence, and the arts but as the veritable sovereign of Gallic culture. She is presented to us in the mode of the theater, her domain. The draperies part, as in a "discovery scene," to reveal a character on stage, and the curtains rise well above her head, emphasizing her exalted status.

Pompadour's elegant languor also illustrates the period concept of *honnêteté*, an ideal of the aristocracy and upper bourgeoisie that existed apart from the demands of court life. *Honnêteté* was characterized by the studied cultivation of refined "conspicuous leisure," the practice of taking refuge from the mundane life and onerous duties at court by indulging in luxurious repose, the ultimate state of happiness in eighteenth-century French letters and thought. These escapees withdrew into cultivated, private leisure and in doing so shaped a superior, noble identity, as the aristocratic Pompadour does in her opulent boudoir.[43]

Her stylish repose is underscored by the careless disposition, typical of Boucher's works, of her accouterments of learning and accomplishment. The uniqueness of the commission notwithstanding, Boucher reconfigured the signature intellectual emblems he essayed in the Louvre sketch. Here again is the hybrid bookcase, now emblazoned with a single tower of her coat of arms, giving her library an aristocratic stamp.

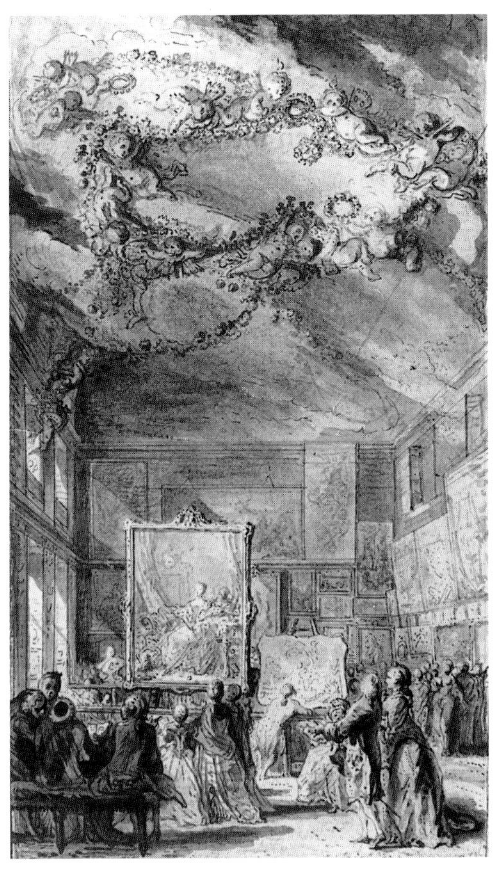

FIGURE 7.
Gabriel de Saint-Aubin, *Drawing of Boucher's Portrait of Mme de Pompadour at the Salon of 1757.* From Du Perron, *Discours sur la peinture et sur l'architecture,* 1758. Waddesdon Manor, The National Trust (photo: Courtauld Institute of Art).

On top of the bookcase is a clock. At first glance, the time reads 3:40, but upon closer scrutiny, we notice that the roman numerals designating the hour are painted backward, consonant with their reflection in the mirror behind the marquise. If the reflection is reversed and we read the clock accurately, the time is 8:20—doubtless in the evening, since the marquise is fully dressed (at 8:20 in the morning she would have been either asleep or, if up, garbed in her dressing gown, as she is in Boucher's Fogg portrait; see Plate 1). This exactitude is unusual in Boucher's portraits of the marquise, and the time may only be conventional, as it is on many period clocks that register 8:20; but it may also have carried special significance for Pompadour.

But how do we decode the meaning of the hour in the Munich portrait—if we can decode it at all? Its significance may have been known only to Pompadour and Boucher. Nevertheless, we know that the portrait was painted in 1756—on the lower shelf of Pompadour's writing table is inscribed "f. Boucher 1756." And we are virtually certain that it was commissioned to commemorate Pompadour's elevation to lady-in-waiting on Sunday, February 8, 1756, perhaps the most important moment of her life at court. We know her approximate schedule on that day. She was presented to the queen after vespers, that is, after 6:00 P.M., and attended Marie Leczinska at a banquet. At court, supper was served around 9:00 or 10:00 P.M. The duc de Croÿ, who was at court that evening, tells us that Pompadour "was very beautifully adorned that night and she attended the Queen with much composure, as if she had never done anything else."[44]

Thus we can speculate that Boucher portrayed Pompadour at a moment following her elevation and before supper when, at the height of aristocratic self-confidence, self-satisfaction, and "supreme grandeur and omnipotence," she withdrew to her library-boudoir to luxuriate in her new position and enjoy the activities she loved best: reading, reflection, and letter writing, the latter of which she frequently attended to in the evening.[45] Her outward gaze suggests an attitude of reflection prompted by what she has been reading; this contemplative attitude epitomizes Pompadour as the quintessential Enlightenment savante.

Fashioned as an emblem in grisaille, the rococo clock is configured as a lyre and embellished with a laurel, signifying two of Pompadour's interests, music and poetry. No such clock can be located in descriptions of Pompadour's effects; thus Boucher may well have invented it for this occasion and imbued it with iconographic significance. In a contemporaneous edition of Ripa's *Iconologia* (1758–60), in fact, Music is personified in a manner similar to Boucher's image of Pompadour in the Munich portrait: a beautifully dressed, seated woman accompanied by a lyre, her elegant garb and recumbent posture emblematizing music as a pleasurable and relaxing activity. Ripa's Poetry is personified by a beautiful woman crowned with laurel and holding a lyre, one the symbol of harmonious sound, the other, of eternal fame.[46]

Pompadour herself engraved images of lyres and laurels encoding the genii of music and poetry in her large *Suite d'Estampes gravées par Madame la Marquise de Pompadour, d'après les Pierres gravées de Guay, Graveur du Roy* (the *Suite of Engravings by Madame the Marquise de Pompadour after the Engraved Gems of Guay, En-*

graver to the King, 1755, 1782; Figs. 8, 9), another leaf of which is depicted at the left of the portrait, strewn among her effects.[47] Part of the grisaille emblem also contains a typical Boucher Cupid on a bed of roses next to the clock. In a painting comprising part of a program of the arts and sciences commissioned for Pompadour's library at her château de Crécy (ca. 1750–52), Boucher earlier fashioned the allegory of Poetry as a Cupid-like child, garlanded with roses, who appears along with a lyre.[48]

In the Munich portrait, then, Pompadour may be seen as the supreme devotee of music and poetry, the arts most central to her interests and amply represented in her library, which in her likeness is symbolized by the bookcase that supports them.[49]

The Cupid; the mirror behind Pompadour; the pearl bracelet she wears; the roses that embellish her dress; the pencil holder and the burin in the foreground; and the books on the shelf of her writing table at the right—all of these emblems may well confer another identity on the marquise, that of a Venus, at least in the mundane eighteenth-century idiom. These attributes appear in Boucher's *Venus at Her Toilette* (New York, Metropolitan Museum of Art, 1751), which hung in Pompadour's bathroom at her château de Bellevue.[50] Some of them emblematize Pompadour as an earthly incarnation of the goddess of love and beauty in Boucher's 1758 Fogg portrait (see Plate 1).

In fact, the pearl bracelet she wears on her right arm in the Munich portrait is the one she wears in the Fogg likeness, except that she has the cameo "of Louis XV turned in to be closer to the veins—that is to intensify the circulatory link from her heart to the king."[51] She turns it inward also because it would have been unseemly, at this moment of her piety as lady-in-waiting, to display her affection for the king by wearing the cameo image openly.

The eighteenth century liberally deified beautiful women, especially powerful ones like Mme de Pompadour, and the marquise had more than her share of such compliments. She apparently identified with the goddess of love and beauty, for she delighted in playing the part of Venus in a heroic ballet in her Théâtre des Petits Appartements at Versailles, and she was apotheosized as a Venus by Voltaire and other members of her coterie.[52] One of the critics of the Salon of 1757, in which the portrait was exhibited, also lauded Pompadour as an astute Venus who patronized Boucher. Here she is presented, with Boucher's light touch, as the embodiment of perfect beauty and learning, playing to the hilt the role of the belle savante.

The Munich portrait anticipates Pompadour's languorous pose in Boucher's lyrical Victoria and Albert painting (signed and dated 1758, 52.4 × 57.8 cm; Plate 5), his third important femme savante portrait of the marquise. Here Pompadour enacts the pastoral heroine she made famous on stage. She reclines in a clearing before an abundant but spatially ambiguous screen of trees and luxuriant foliage indicating a wood in springtime. An amalgam of artifice and nature, this picturesque backdrop is the stuff of Boucher's theatrically inspired stage sets in his many painted pastorals.

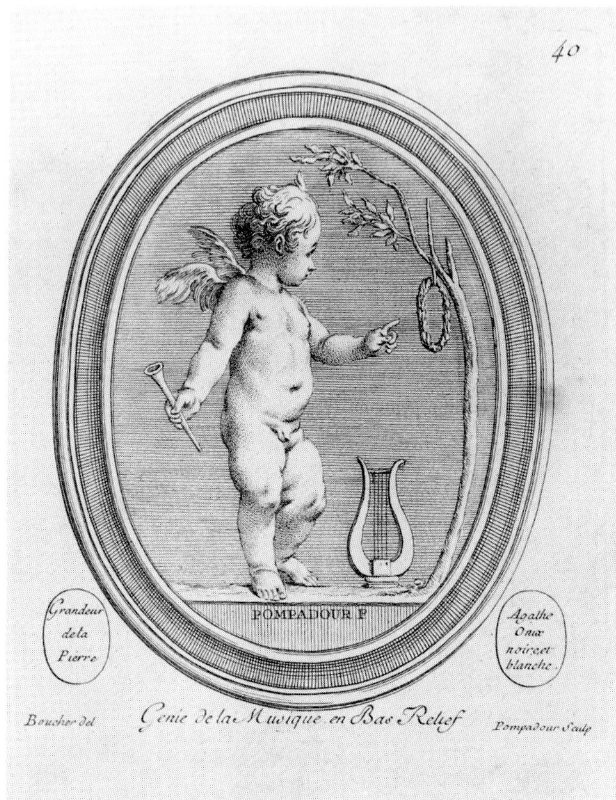

FIGURE 8.
Mme de Pompadour after François Boucher, *Genie de la Musique en Bas Relief*, 1782. New York, Print Collection, The New York Public Library.

This screen of burgeoning foliage throws into relief Pompadour's pyramidal form; her capacious dress is modeled by a limpid light raking downward through the trees from the upper left. The portrait captures her self-described "reflective" disposition. She meditates on what appears to be one of the many volumes of pastoral literature, probably poetry, in her vast library. To emphasize her love of reading, her left arm rests on books dog-eared from use, rare marbled paperbacks that only a cognoscente would own.[53]

Honnêteté and noble leisure also permeate this tranquil portrait. These literary concepts described a world of serenity abstracted from the life of politics and the struggle for advancement, a life that Pompadour knew all too well. These principles and their pastoral embodiment reflected the desire to escape the formal display at court that cloaked the solicitations of favor and office. The gardens, parks, and woods were aesthetically appealing and stylish retreats. Pompadour could be reading a vol-

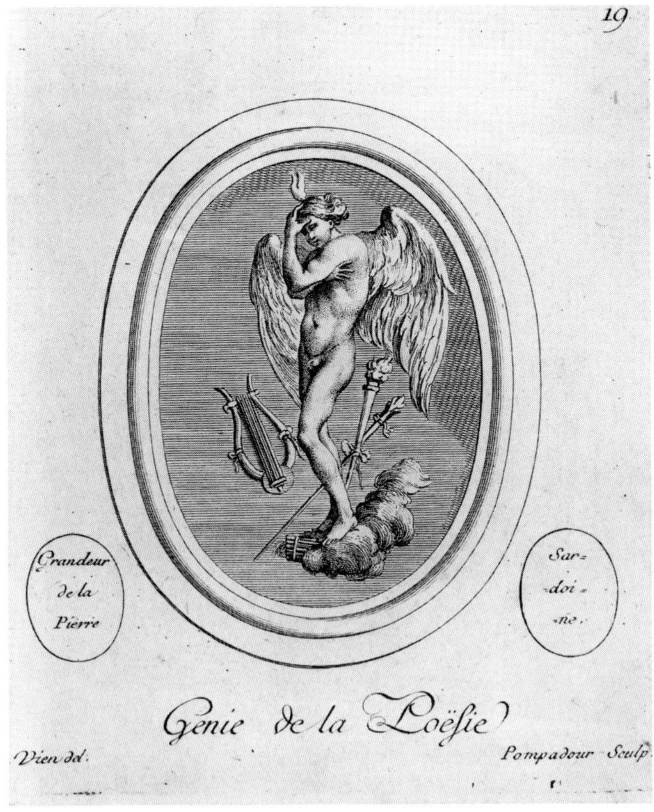

FIGURE 9.
Mme de Pompadour after Joseph-Marie Vien, *Genie de la Poësie*, 1782. New York, Print Collection, The New York Public Library.

ume of pastoral verse by a member of her literary coterie celebrating the ideals of *honnêteté* and noble leisure. In a literary equivalent of Boucher's portrait, written years earlier, in 1745, the abbé de Bernis, her "eternal friend," lyricized the youthful Pompadour herself as an incarnation of noble repose: "But I saw her in a solitary wood / Where the young Pompadour goes to dream." And Charles-Jean François Hénault, the esteemed historian, president of the French Academy, and Pompadour's social acquaintance, wrote of an ideal pastoral heroine like the marquise: "We saw her, she dreamed under these elms. / It was there that her voice attracted the birds."[54]

These literary ideas were not lost on Boucher, the master of the painted pastoral and friend of writers;[55] he constructs his portrait of Mme de Pompadour with the visual poetics of the pastoral and *honnêteté* in mind. He also understood her personality, her desire to withdraw from the banalities and pressures of the court. She expressed this longing to her confidante Mme de Lutzelbourg as early as 1749, just four years after she became the king's mistress. (Marie-Ursule de Klinglin, comtesse de Lutzelbourg, thirty-eight years Pompadour's senior, shared the marquise's passion for the theater. She was an intelligent and cultivated Alsatian—her husband had been governor of Strasbourg—who also corresponded with Voltaire.) Pompadour wrote to her: "The life I lead is terrible; I hardly have a minute to myself: rehearsals and performances, and twice a week continual trips to the Petit château as well as La Muette, etc. Considerable and indispensable duties." And again in the same year, she complained to Vandières: "The older I get, my dear brother, . . . the more my reflections are philosophical. . . . Excepting the happiness of being with the king, who certainly consoles me about everything, the rest is merely a web of wickedness, platitudes, in short, of all the miseries of which wretched human beings are capable. A fine subject for reflections, above all for someone born as reflective as I." In December 1751, she renounced the hunt with her consort because, as she wrote to Mme de Lutzelbourg, "I need some time to think." In 1755 she was so disgusted with the court that she wrote to the king for permission to withdraw altogether. And in the year that the Munich portrait was painted, she reiterated to her friend the duc de Choiseuil, "Were I to follow my taste for freedom and quiet, I would long ago have left a land where slavery has no charm, when passions no longer hold one. But I know that, out of gratitude to the King, I must sacrifice this precious liberty." There is a distinct possibility that Louis XV bestowed the honor of lady-in-waiting on Pompadour early the next year in order to keep her by his side in her indispensable role as cultural adviser and counselor. Like the literary escapees who found their repose in the country, Pompadour found leisure and tranquillity in the forest of Compiègne: "I pass there half my life with great satisfaction," she confided to Vandières on June 15, 1750.[56] Eight years later, Boucher evoked her love of pastoral repose in the Victoria and Albert portrait, one of his most poetic and sympathetic paintings.

François-Hubert Drouais returned Pompadour to court in the last great femme savante portrait of her (London, National Gallery; Fig. 10). An inscription on the portrait tells us: "Painted by Drouais the younger / the head in April 1763: and the painting finished in May 1764," a month after the marquise's death. We know virtually nothing about Pompadour's relationship to her last portraitist. But because of her chronic illness and resultant infirmity, we can safely assume that she had very little contact with Drouais, save for a few sittings during which he made studies of her face and head that he developed on a separate canvas and subsequently affixed onto the larger surface.

In Drouais's naturalistic canvas, Pompadour plays her valedictory role as the "mature woman" of the eighteenth century, a construct in cultural circulation.[57] Her youth and beauty spent—the eighteenth-century woman was considered undesirable to men and society at thirty or younger—the forty-two-year-old Pompadour is enshrined by her perceptive portraitist as the grande dame of arts and letters. Like

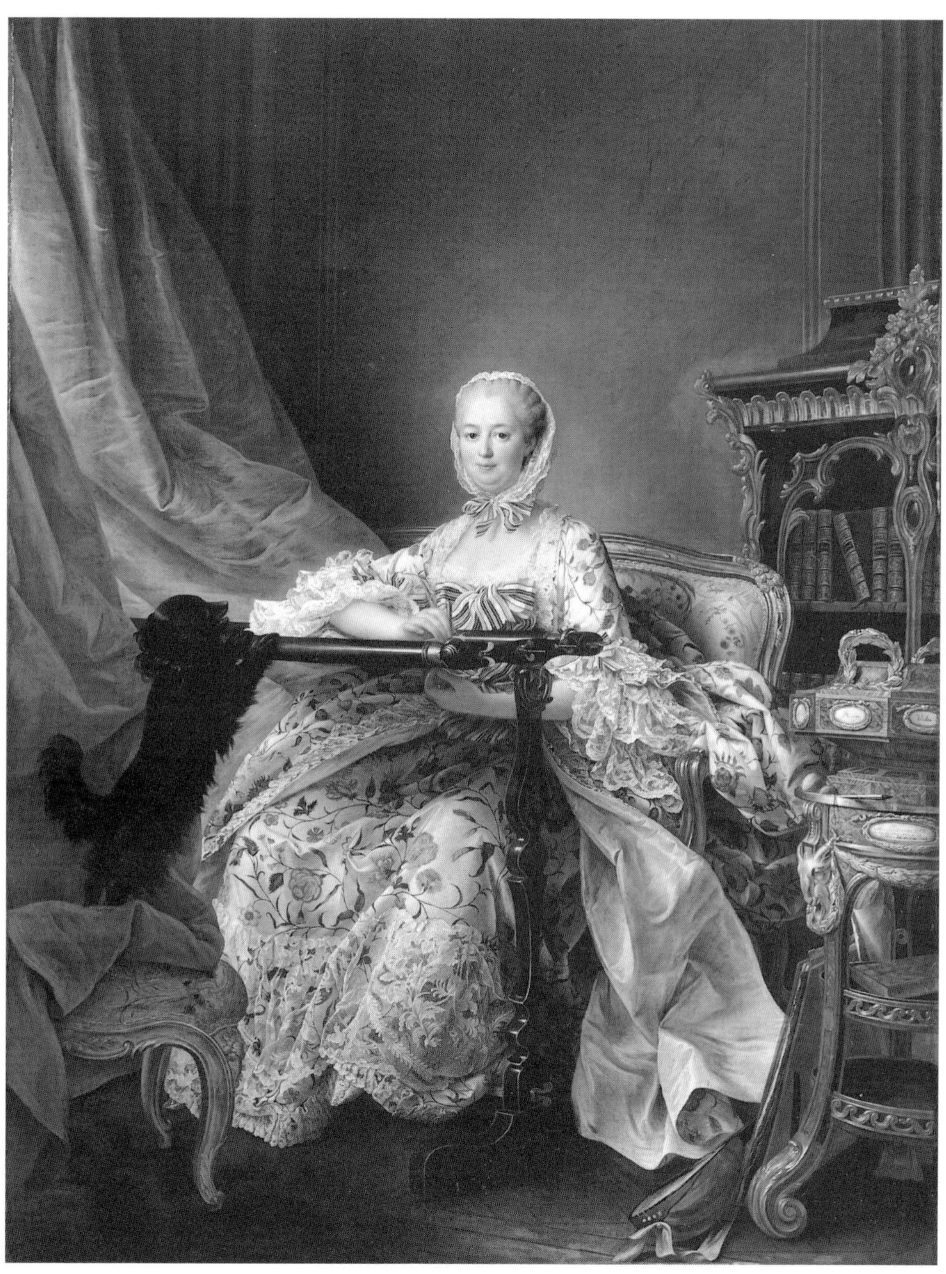

FIGURE 10.
François-Hubert Drouais, *Portrait of Mme de Pompadour*, 1763–64. London, The National Gallery (reproduced by courtesy of the Trustees).

her venerable sisters in period literature, she is ensconced in her role as an aging intellectual, and she seems to have been comfortable with this identity. In this role she fulfills society's expectations of a matronly asexual mistress of learning: from the pencil holder, the nearby portfolio of engravings, the books in the bookcase, and the skeins of yarn on her classically simple table with a rotating top, we infer her seasoned intelligence and artistry. Empowered by her sagacity, she is enthroned at her tapestry frame, where, according to the duc de Croÿ, she received ambassadors: "Thus one passed from her toilette to her loom . . . and she would equal or surpass Mme de Maintenon, whom she had been imitating carefully for quite some time." This is only one way in which she mimicked her royal predecessor.[58]

Drouais's life-sized portrait (214 × 157 cm), which resonates with Aved's naturalistic full-length likeness of Mme Crozat (Montpellier, Musée Fabre, 1741),[59] combines the magisterial court portrait format with an array of meticulously rendered and glossily treated genre elements that comment on Pompadour's artistic and intellectual tastes. The light, which streams into the room from an implied window at the left, vigorously models the marquise, picks out a panoply of textures, and creates a credible space. Again, we may assume that the bright light that illuminates Pompadour's high forehead symbolizes her intellectual acuity.

In Drouais's portrait the loom intervenes between Pompadour and us, her respectful supplicants, setting up an effective distance and underscoring her high status. She is exalted by the low viewpoint of the beholder, who, like her visitor Meinières, is "full of astonishment and admiration" at her "hauteur";[60] by the majestic full-length format; and by the lofty swag of drapery rising above her at the left. As the grande dame, the marquise is still conscious of beauty and fashion; the duc de Croÿ remarked that in her maturity she was still "strikingly decked out."[61] She continues to use maquillage, a mélange of red and white makeup, but applies it more heavily than in her youth, for it disguises the ravages of time and ill health as well as signifying her status at court. She wears a painted silk sack dress, a loose-fitting dress then in fashion whose sweeping overdress and extravagant lace cuffs give it a queenly flourish. Her double chin, gray powdered hair, and matronly lace cap bespeak her age, but Pompadour gazes at her interlocutor with an expression of dignity and will, qualities that helped to elevate her from the bourgeoisie to aristocratic heights.

Because we have little contemporary documentation of the portraits and no knowledge of their whereabouts during Pompadour's lifetime, we have to assume that they were kept in Pompadour's domiciles and were seen only by members of her inner circle.[62] To understand how her contemporaries responded to them, we must rely on the criticism of the Salons of 1755 (for La Tour's portrait) and 1757 (for Boucher's), and on the contemporaneous critique of Drouais's portrait, which was shown at the Palais des Tuileries in 1764.

In the Salon of 1755, La Tour's pastel was exhibited, tellingly, next to Nattier's posthumous portrait of Louis XV's daughter, *Mme Henriette Playing the Bass Viol* (Versailles, Musée National du Château; Fig. 11). On the other side of Nattier's portrait appeared Tocqué's likeness of Pompadour's brother, the marquis de Marigny, the director of royal works and co-patron, with Pompadour, of the Ecole Militaire, its plan on his desk at the left (Versailles, Musée National du Château; Fig. 12). Salon audiences perhaps saw the consanguinity of this painted trio.[63] Employing the formal rhetoric of the court portrait—the stately format, the verticality of the architecture, the swag of drapery heightening the status of the subjects—the three works focus on intellectual, talented personages connected with the crown.

Critics in 1755 saw La Tour's pastel of Pompadour as depicting a great patroness, muse, philosophe, savante, and, primarily, beautiful woman (see Plate 3). The author of the *Lettre sur Le Salon de 1755, Adressée à ceux qui la liront* (*Letter on the Salon of 1755, Addressed to Those Who Will Read It*), for instance, praises Pompadour as guardian of Enlightenment culture: "It is a work that inspires feelings of admiration and gratitude for its author; one is enchanted to see the arts make such great efforts for someone who protects them with so much generosity, discernment, and greatness."[64]

The reviewer of the *Lettre A Un Partisan Du Bon Goût . . .* (*Letter to a Partisan of Good Taste*) praises Pompadour as a beautiful woman, a muse, and a protectress. For him, she reincarnates "the beautiful Laura, who by the delicacy of her taste inspires our 'modern Petrarchs'": not only Voltaire, Montesquieu, Diderot, and d'Alembert, the gifted authors of the volumes on her console table, but presumably also La Tour himself, who benefits from her inspirational patronage. In this male critic's eyes, Pompadour's image combines "intellect and graces," "nobility worthy of respect," and "enchanting sweetness,"[65] phrases in which he salutes her womanly attractiveness and her intellectual force, in life as well as in the pastel.

Another reviewer takes issue with his colleague's unequivocal praise of La Tour's pastel, condemning the artist's lack of verisimilitude. On the one hand, this writer sees Pompadour as the consummately beautiful devotee and patron of learning, as "Laura, lover of the arts who cherish her"; on the other hand, he asserts that "no one recognizes Laura under this large and beautiful glass" (the portrait was exhibited behind glass). He charges La Tour with robbing from the original all her beauties and with failing to imbue nature with the graces obligatory in a representation of a beautiful woman. He contrasts La Tour's generalized image with Carle Van Loo's overdoor depicting Pompadour as a sultana drinking coffee (see Fig. 4), exhibited in the same salon: she "more closely resembles the beautiful Laura."[66]

Apparently convinced that his fellow reviewer had a point about the lack of likeness in the pastel, the author of the *Lettre A Un Partisan Du Bon Goût* responded to his colleague's critique. Agreeing that mimesis is not La Tour's forte—"If the Sul-

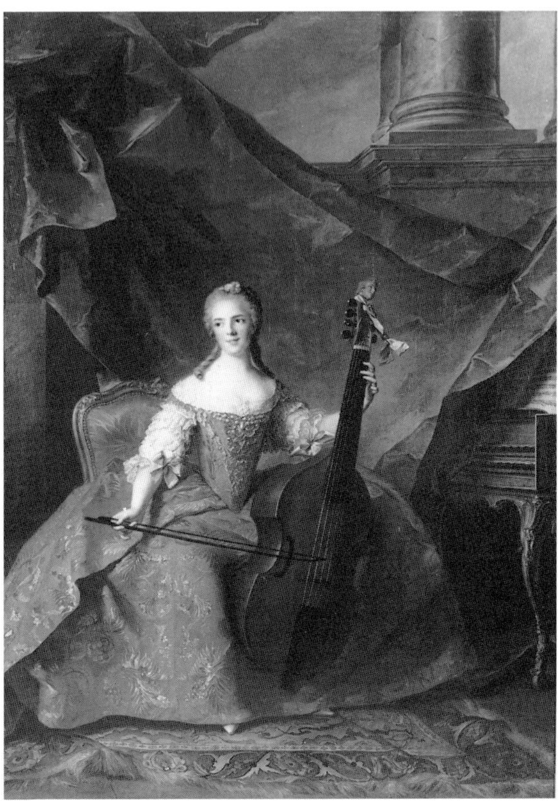

FIGURE 11.
Jean-Marc Nattier, *Portrait of Mme Henriette Playing the Bass Viol*, 1754. Versailles, Musée National du Château (photo: RMN).

tan is a good resemblance, the pastel is not"—he censures the artist for a host of faults in representation:

> It is true that this pastel has not been posed by the painter to advantage. One sees only a three-quarter-view of the head, which should have been shown full-face. The eyes are lost and that results in an air of distraction, which does not accord with the graces. Nor is the coiffure better conceived. The hair is raised up from behind and is not powdered. Even though most women do their hair in this fashion, it would have been better to give the head a more picturesque ornament. One would say that M. de la Tour proposed to make

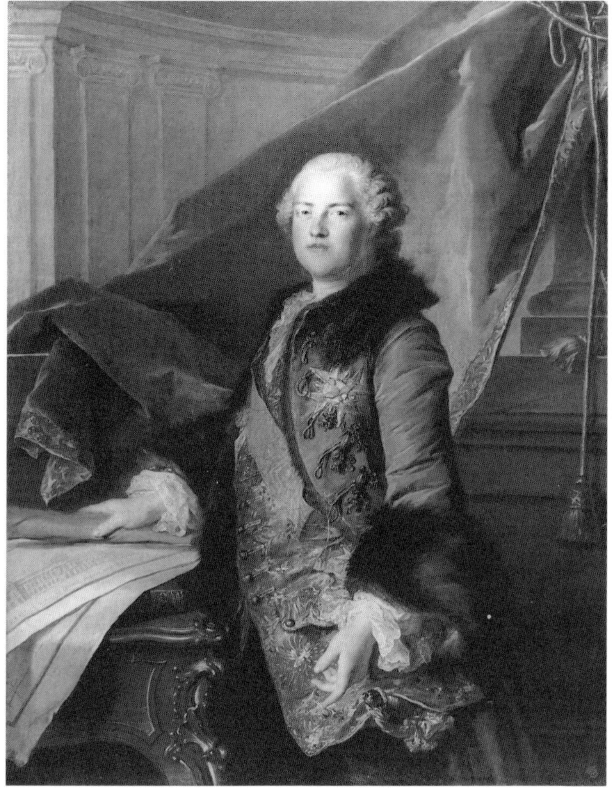

FIGURE 12.
Louis Tocqué, *Portrait of the Marquis de Marigny*, 1755. Versailles, Musée National du Château (photo: RMN).

the portrait of a Philosophe. Didn't he know that one should eschew distraction and plainness when one wants to represent a beautiful woman? This able painter had too much confidence in his art. He believed inopportunely that he would be able to render nature under the least favorable aspect, without making it lose its most precious embellishments. In order that his bold project not escape viewers, he took care to place very weighty tomes on a table in this picture. Such neighbors are incompatible with what is pleasing; their proximity is contagious. In the presence of the *Encyclopédie*, one is compelled to assume a grave and severe air.[67]

This writer's harsh assessment of the pastel evinces gendered expectations of the portrayal of a beautiful woman that conflict with Pompadour and La Tour's idea of a serious eighteenth-century philosophe. The critic interprets Pompadour's musing on her score, her head turned to the left (the posture of superior contemplation she assumes in all of her portraits), as distraction, inappropriate to the portrayal of a comely woman. He would have Pompadour deny the inherently reflective nature she and her portraitist reveal in her pose. In accordance with society's, particularly men's, expectations of women, she should conform to the graces by confronting the beholder and should be "agréable" (pleasing) by embellishing herself with jewelry (of which, incidentally, Pompadour had plenty) and powdering her hair (it is, in fact, lightly powdered). This male construct of a coquette, decidedly unserious, never reads books, especially not the daunting *Encyclopédie*.

The term "graces," which the authors of the *Réponse A une Lettre adressée à un Partisan du bon goût* and *Seconde Lettre à un partisan du bon goût* employ in their reviews, abounds in period criticism, poetry, novels, and versified engravings praising beautiful women. We should know its meaning. In the Enlightenment, if a woman's physical appearance was molded by the Graces, she was comely and also exuded charm, attractiveness, gracefulness, and gentleness. If she was well enough endowed to merit the rank of the fourth grace, a human incarnation of Venus's companions, she was also pleasing, primarily if not exclusively to men.[68]

Voltaire defines and elaborates on the term "grace" in the seventh volume of the *Encyclopédie*, whose fourth tome sits prominently on Pompadour's console table in La Tour's pastel. According to Voltaire, "A beautiful person will not have any graces at all in her face if her mouth is closed, without a smile; if her eyes lack sweetness. The serious is never gracious; it does not attract at all. It approaches the severe too much, which repels."[69]

Like Voltaire, the male critic of La Tour's pastel cannot reconcile a graceful woman with a serious female "philosophe," who is accompanied by great books (including *La Henriade,* Voltaire's own philosophic work, which occupies a conspicuous place on Pompadour's desk). The presence of intellectual volumes in a portrait of a lovely woman is incongruous and jarring. But Pompadour the patron and La Tour the portraitist, both familiar with Enlightenment constructs of feminine beauty, had more progressive ideas about the femme philosophe. For them the intelligent woman happily combined comeliness and bookishness: her physical endowments need not detract from her seriousness and dedication to knowledge.

Other reviewers had no problem with the earnestness and high-mindedness of La Tour's portrait. One of them, recognizing that the pastel could be appreciated only by an informed public—"les gens d'art" (the people of art, or the cognoscenti)—recognized its sitter's "tête Savante" (savante head).[70] Another critic noted that La Tour's "choice of the simple and the serious enhanced the nobility" of his subject.

But this nobility had to be feminized by "an agreeable head,"[71] appropriate to a femme savante/philosophe.

Boucher's Munich portrait (see Plate 4) was better received than its predecessor, save by Baron Grimm, who censured it as "the same portrait done by M. de La Tour, and exhibited two years ago, [which] was much criticized. This seems to me bad in quite a different way; detestable in its color, it is so laden with ornaments, pompons and all sorts of frills, that it must hurt the eyes of everyone of taste."[72]

What Grimm interpreted as odious, the reviewer of the Salon's official journal, the *Mercure de France*, praised as natural—indeed essential—attributes of the beautiful devotee of learning: "The Portrait of Madame la Marquise de Pompadour, by M. Boucher, is indeed worthy of his brush! What graces! What richness! What ornaments! Books, drawings and other accessories indicate the taste of Madame la Marquise de Pompadour for the sciences and the arts that she loves and cultivates with success, those to whose study she knows how to consecrate her useful moments." For this critic Boucher was the supreme "Painter of the Graces [who] has only rendered nature, without taking the trouble of embellishing or flattering his model."[73] What Grimm despised as rococo excess and the modern viewer would construe as flattery and idealization, this critic admired as ingenuous naturalism. The sobriquet for Boucher, "the Painter of the Graces," need not mislead us; the term "Graces" at the time also denoted artless beauty and charm.[74]

E.-C. Fréron, the reviewer of the journal *L'Année Littéraire*, saluted Boucher as the master "*Venus* and her Court have chosen for their Painter," an extravagant compliment to Pompadour, whom Boucher, as I have suggested, constructed as an earthly Venus. For Fréron, this modern goddess of love was pictured by her Apelles with a noble, simple, and pleasant attitude and with a head characterized by beauty, graces, and delicacy—in short, the epitome of comeliness and learning, the ideal femme savante.[75]

The sober Grimm, an exponent of naturalism, finally found a portrait of Pompadour that pleased him: Drouais's tableau, exhibited in the Palais des Tuileries after the marquise's death in 1764 (see Fig. 10). Grimm focused respectfully on, in his words, "this celebrated woman," whom he described "working at an embroidery frame in a cabinet in which one sees . . . books, implements of painting and music, etc." As her acquaintance, Grimm perspicaciously paid tribute to Pompadour's peculiar meditative air—"[elle] parait mediter"—appropriate to a femme savante/philosophe. Grimm believed that Drouais's representation outstripped those of Pompadour's other portraitists, since he was uniquely capable of seizing women's likenesses "without jeopardizing the delicacy and grace that make the charm of their physiognomy."[76] In Pompadour's portrait Grimm saw the epitome of the Enlightenment femme savante.

In their femme savante portraits, Boucher and La Tour did not intend realistic portrayals. Following the vogue of the time, they paid tribute to Pompadour's legendary but past beauty. According to contemporaries, she was at the summit of her beauty when she became the king's favorite in 1745. She was rather tall, with an oval face, a superb complexion, and splendid arms and hands. Agreeably curved and rounded, she moved with uncommon grace. Her brilliant eyes, her most notable feature, reflected her vivacity and intelligence.[77] When Boucher and La Tour fashioned her portraits, waning health had dimmed her legendary beauty: her figure had become gaunt, and her complexion, rather than white and smooth, as imaged in her portraits, was sallow and wan.[78] The pristine visage they represented was factitious, created by the application of a white resin heightened by florid rouge. This makeup at once disguised her fading beauty, signified her status at court, and mimicked the poetic red-and-white complexions of Laura and Venus, Pompadour's fictional counterparts, recognized by Salon critics.[79] The criticism of Boucher and La Tour for failing to capture Pompadour's likeness misses the portraitists' purpose of shaping a rococo paragon. We sense a dichotomy between such idealization and the serious images of the studious woman in the savante portraits, but the equivocation was forced on Pompadour and her portraitists by the prevailing clichés about perfect femininity. The femme savante in the eighteenth century was expected to be the amalgam of learning and glamour.

In fashioning their pictorial encomia, Boucher and La Tour, and Nattier before them (see Fig. 3), who was dubbed by a contemporary "the pupil of the Graces, the painter of beauty,"[80] followed a visual poetics that corresponded to literary conventions of beauty written by, to use the phrase of the author of the *Lettre A Un Partisan Du Bon Goût*, "our modern Petrarchs." These were eighteenth-century society poets and novelists who perpetuated the tradition of idealized description codified by Petrarch and the Petrarchans in the three previous centuries. Pompadour knew many of these littérateurs, including Voltaire and Bernis, who worked in the tradition, and Boucher and La Tour moved in the cultivated circles they frequented.[81] Prevailing notions of ideal beauty issued from the alliance of "the sister arts," promulgated by eighteenth-century critics, and these ideas sprang from and were nourished by the same cultural matrix.[82]

Like her literary sisters, Pompadour is idealized and generalized, endowed with a softly contoured, fluid, and supple figure, which swells and ebbs in the right places.[83] Boucher himself, "the Painter of the Graces" and the official portraitist of the Venus-like Pompadour, subscribed to this model of beauty: "One should hardly be able to imagine that a woman's body contains any bones; without being fat, they must be rounded, [yet] delicate and slim-waisted, without being skinny."[84]

Pompadour's costumes enhance this ideal pliancy and softness. They are versions of haute couture in the style known as the "open gown," or the "gown *à la françoise,*" whose fullness at the hips is created by side hoops and at the arms by sleeves pushed up with jeweled ribbon ties (in the Louvre sketch and the Victoria and Albert portrait) or triple lace ruffles (in the other portraits). This amplitude contrasts with a tapered ribbon-bowed or tightly laced stomacher, which emphasizes the slimness of the waist and highlights the alluring décolletage. The softness of Pompadour's figure is also underscored by the sumptuous silks she wears in all of her fashion plates, and especially in La Tour's and Drouais's portraits, in which her dresses—of figured silk and Chinese silk, respectively—are embellished with meandering floral designs.[85]

Pompadour's hands, which seem boneless, in accordance with Boucher's paradigm, signify delicacy, grace, and aristocratic composure. They visually poeticize Laura's "bella man," for they are "a little long," with slender fingers "a little red."

Pompadour also has the face of the ideal eighteenth-century woman. It is a perfect oval (as it allegedly was in life, according to contemporaries), rounded off by a slightly fleshy chin. Her eyes are large and sparkling, her eyebrows perfectly arched, her nose straight and regular, and her lips glistening with a vermilion tint. Her strikingly white skin is, in Petrarchan terms, like porcelain or alabaster. Her complexion radiates "lilies and roses," a metaphor concretized in Boucher's portraits by the pinkish white roses in the foreground, and in the Munich likeness by the red roses on the shelf of her writing table.[86]

The roses also feminize her learning. This cerebral beauty is never encumbered by her books; she masters all branches of learning with delicacy and finesse and perpetually exudes an air of freshness and youth. This belle savante, the Pompadour of the portraits, is a compelling fiction, a source of pleasure to anyone willing to suspend disbelief, and a fitting representation of that rare combination of beauty and wisdom that Pompadour strove to embody—and in her portraits did.

2

EDUCATING AND DEFENDING THE FEMME SAVANTE

Pompadour's femme savante portraits are not merely agreeable fantasies. The savante persona and the attributes of learning suggest her unusual education, the best a woman could obtain in the eighteenth century. A patriarchal society with a low opinion of a woman's mental capacity limited her access to solid primary and secondary schooling and afforded her no opportunity to attend university. By contrast, boys of the upper classes received a much more substantial formal education—a grounding in Latin grammar, literature, and civilization, as well as rhetoric, vernacular literature, philosophy, the physical and natural sciences, mathematics, history, theology, and music.[1] Armed with this early training and a higher education, men entered into professions and assumed positions of power denied to women.

Pompadour's road to learning was by necessity slow because of her gender. Her education began at the Ursuline convent at Poissy, where from ages six to nine (1727–30) she learned the rudiments of knowledge.[2] The nuns at Poissy, renowned for their teaching, introduced girls like Jeanne-Antoinette Poisson to the *arts d'agrément* (the arts of pleasing, including drawing, music, and singing), with which girls of the aristocracy and the haute bourgeoisie embellished themselves in order to ensnare a husband of rank and means. Pompadour's convent at Poissy, like all other religious schools in the eighteenth century, was under the sway of Mme de Maintenon's Maison Royale de Saint-Cyr, the religious boarding school founded in 1686 that educated the impecunious daughters of the nobility and army officers. The curriculum at Poissy echoed, with some variations, the class structure and pedagogy of Saint-Cyr. Girls aged five to ten in the beginning "classe rouge" studied reading, writing, arithmetic, grammar, Latin, and religious history. In the next class, the "classe verte," girls up to age fourteen studied music, history (particularly French history), geography, and mythology, while in the "classe jaune," fourteen- to sixteen-year-olds deepened their knowledge of music, singing, dancing, religion, and the French language and took drawing lessons. The eldest, in the "classe bleue," crowned their instruction with more geography, more French language, and history and perfected the *arts d'agrément.*[3]

While her educational experience at Poissy hardly augured her later cultural interests and her persona of learned woman, it did instill in the young, sensitive, and receptive Mlle Poisson a love of learning. It also supplied her with embryonic skills that she amplified in her teens with her Parisian tutors and during her maturity as Mme d'Etioles and as the marquise de Pompadour.

In fact, some facets of a woman's early education à la Saint-Cyr and Poissy can be seen emblematized in Pompadour's savante portraits, homages to Enlightenment female education. That Pompadour was deeply interested in education is clear from the volumes on the subject in her library. Drawing, one of the major *arts d'agrément* at convent schools, is encoded by the pencil holder in most of her portraits. While we are uncertain whether Pompadour had lessons in drawing, either at Poissy or at another stage of her life, we know that around 1750 she learned the art of engraving from Boucher and the engraver Charles-Nicolas Cochin.[4] Engraving is emblematized in her likenesses by the burin and by her portfolio of prints. Geography, another staple of convent curricula, is suggested by the globes in Boucher's Louvre sketch and in La Tour's pastel. Globes such as these were standard elements of any educated woman's library.

Saint-Cyr and Poissy also nurtured the activity that became Pompadour's favorite pastime and the balm of her frenetic life at court: "Next to the pleasure of being with you and my other friends, I know of none greater than reading," the marquise later confided in a missive to her close friend Mme de Lutzelbourg.[5] All of the portraits express Pompadour's love of books and reading by the volumes that she holds or that accompany her.

History, particularly the history of France, was also taught in the convent schools, and although Jeanne-Antoinette was too young to immerse herself in it, she became infatuated with the French monarchy during her girlhood. She later developed this interest by reading voraciously on the subject, either consciously or unconsciously preparing herself for her role as Louis XV's learned companion. Books on the history of France, its kings and its mistresses, fictional and nonfictional, constituted a significant portion of her library.[6] Some of the books in her portraits, notably *La Henriade,* Voltaire's historical epic of Henri IV's reign, signify her devotion to Gallic history.

Having very likely received musical instruction at Poissy and with sophisticated tutoring in music during her teens in Paris, Mlle Poisson blossomed into an accomplished harpsichordist and singer and later, at Versailles, into one of the leading singer-actresses of her day. Not surprisingly, then, her portraits highlight her musical proficiency. She touches her gilt-wood rococo harpsichord in Boucher's Louvre sketch; in La Tour's pastel she fingers a score vaguely notated for an eight-stringed guitar, which together with another score rests on a couch at the left;[7] and in Drouais's canvas, she is attended by her mandolin at the right. Musical sheets for voice are strewn among her effects at the left in Boucher's Munich portrait (Fig. 13).

The embryonic knowledge Pompadour acquired at Poissy was amplified during her teens when she entered the beau monde of Paris. Her pedagogical ciceroni were her mother and Lenormant de Tournehem, who were attuned to Jeanne-Antoinette's sensibility and saw to it that she was trained in the performance arts, traditionally a woman's forte. The mother and the putative father settled for no less than the most distinguished teachers for their lovely, intelligent daughter. They engaged the actor Jean-Baptiste Simon Sauvé Lanoue and the celebrated tragic playwright Prosper Jolyot de Crébillon (Crébillon Père) to nurture Mlle Poisson's elocution and declamation; the seasoned master Guibaudet to teach her dance and deportment; and the illustrious countertenor, composer, and musician Pierre Jélyotte to instruct her on the harpsichord and foster her light, crystalline voice.

Poisson received the musical training typical for girls of the haute bourgeoisie and the aristocracy in the eighteenth century, for whom music was a central educational endowment and the favorite social accomplishment. Because of their excellent education in music, some of these young women became highly accomplished amateurs and professionals who could compete successfully with men. They frequently could play two or more instruments and were instructed on "feminine-gendered instruments" that advantageously displayed the female form and enabled women to parade their elegance and grace.[8] The guitar (popular in the 1750s) in La Tour's pastel and the mandolin (all the rage in the 1760s) in Drouais's tableau refer to Pompadour's two talents, the singing and dancing that these instruments accompanied. The most captivating feminine-gendered instrument was the voice, and Boucher alludes to Pompadour's mellifluous singing by the musical sheet scored for voice that rests among her accouterments at the left of the Munich canvas.

The harpsichord, the queen of the "female" instruments, was the primary vehicle for women in the first half of the eighteenth century. Because of its expense, it was also an icon of distinction. In Boucher's Louvre sketch, surely the fine harpsichord that Pompadour touches, in the manner François Couperin prescribed in *L'Art de toucher le clavesin* (*The Art of Touching the Harpsichord*, 1717), not only blazons the marquise's musical proficiency but also encodes her high rank, her breeding, and her role as a cultivated woman. Boucher's oil sketch highlights, too, her exquisite physical endowments: the glass of fashion and the epitome of youthful beauty and grace, she wears a sumptuous champagne-colored open gown inspired by Rubens or Van Dyck, the slimness of her figure, emphasized by her tightly laced bodice, contrasting with the capacious folds of her dress. Her alluring décolletage, revealing a breast white as porcelain, is topped by her modish lace ruff and piquantly set off by a spray of roses.[9] Together with the signature Pompadour pompon in her hair, the bouquet provides a metaphor for the rosy éclat of her complexion, as the modern Petrarchs would have it. Turning away from her harpsichord while gracefully touching one of its keys with the studied casualness of an aristocratic *honnête femme*, Pompadour gazes outside the portrait, presumably at an invisible source of musical inspiration. In her portraits she is the embodiment of talent, beauty, and elegance; she fashioned herself and was fashioned by Boucher as the worthy companion of the crown. In this regard, here and to a lesser extent in her other savante portraits, Pompadour situates herself squarely in a stellar lineage of noble French consorts who were performers, patrons, and connoisseurs of music. From Marguérite de Valois, through Marie de' Medici and Anne of Austria, to the marquises de Montespan and de Maintenon, wives and mistresses of the French kings distinguished themselves in this arena.[10] Pompadour, as I have noted, knew her Gallic history as well as her music.

Pompadour took all learning seriously. Concurrently with her instruction in the performing arts, she amplified her education by reading extensively in the substantial library of her wealthy, ennobled godfather, Jean-Pâris de Montmartel. Later, when she became Mme d'Etioles, she began amassing her own library. From 1745, when she became the marquise de Pompadour, until her death in 1764, she continued to augment this library, which in 1764 consisted of an astonishing 3,525 volumes. This was an encyclopedic collection that ranged from books on jurisprudence, medicine, science, mathematics, rhetoric, grammar, philosophy, theology, political science, education, and fine arts to her favorite subjects: music, theater, French history, essays, memoirs, novels, and poetry from antiquity to modern times.[11] The library, which is emblematized by the books and the bookcases, together with other trappings of learning in Pompadour's portraits, could only have been assembled by a woman passionately devoted to knowledge.

Pompadour's contemporaries lauded her capacious mind and her erudition. The Parisian diarist and attorney François Barbier, a reliable chronicler of the epoch, declared unequivocally that the twenty-one-year-old "Woman of Etioles . . . had all the education possible" and "an education recherchée." Voltaire himself, in a letter of 1745 to Charles-Jean François Hénault, wrote: "She had read more at her age than any old woman in the country where she is going to reign and where it is proper to wish that she reign. She had read nearly all the good books, save yours; she feared feeling obliged to learn it by heart."[12]

Along with other extraordinary women of the age, several of whom will be treated in this study, Pompadour overcame—through intelligence, ambition, and tenacity—a major impediment, the predominant patriarchal view of a woman's limited mental capacity.[13] This jaundiced attitude was ubiquitous: it infiltrated the flagrantly insufficient curricula of convents; it manifested itself in the barring of women from all institutions of higher learning; and it thus thwarted women from entering the professions and playing a meaningful part in public life. "But of all studies, the most necessary and the most natural to women is the study of men," wrote the self-described "feminist" Boudier de Villemert, author of the ironically titled *Nouvel Ami des femmes* (*The New Friend of Women*, 1779),[14] concealing the tacit goal of the male ruling class during Pompadour's time: the disempowerment and marginalization of the second sex that kept women in their place as delightful but ineffectual embellishments of men.

But the fortunate few, like Pompadour, who managed to learn were buttressed not only by their unflappability but also by advantageous circumstances—class, privilege, means, familial and societal connections. These gave them opportunities to be tutored by qualified masters, leisure to amplify their knowledge through reading, and entrance to the network of the intellectual salon—all of which helped them to complete their education. These privileged women, Pompadour among them, were regarded as exceptions to the rule of female inferiority.

Education, the only way to redress the injustices perpetrated against women, was the subject of debate in Enlightenment intellectual salons and a central theme in the writings of almost all authors, male and female.[15] Among these writings were tracts belonging to the Women's Quarrel, a literary and sociocultural discourse that was codified in the Renaissance, gained momentum in the seventeenth century, and persisted with force during Pompadour's time. The Quarrel concerned the relative merits or blemishes of the sexes, whether women should be educated and, if so, what the extent of their training should be.[16] By the time Pompadour's savante portraits were fashioned, the liberal participants in the Quarrel argued that a woman had a right to untrammeled learning. In Pompadour's library were volumes devoted to the discourse, and under her protection were philosophes who composed some of the Quarrel texts.[17] Pompadour's learned woman portraits were conceived and executed at the most vociferous moment of the *querelle*, and the portraits themselves quietly participate in the debate.

The Women's Quarrel resounded within Pompadour's own coterie. Surely she knew the article "Des Femmes," written around 1745 by her great friend and counselor the abbé de Bernis, who at this time was by her side on her estate at Etioles and then at Versailles when she became Louis XV's titular mistress.[18] Bernis muses:

> I have also heard posed the question of the superiority of men over women. When one has considered well on it, I imagine that one must think that the superiority of men is based only on the force of their organs and a better education. . . . The force of the body had to give men real superiority, which is that of domination. They have been the masters they have been obliged to

be: the strong always subdues the weak. . . . If to this physical advantage one joins that of a more enlightened and more extensive education, one will easily understand that men, superior in force, must be superior in knowledge.[19]

But Bernis, while understanding and sympathizing with the dilemma of women, unfortunately offers no recipe for changing their situation; as a man, he accepts the status quo.

Many of the philosophes who championed unfettered intellectual inquiry, often with the approbation and protection of Mme de Pompadour, embraced the feminist cause, defending a woman's right to an encyclopedic education and her freedom to enter and participate in the professions.[20]

D'Alembert, a coeditor of the *Encyclopédie*, the fourth volume of which is placed prominently on Pompadour's console table in La Tour's pastel, took up the issue, indignantly reproaching Rousseau for his inveterate misogyny and censuring "the slavery and the kind of degradation into which we have plunged women, the shackles that we place on their mind and soul . . . [and] finally the disastrous, I would say almost murderous, education, which we prescribe for them without permitting them to have another."[21] In 1756, the year of Boucher's Munich portrait of the marquise, the journalist and literary critic Baron Grimm, a habitué of Pompadour's salon, joined forces with d'Alembert against the incorrigible Rousseau by asserting: "All that can be said further against women is equally destitute of reason and philosophy; all the defects with which they are reproached are the work of man, of society, and of an ill-regulated education."[22] The sensationalist epistemologist Helvétius, who gathered with other radical thinkers at Versailles under the oblique patronage of Pompadour and who believed in the omnipotence of education, opined that since men and women were born without ideas, the contents of their minds could be ascribed only to education; if both sexes were given an equal education, the results would be identical.[23]

But Montesquieu, whose *De l'Esprit des Lois* is highlighted as one of Pompadour's favorite books in La Tour's pastel, spoke most eloquently on the subject. In the *Persian Letters*, the 1730 edition of which Pompadour owned, Montesquieu arms women with their most potent weapon in their battle against the tyrannical force of men: beauty, their natural superiority; if their fairness were enhanced by a worthy education, women would be empowered and would neutralize the oppressive hegemony of men.[24] These attributes of beauty and education define the Enlightenment exemplar of womanhood: the belle savante.

This liberal strain of the Quarrel had been inaugurated by Poullain de La Barre (1647–1723), arguably the most revolutionary feminist of all time. In his groundbreaking treatise, *De l'Egalité des deux Sexes* (*The Equality of the Two Sexes*, 1673 and

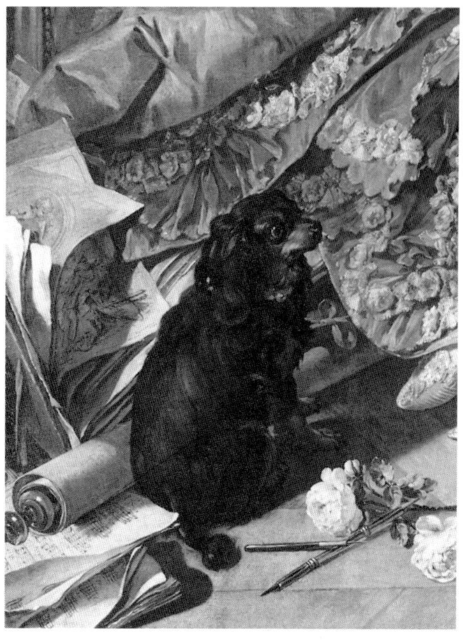

FIGURE 13.
François Boucher, *Portrait of Mme de Pompadour* (detail), 1756. Munich, Alte Pinakothek (photo: Bayerische Staatsgemäldesammlungen).

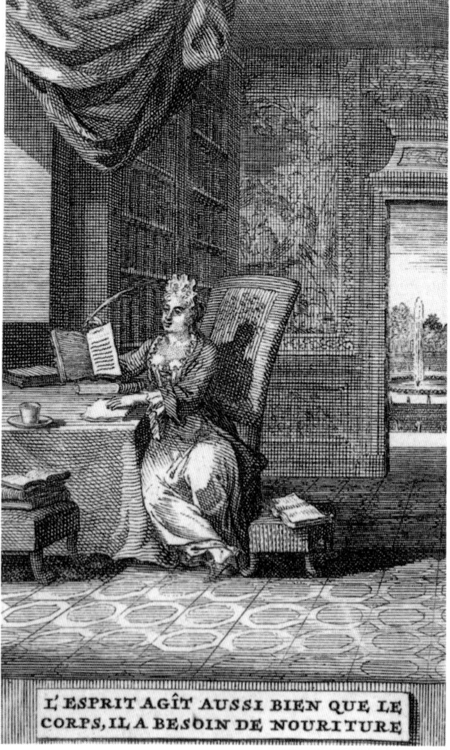

FIGURE 14.
Anonymous, *Frontispiece to Les Femmes sçavantes*, 1718. Cincinnati, Langsam Library, University of Cincinnati.

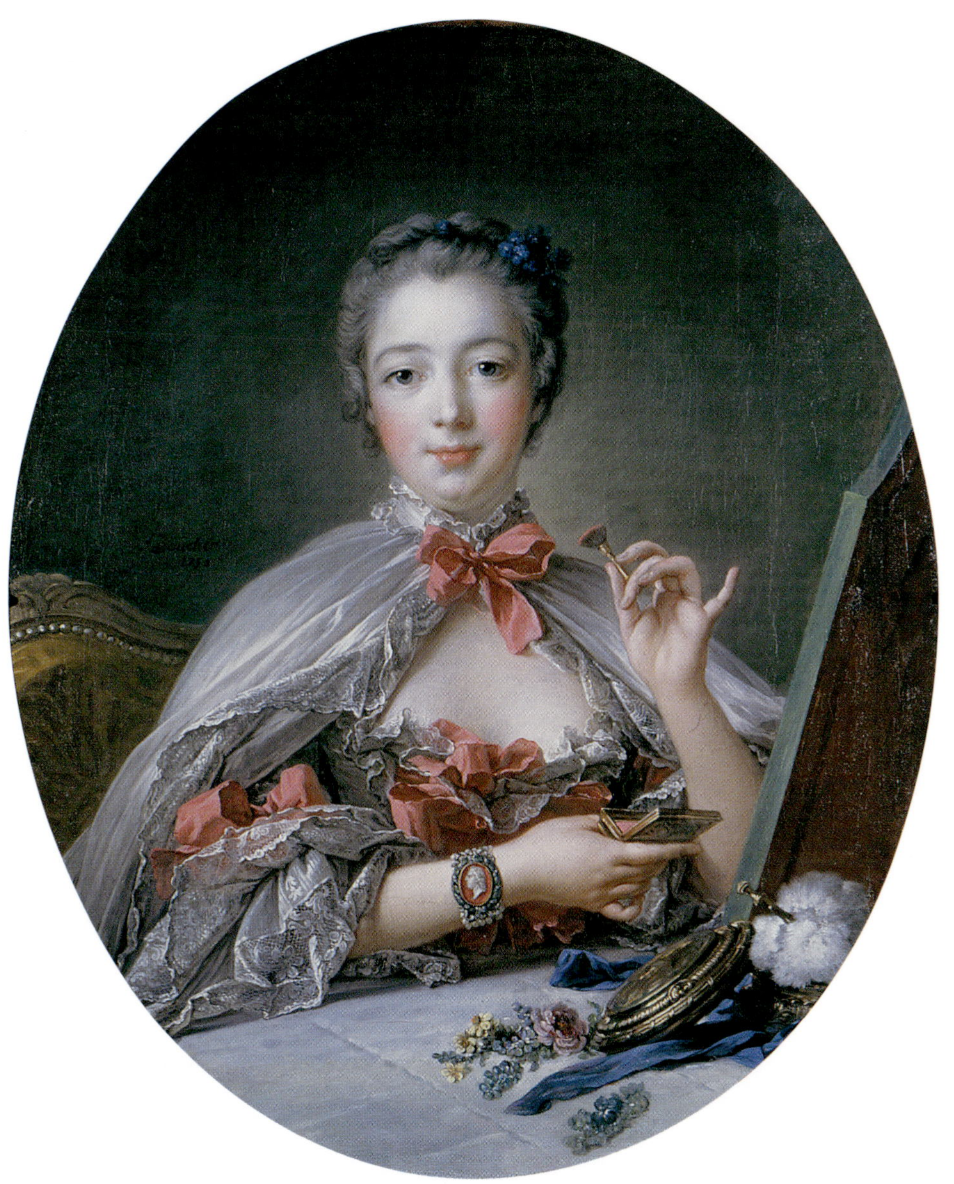

PLATE 1.
François Boucher, *Portrait of Mme de Pompadour at Her Toilette*, 1758. Courtesy of the Fogg Art Museum, Harvard University Art Museums, Bequest of Charles E. Dunlap.

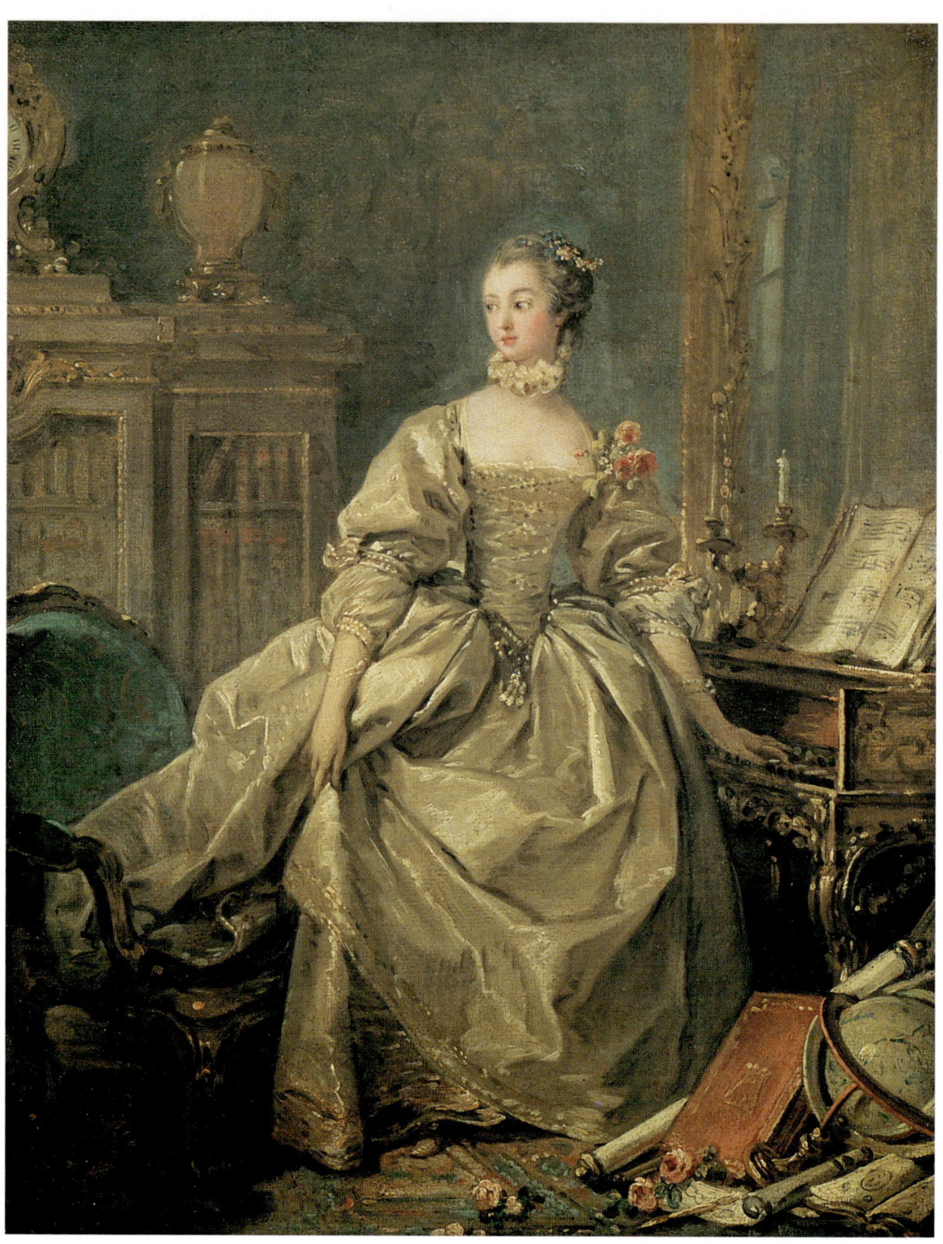

PLATE 2.
François Boucher, *Portrait of Mme de Pompadour*, 1750. Paris, Musée du Louvre (photo: RMN-Arnaudet).

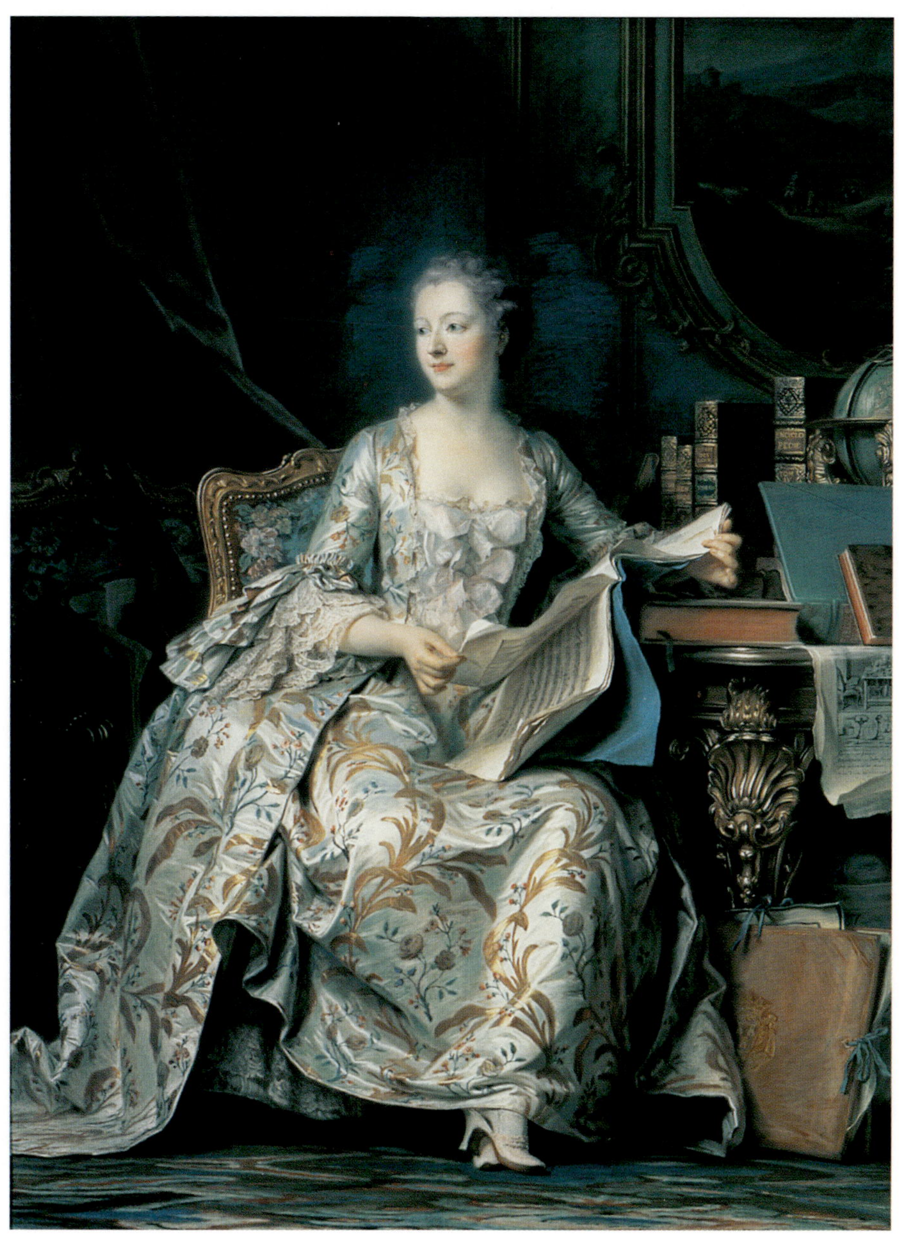

PLATE 3.
Maurice-Quentin de La Tour, *Portrait of Mme de Pompadour*, 1755. Paris, Musée du Louvre (photo: RMN-Gérard Blot).

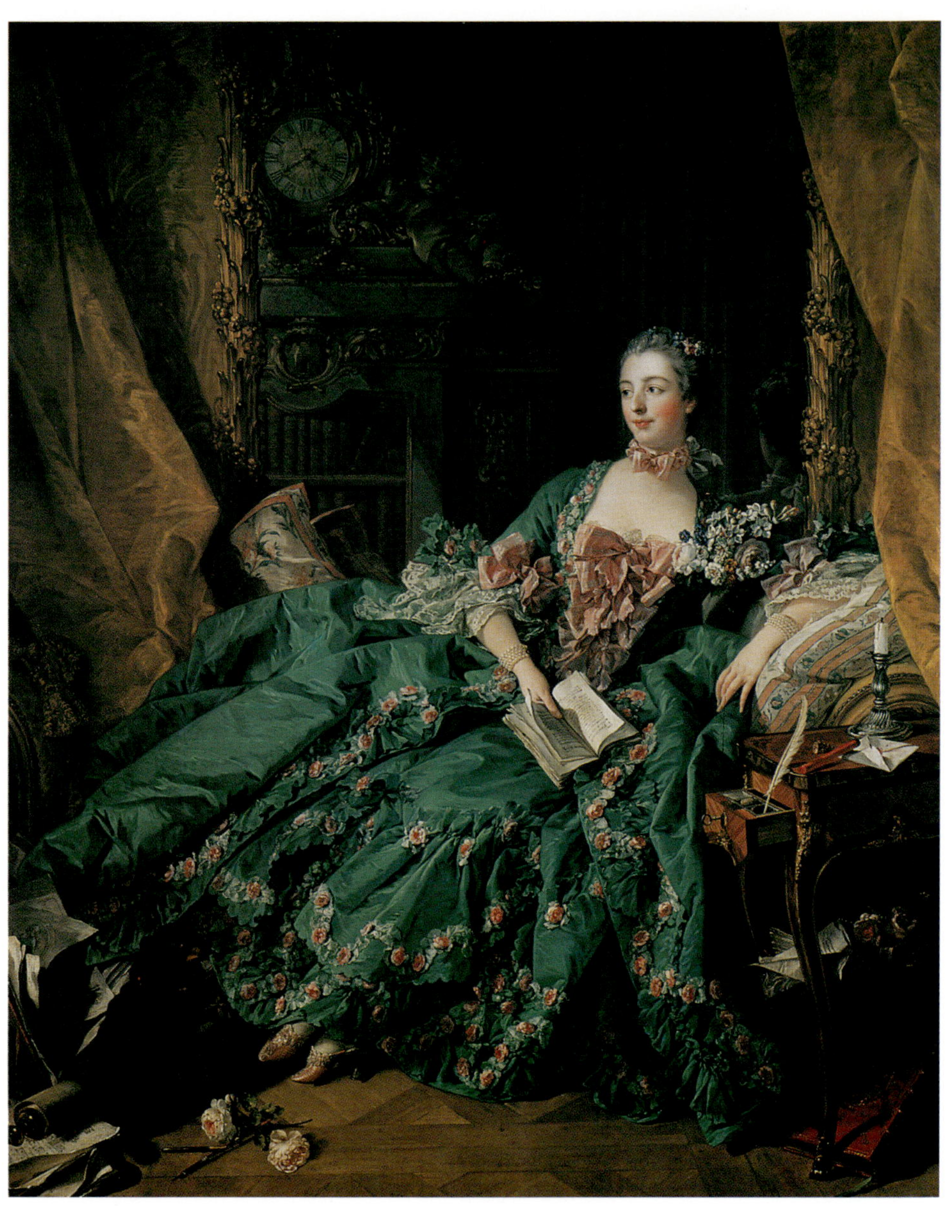

PLATE 4.
François Boucher, *Portrait of Mme de Pompadour*, 1756. Munich, Alte Pinakothek (photo: Kunstdia-Archiv ARTOTHEK, D-Peissenberg).

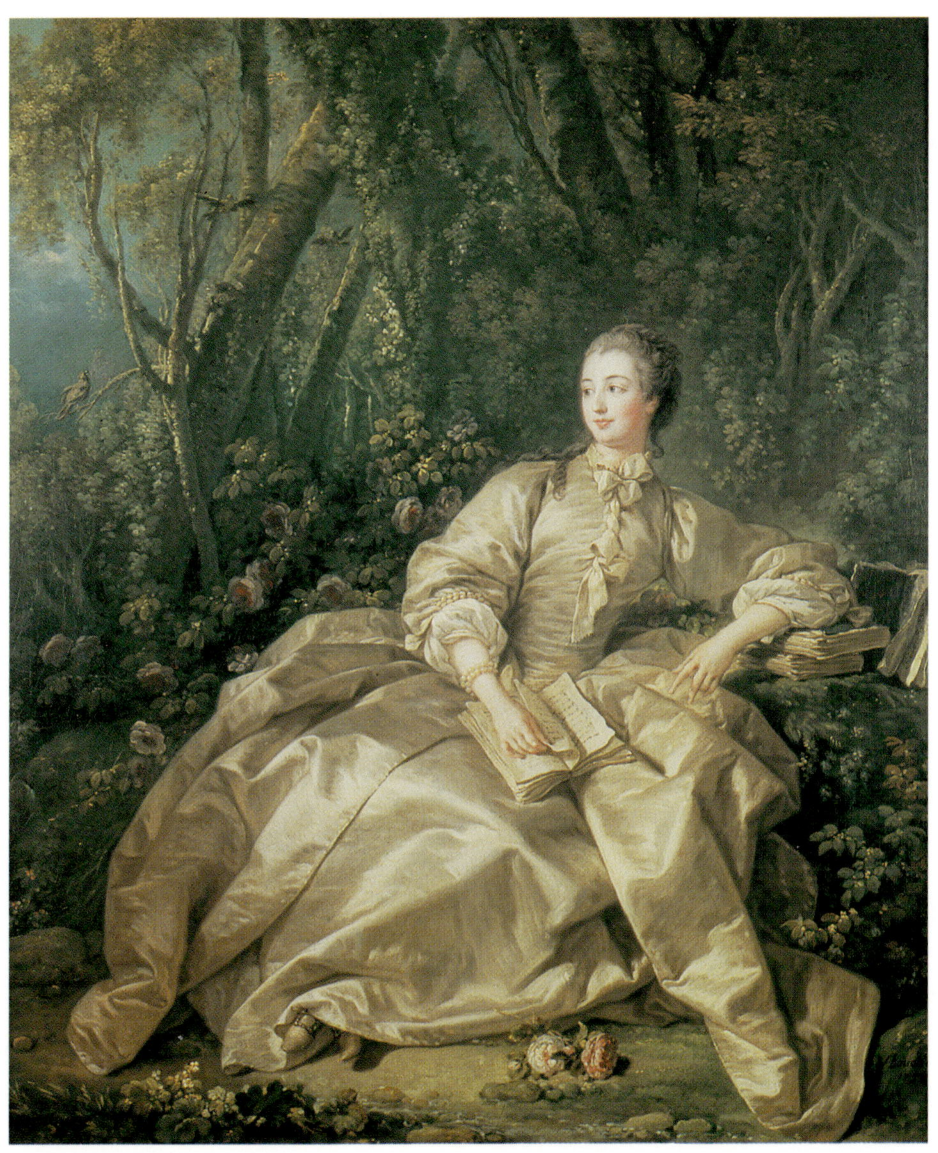

PLATE 5.
François Boucher, *Portrait of Mme de Pompadour*, 1758. London, The Victoria and Albert Museum (photo: V&A Picture Library).

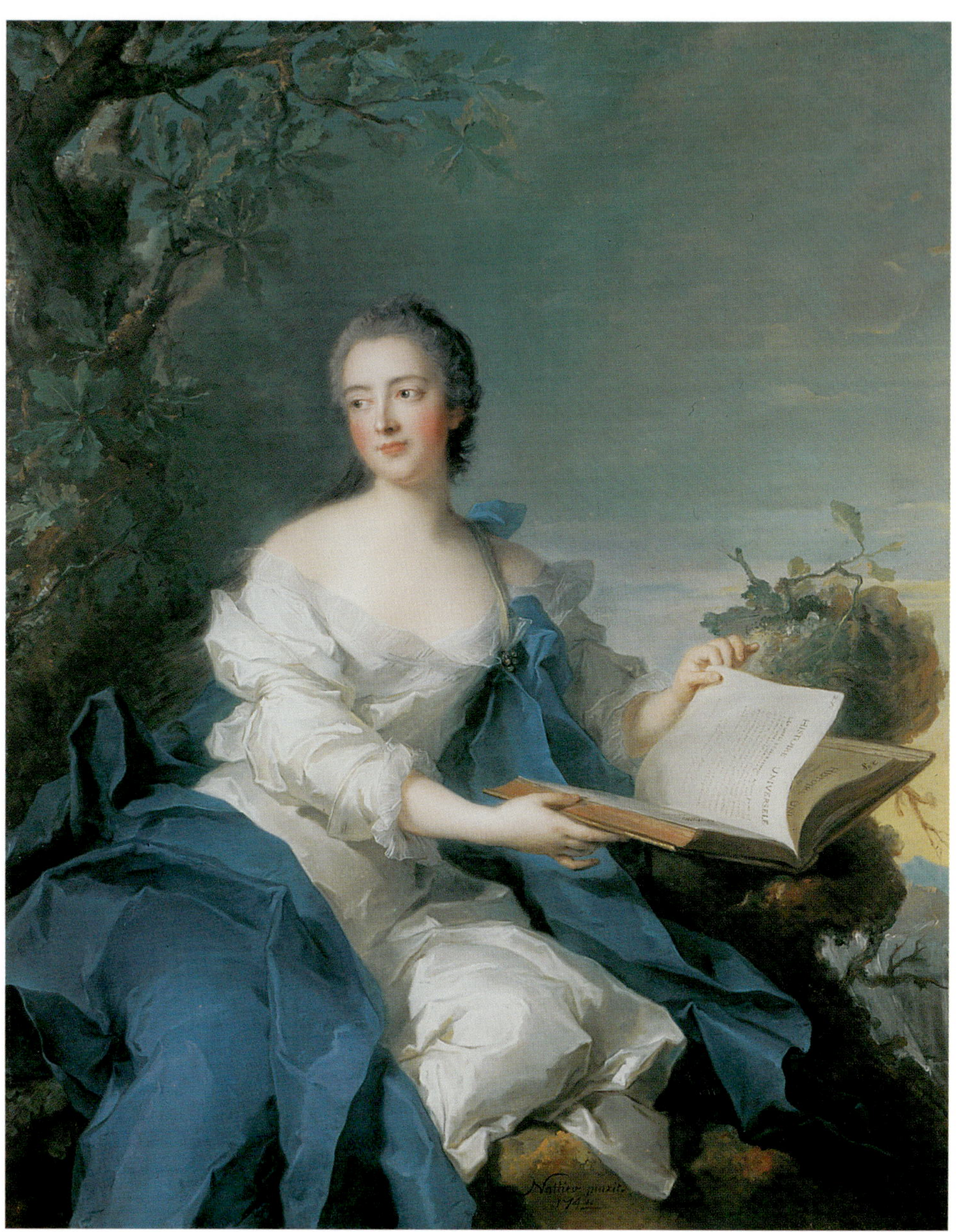

PLATE 6.
Jean-Marc Nattier, *Portrait of the Princesse de Rohan Holding a Book*, 1741. The Toledo Museum of Art, gift of Edward Drummond Libbey.

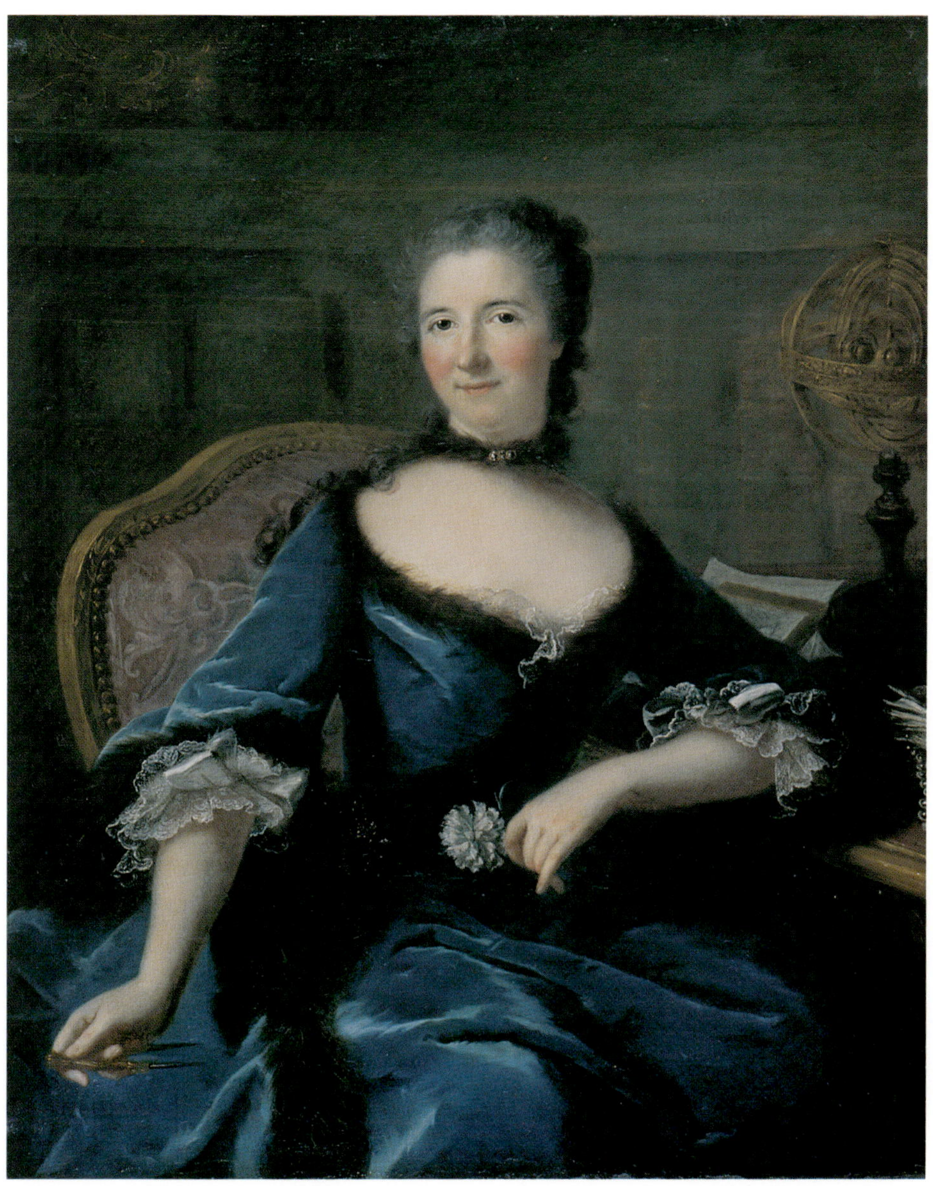

PLATE 7.
Marianne Loir, *Portrait of the Marquise du Châtelet*, ca. 1745–49. Bordeaux, Musée des Beaux-Arts.

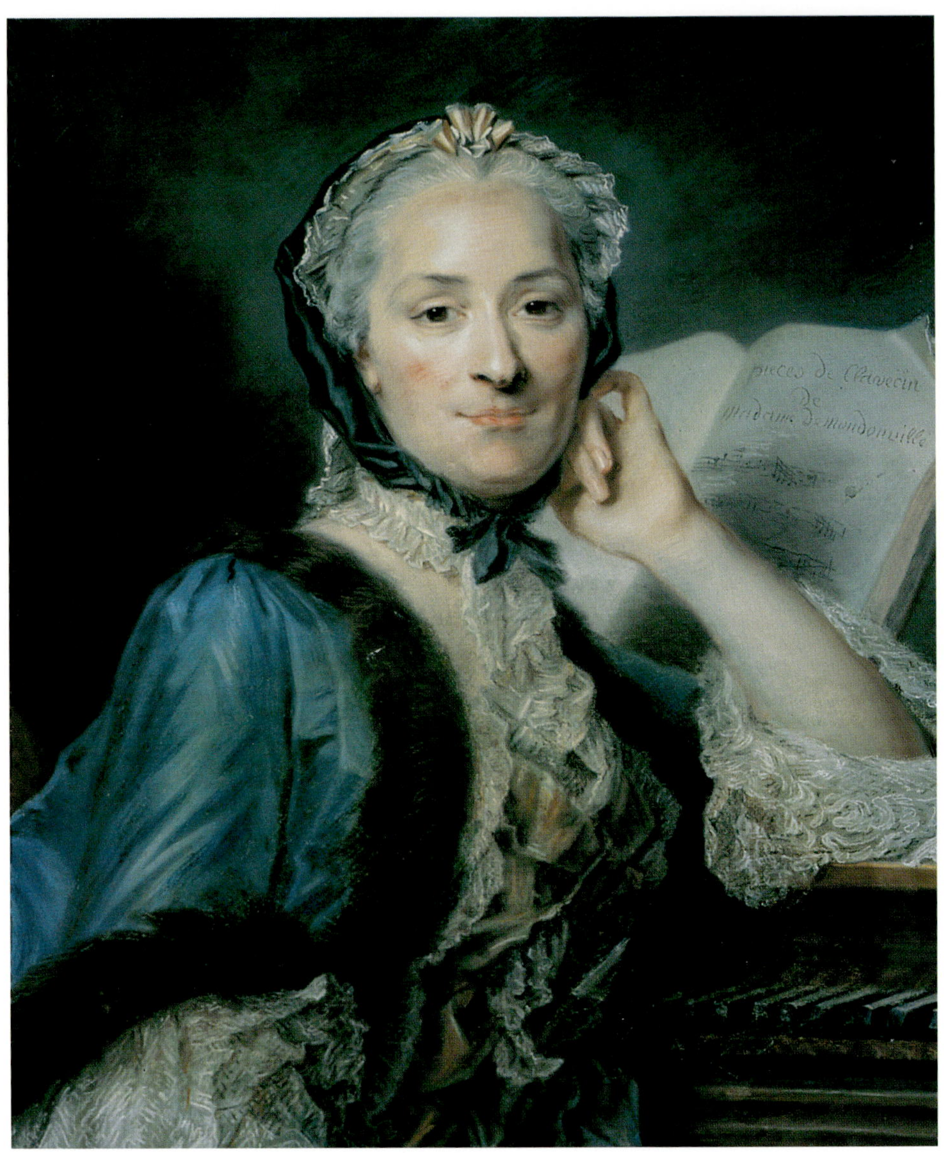

PLATE 8.
Maurice-Quentin de La Tour, *Portrait of Anne-Jeanne Boucon, Mme de Mondonville*, 1753. The Saint Louis Art Museum.

many subsequent editions), he proclaims the unthinkable notion that "the mind has no sex." Denouncing the idea of women's innate inferiority as a fiction issuing from mere custom and casual observation, Poullain audaciously argues that any faults women are accused of either are imagined or derive entirely from the education they are given. Poullain asserts: "Considering the two sexes in general, we recognize that one has as much aptitude as the other . . . [and] that women, considered according to the principles of sound philosophy, are as capable as men of all kinds of knowledge." He repudiates any exclusion of women from the sphere of the intellectual and promotes their unfettered application to learning and their entry into all of the professions. *De l'Egalité des deux Sexes* was written not by a contemporary feminist but by a Cartesian working during the most repressively patriarchal period of the ancien régime, the reign of Louis XIV.[25]

Having concluded that a poor education is the principal cause of the weak position of women, Poullain published, in 1674, *De l'Education des dames* (*Of the Education of Women*), the logical sequel to *De l'Egalité des deux Sexes.* He proposes an egalitarian and encyclopedic program of study that would raise women up to the intellectual level of men. Poullain argues that women should be permitted to learn everything and provides them with a Cartesian method to cultivate a critical mind. Armed with these resources, women would become free to control their own destinies.[26]

Poullain's revolutionary ideas on education spawned other volumes that expanded and detailed the pedagogical program he outlined. The most comprehensive was *Les Femmes sçavantes* (*The Learned Women, or the Women's Library, which Treats the Fields of Learning that Suit Women, the Conduct of their Studies, the Books that They are Able to Read, and the History of Those Who have Excelled in the Sciences*, 1718), by "Monsieur N.C." In this ambitious, sympathetic, and respectful guide, we learn that Sorbonne-quality education begins in early childhood. Between the ages of three and seven, a girl should not only learn to read and write but also study several languages. At age ten or twelve, she should devote herself to grammar and arithmetic, and at fifteen, after she has mastered the basics, she is enjoined to apply herself to rhetoric, poetry, philosophy, theology, and much more.[27]

The comprehensive library prescribed by the author of *Les Femmes sçavantes*—dictionaries, prints, poetry, drama, history, and books on science, rhetoric, geography, music, and painting—is strikingly similar to Mme de Pompadour's. One is tempted to think that Pompadour had *Les Femmes sçavantes* in hand when forming her collection. She would have been struck by its counsel to an educated woman to combine her reading with meditation.[28] She also would have noticed its frontispiece (Fig. 14)—admittedly banal, as frontispieces usually are—which pictures a fashionably clad savante in her study, presumably reflecting on a book culled from the library behind her. Prosaic as it is, the engraving nevertheless anticipates by a number of years the visual poetics of Boucher's Munich and Victoria and Albert portraits, whose principal theme is Pompadour's self-proclaimed indulgence in "philosophical reflections." As Pompadour herself put it, she was born "réfléchissante."[29]

Advocates of the belle savante reasoned that a woman has an intellectual advantage because she is blessed at birth with cold and moist humors, which facilitate learning. The theory of the humors, which traces back through Renaissance to medieval physiology, reasoned that a person's character and health were determined by the configuration of the four fluids in the body: blood, phlegm, choler, and black bile; accordingly, one's disposition might be sanguine, phlegmatic, choleric, or melancholy.[30] This seemingly anachronistic theory, ubiquitous in the Women's Quarrel, is promulgated by C. M. D. Noël in *Le Triomphe des femmes* (*The Triumph of Women, Where it is Shown by Many and Powerful Reasons, that the Female Sex is More Noble and More Perfect than the Male*, 1698). Noël concurs with Poullain's enlightened ideas regarding women's education and goes beyond them. Women's moist, humid complexion, he says, "is the property of memory, and it is in the memory that all our learning is stamped and preserved; it is therefore accurate to say that humid people have a greater disposition to the sciences." In the eighteenth century, "les sciences" meant learning. According to Noël, women are quicker, as well as more brilliant, cerebral, and reasonable than men, because women's aqueous constitution disengages them from matter, which weighs down and stultifies men.[31]

Some of the most compelling and persuasive discourses in the Quarrel were written by representatives of the gender that had the greatest stake in the outcome. In 1719 an anonymous woman wrote, "for the defense and justification of [her] sex," *Le Triomphe du beau-sexe sur les hommes* (*The Triumph of the Fair Sex Over Men, in Which One Shows the Advantages and Prerogatives that Render Women Superior to Men, by Incontestable Proofs*). This feminist inveighs against those who have disempowered her gender: "The envy and slander of men toward women have often made them try to usurp from our sex the loftiest qualities that belong to it, among which are those of judgment, penetration, speaking well, and writing delicately, even with soundness." She responds to men who accuse learned women of coquetry: "Surely it is not reading good books, nor application to learning that makes coquettes. . . . [I]n every era there have been femmes savantes, of a superior mind, and our sex has all the requisite qualities to be able to keep apace, at the very least, with men of merit, in the career of studying *belles lettres*." After detailing the indignities visited upon women and the obstacles that they encounter on their road to knowledge, the author concludes that "it is surprising that one is able to find a single fille or femme savante."[32]

In 1750, the year of the genesis of Boucher's first portrait of Pompadour, two important defenses of womankind written by women appeared in print: Mlle Archambault's *Dissertation sur la question, lequel de l'homme ou de la femme est plus capable de constance? Ou la cause des dames* (*Dissertation on the Question Whether Man or Woman Is More Capable of Perseverance; or, the Cause of Women*)[33] and Mme de

Puisieux's *La Femme n'est pas inférieure à l'homme* (*Woman Is Not Inferior to Man*),[34] reprinted in 1751 as *Le Triomphe des dames* (*The Triumph of Women*). Puisieux's incendiary manifesto, safely cloaked in her husband's identity, was influenced by Poullain de La Barre. After echoing Poullain's maxim that the mind has no sex and his assertion of "a perfect equality between the two sexes," Puisieux takes up the cause of highly qualified but jobless academics:

> Why has not one seen women, why do they still not see women who deserve to have a place among savants, and who are more capable of teaching the sciences [knowledge] than those who presently fill most of the chairs at universities? The century in which we live has produced as many of them as any other up to the present, their modesty preventing them from parading it publicly.[35]

In conservative circles during the Age of Enlightenment, "the indecency of knowledge"[36] discouraged women of intellectual aspirations. In the mid–seventeenth century, Madeleine de Scudéry, the most illustrious femme savante of her time, had admonished women of the intellectual salons to dissemble their learning, for an overt display of erudition violated the decorum and modesty expected of the demure sex. Later in the century, the repressive cleric and pedagogue Fénelon gave the warning a moral dimension, charging women who lusted after knowledge with outright indecency. Both Puisieux and the female author of *Le Triomphe du beau-sexe sur les hommes* responded to this entrenched, repressive view of intelligent women.

They do so with Poullain's *De l'Education des dames* in hand. Subverting the cultural construct of female modesty and reserve, Poullain declares: "There is, in my opinion, nothing more pernicious than false humility. . . . Observe all, look at all and listen to all without scruple. Examine all, judge all, reason above all. . . . You have a mind; use it, and sacrifice it blindly to no one."[37] Thanks to Poullain and his eighteenth-century disciples, becoming a learned woman no longer meant suffering the frustration of taciturnity or the accusation of lasciviousness.

Because of her allegedly cold and moist humor, the femme savante ideal came to be generally defined, not only in the tracts but also in belles lettres and fashionable society, by such modish epithets as "fine," "graceful," "delicate," "lively," "imaginative," "subtle," "penetrating," and "reflective." For example, Graillard de Graville, the author of *L'Ami des filles* (*The Friend of Girls*), a tract that Pompadour owned and presumably read, asserted that the fair sex "has naturally a finer, livelier, more penetrating, I dare say more reflective mind than ours." These qualities, according to Graillard, characterize a being of perfect beauty and reason devoted to the arts and sciences and uniting the attractions of the Graces and the charms of the Muses.[38]

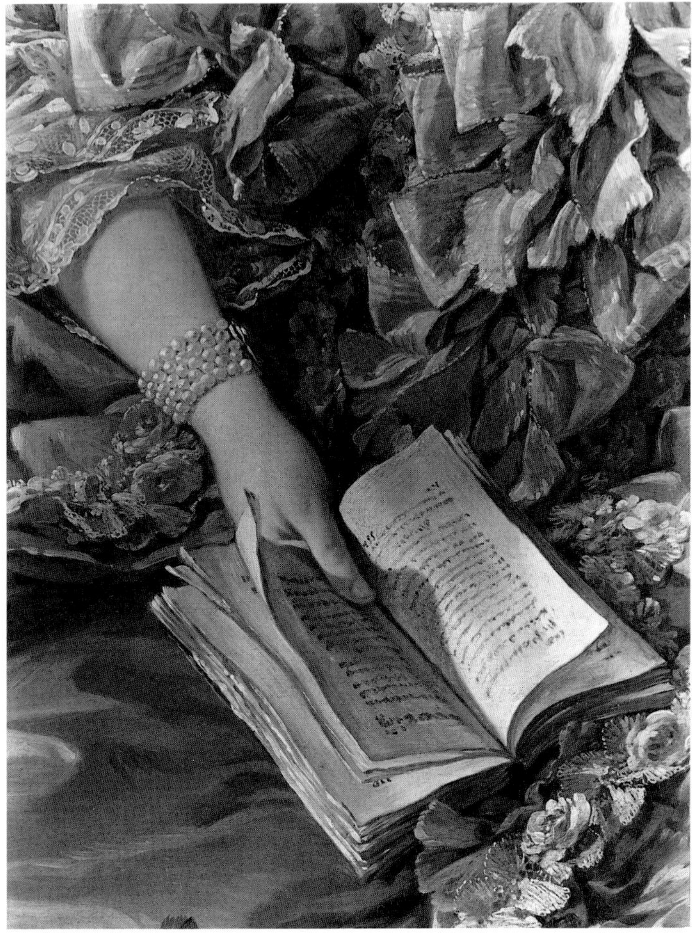

FIGURE 15.
François Boucher, *Portrait of Mme de Pompadour* (detail), 1756. Munich, Alte Pinakothek (photo: Bayerische Staatsgemäldesammlungen).

In Dom Caffiaux's voluminous treatise, *Défenses du beau sexe* (*Defenses of the Fair Sex*, 1753), these feminine epithets abound and describe an educated woman who is quintessentially French. For Caffiaux, the savante not only excels in all fields of knowledge but also dresses her erudition "à la françois," that is, with "an air of liberty and ease."[39] The Gallic femme savante is thus the apogee of all knowledge and reason, all refinement, all beauty and grace, a woman never seen in any culture or any century prior to the Enlightenment.

This ideal, embraced by the champions of women, is what guided La Tour and Boucher, the "Painter of the Graces," in constructing Pompadour's pictorial persona. Pompadour gracefully touches her harpsichord, looking off to the left with a lively visage, delicately fingers a musical score or a page in a book, or finely couches a volume in her lap (Fig. 15), reflecting on its contents. Her humid complexion and "exquisite organs" (à la Mme de Puisieux) have generated her tall, attenuated figure, delicate features, and ethereal beauty. In all of her portraits, Pompadour dresses "à la françois," particularly in Boucher's Munich tableau, in which she is garbed in her *robe à la françoise,* a gown of green silk taffeta decorated with lace and pink rose garlands, its bodice embellished with a row of ribbon bows of pink and silver striped silk.[40]

A perfect beauty who unites the attractions of the Graces and the charms of the Muses, Pompadour presides over the arts and sciences, over France's culture, with the Gallic femme savante's distinctive air of liberty and ease. A person of great achievement, she personifies the Enlightenment. In her portraits, she presents herself as the learned woman par excellence, unabashedly parading her erudition and accomplishments.

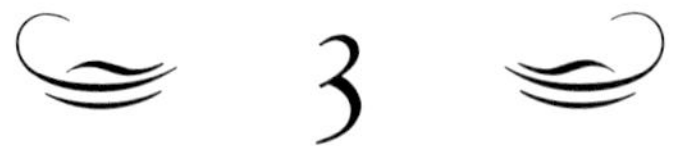

THE NEW MONTESPAN / THE NEW MAINTENON

Issuing from a long-standing literary and sociocultural discourse, the concept of the femme savante informing Pompadour's portraits was first embodied, during the reign of Louis XIV, in numerous fashion plates—*gravures de mode*—depicting women of leisure and class engaged in intellectual activities. Among the earliest prototypes are the engravings paying tribute to Mme de Montespan and Mme de Maintenon, the consorts of Louis XIV and Pompadour's predecessors in courtly and cultural pursuits. Another set of savante representations belongs to a fertile strain of engraved encomia to France's most illustrious learned women, intellectuals who enriched their country's cultural legacy. At first glance, these divergent traditions of engravings, along with painted portraits of educated women, which I will discuss in chapter 4, would seem to conflict: the fashion plates privileging the allure of talented women, the engravings and paintings of intellectual women foregrounding their erudition, sometimes at the expense of their comeliness. But these ostensibly opposing strains coalesce harmoniously in Pompadour's portraits to shape the ideal belle savante, as the eighteenth century understood her—and demanded of her. Surprisingly, most of the prints treated in this chapter are hitherto unpublished, and none has been discussed in connection with Pompadour's likenesses.

Boucher and Pompadour found inspiration in these precedent engravings. Engravers themselves, they were familiar with the print market on which they drew for Boucher's *Portrait of the Marquise at Her Toilette* (see Plate 1).[1] Pompadour's images were the apogee of an already solidly established and influential visual and iconographic tradition. In life, Pompadour reinvented herself in the image of Montespan and Maintenon. In art, she and her portraitists created her persona out of the pictorial conventions of the femme savante.

Pompadour's personae as reader, writer, and musician were anticipated generally in late seventeenth- and early eighteenth-century fashion plates, engravings depict-

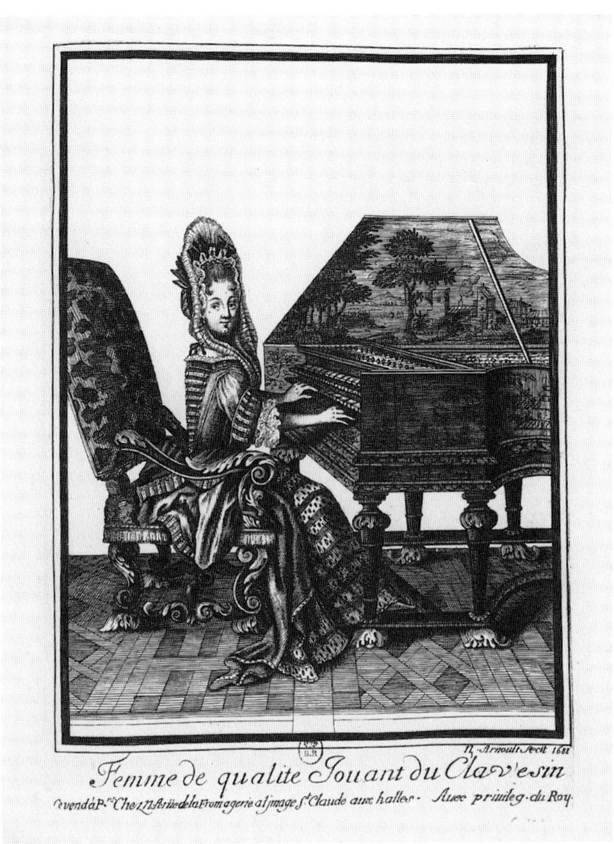

FIGURE 16.
Nicolas Arnoult, *Femme de qualité Jouant du Clav'esin*, 1688. Paris, Bibliothèque Nationale, Département des Estampes.

ing the fashions and diversions of the upper classes during the later reign of Louis XIV. In these prints, the ideal savante is an amalgam of learning and glamour.

Nicolas Arnoult's *Femme de qualité Jouant du Clav'esin* (*Woman of Quality Playing Her Harpsichord*, 1688; Fig. 16) reflects the importance of music in the education of upper-class women of the period.[2] While this modish keyboardist is obviously proficient enough to master her two-manual harpsichord, her mind is not completely on her work; she is as interested in presenting herself as a fashion plate to the beholder as she is in touching the notes of what may be the latest Lully sonata. She is the site where elegance and talent converge.

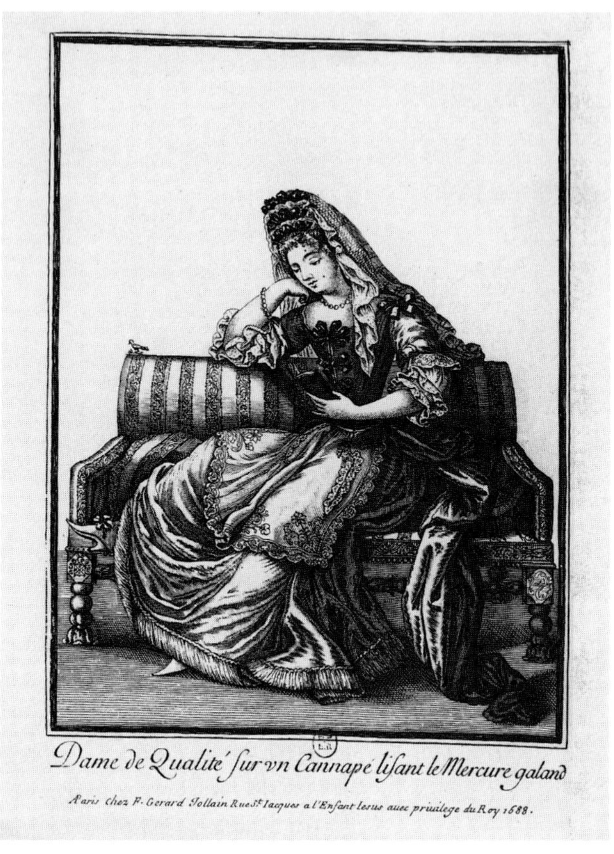

FIGURE 17.
François-Gérard Jollain, *Dame de Qualité sur vn Cannapé lisant le Mercure galand*, 1688. Paris, Bibliothèque Nationale, Département des Estampes.

The sheer profusion of portrayals of accomplished and learned women in the fashion plates not only establishes an iconography that prefigures Pompadour's savante likenesses but also documents the ferment of feminism in the seventeenth century, a movement that animated defenders of women's intellectual parity in the Women's Quarrel and introduced them into salons as arbiters of culture.[3] The subject of François-Gérard Jollain's *Dame de Qualité sur vn Cannapé lisant le Mercure galand* (*Woman of Quality on a Couch Reading the Mercure Galant,* 1688; Fig. 17)

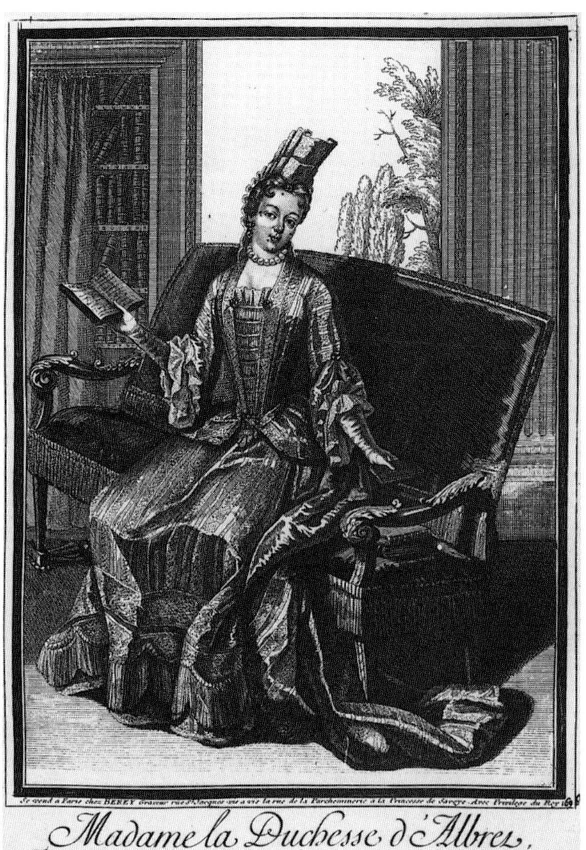

FIGURE 18.
Claude-Auguste Berey, *Portrait of Madame la Duchesse d'Albres,* 1690. Paris, Bibliothèque Nationale, Département des Estampes.

is one of the few studious women in these prints who actually concentrates on her reading; yet her bookishness is feminized by her elaborate dress, her modish hairdo à la Fontanges, and her fashionably nonchalant posture. Her bejeweled right arm postures the thinker, and the long, delicate fingers of her left hand steady her copy of *Le Mercure Galant,* a popular periodical that published literary and scientific works meant to appeal to a female readership, which was expanding as a result of feminist agitation. Mme de Pompadour possessed a complete set of *Le Mercure Galant.*[4]

Among the innumerable engravings of cultivated women are progenitors of Pompadour's portraits. For example, Claude-Auguste Berey's *Madame la Duchesse d'Albres,* an engraved likeness of the leading *précieuse salonnière* (1690; Fig. 18),[5] foreshadows Boucher's *Portrait of Mme de Pompadour* in Munich (see Plate 4): an

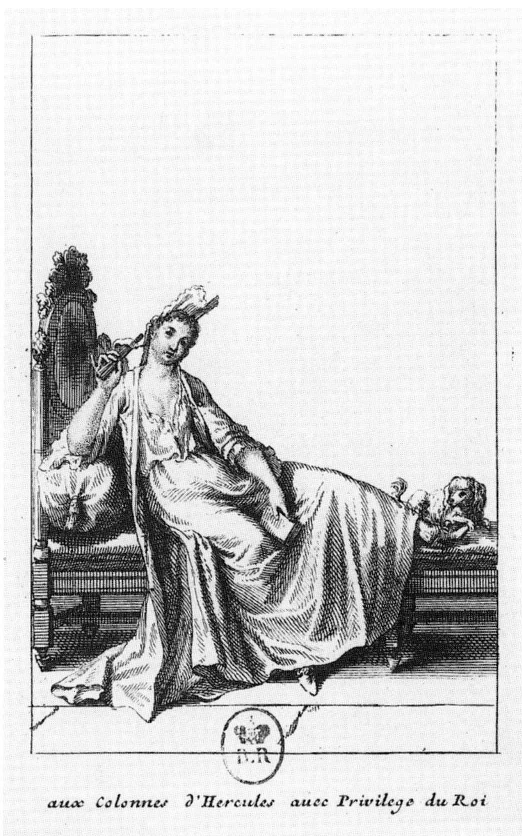

FIGURE 19.
Jean Mariette, *A Modish Reader en négligée*, late seventeenth or early eighteenth century. Paris, Bibliothèque Nationale, Département des Estampes.

opulently garbed, beautiful bibliophile on a couch, holding an open volume that presumably has been culled from the ample library behind her. Erudite as these women are, however, they display rather than peruse their books: the distance from their volumes subtly undermines their seriousness and underscores their feminine allure.

Admittedly somewhat prosaic, an engraving of a modish reader in informal dress (Fig. 19) by Jean Mariette (1660–1742) nevertheless sketches the rudiments that Boucher will later amplify and embellish in the Munich portrait of Pompadour: a self-consciously comely women recumbent on a daybed, one arm propped by a pillow, the other languidly drooped across her body, a book in her hand.[6] These learners are quiescent rather than intense, and as such they conform to the current patriarchal construct of the savante: self-possessed, à la mode, and always beautiful. Each beauty is accompanied by her pet spaniel, in Pompadour's portrait probably

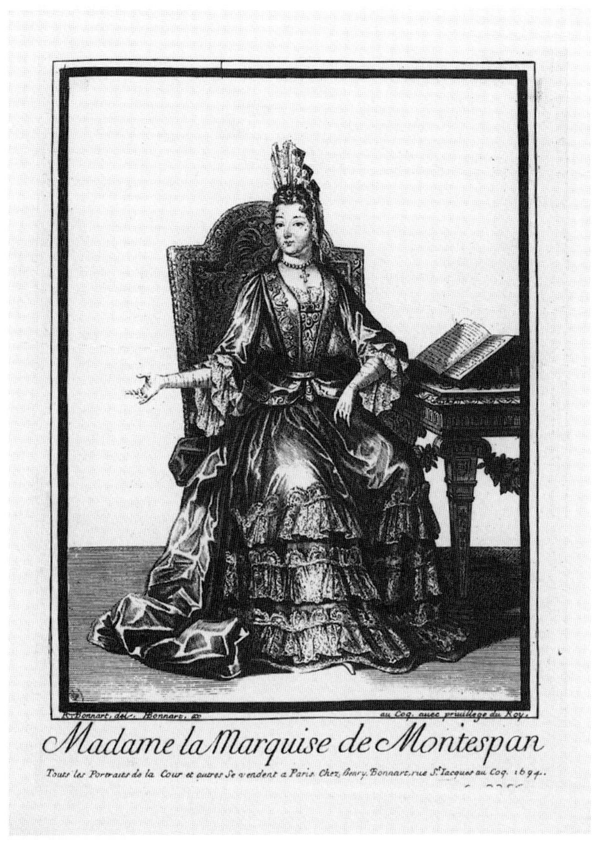

FIGURE 20.
Robert and Henri Bonnart, *Portrait of Mme de Montespan*, 1694. Paris, Bibliothèque Nationale, Département des Estampes.

the ever-constant Inès, who also guards her in Boucher's picture in the Wallace Collection (see Fig. 5).

The fashion plates, not surprisingly, also honor two of the most celebrated intellectual women of the era: Mme de Montespan and Mme de Maintenon, the educated, accomplished, and influential consorts of Louis XIV. The engravers Robert and Henri Bonnart portray the anachronistically glamorous Montespan (she was in her mid-fifties in 1694) as a fashionable reader who has just turned away from her volumes to confront the beholder (1694; Fig. 20).[7] Maintenon appears as a more serious reader in two prints by Antoine Trouvain: in the first (1695; Fig. 21), the restrained, pious intellectual is caught either turning a page or displaying her book to the viewer as a sign of her studious preoccupation and her quality of mind; the second (1705; Fig. 22),[8] which echoes Berey's image of Maintenon's fellow *salonnière*, la duchesse d'Albres, features the mistress-turned-wife

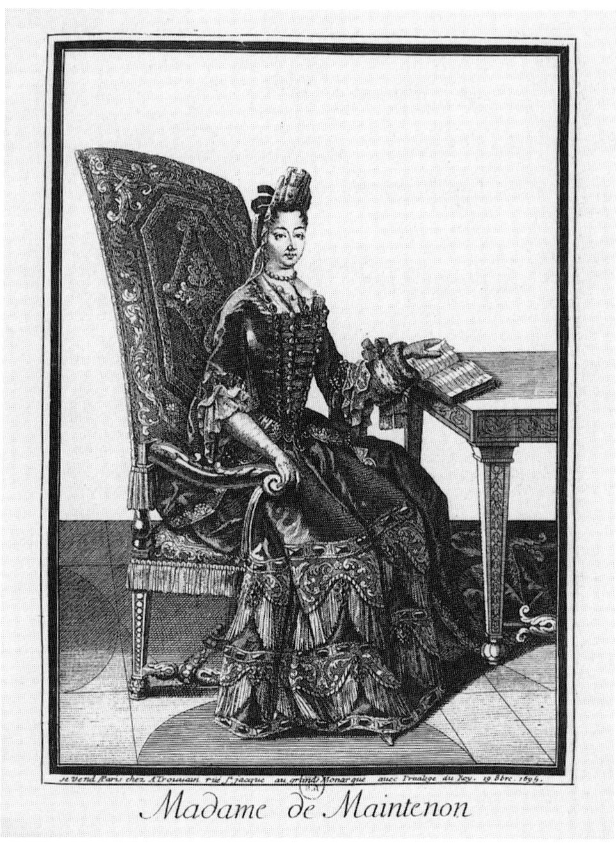

FIGURE 21.
Antoine Trouvain, *Portrait of Mme de Maintenon*, 1695. Paris, Bibliothèque Nationale, Département des Estampes.

of Louis XIV holding (but not reading) two volumes, recommending them to the spectator.

As Boucher was beginning his first portrait of her, Pompadour was reinventing herself as a new Montespan and a new Maintenon. Many of her activities and movements attest to this new persona. Between the end of 1749 and the spring of 1751, when she was on the rise politically, she moved to the prestigious Counselor's apartments on the ground floor of Versailles, lodgings that both Montespan and Maintenon had formerly inhabited. The timing of her move was perfect; at the period

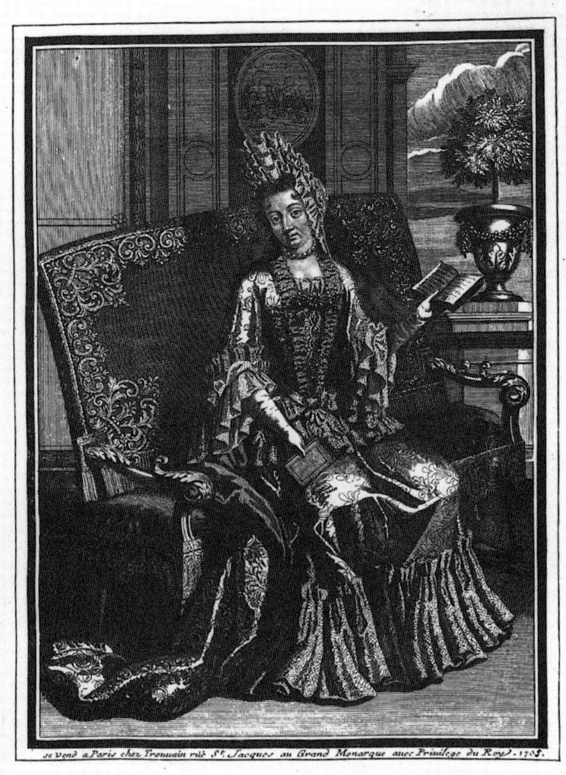

FIGURE 22.
Antoine Trouvain, *Portrait of Mme de Maintenon*, 1705. Paris, Bibliothèque Nationale, Département des Estampes.

when she was transforming from Louis XV's amorous mistress to his platonic friend, she remembered Montespan, who had occupied these quarters after she relinquished her intimacy with Louis XIV and assumed the post of his platonic counselor. Pompadour apparently wished also to reincarnate Maintenon, whose shade she must have imagined keeping her company in her new suite. Rumor had it that she summoned Louis XV's ministers to her new lodgings, consciously mimicking Maintenon, who several decades earlier had given audience to Louis XIV's deputies in the very same locale.[9] Pompadour was a consummate political historian.

Her identification with these royal predecessors continued unabated for a number of years, when she was ascending from marquise to duchess to lady-in-waiting. In 1750 she made a highly publicized pilgrimage to Maintenon's Maison Royale de Saint-Cyr, the model of her school at Poissy, to use it as a paradigm in turn for her and her brother's institution-in-progress for boys, the Ecole Militaire, as well as to hear a performance of the *Idylle de Saint-Cyr*. In a letter of September 18 to Joseph Pâris-Duverney, she rhapsodized about her experience: "The day before yesterday we went to Saint-Cyr. I cannot tell you how touched I was by this establishment, as well as by all therein."[10]

Maintenon was clearly on her mind during the decade when her portraits were painted. In 1752, when she rose to the rank of duchess, she acquired the two-volume edition of the *Lettres de Madame de Maintenon*, published the same year, and in 1756, when she was given the title and privileges of supernumerary lady-in-waiting to Queen Marie Leczinska, she purchased the fifteen-volume edition of the *Lettres de Mme de Maintenon, & Mémoires*, published in 1755 and 1756. In 1755, in the midst of her political ascendancy, she subscribed to the six-volume edition of the *Mémoires de Madame de Maintenon*.[11] Louis XIV's probable morganatic wife and companion was clearly the architect of Pompadour's political project. In the *Mémoires* and the *Lettres* she would have read about Maintenon's curriculum at Saint-Cyr,[12] and would have been struck by its reflection of her own tastes and talents, as they are encoded in her portraits: writing, history, literature, geography, drawing, and music.

Maintenon's legacy as founder and headmistress of Saint-Cyr lived on well into Pompadour's time, not only in eighteenth-century conventual curricula, including that at Pompadour's own Ursuline convent at Poissy, but also in laudatory engravings. For instance, Maintenon is featured as the erudite founder of Saint-Cyr and therefore as a stellar femme savante in Etienne-Jahandier Desrochers's suite of engraved portraits, the *Recueil de Portraits des personnes qui se sont distinguées tant dans les Armes que dans les belles Lettre[s] et les Arts*, published during Pompadour's lifetime (Fig. 23).[13] Desrochers's compendium will be discussed shortly as a major impetus of the learned-woman iconography that pervades Pompadour's portraits.

Pompadour's contemporaries also identified her with Maintenon and Montespan. In 1756, when Boucher painted the Munich portrait to commemorate Pompadour's elevation to lady-in-waiting, Président Hénault remarked that Pompadour's "grand air of reform," commensurate with this exalted office, evoked the memory of the pious Maintenon. This new grandeur prompted Pompadour's contemporaries to associate her also with the dignified devoutness of the older, once-scintillating Montespan. The prince de Ligne reminisced: "I saw Louis XV again with a grand air of Louis XIV, and madame de Pompadour with that of madame de Montespan."[14]

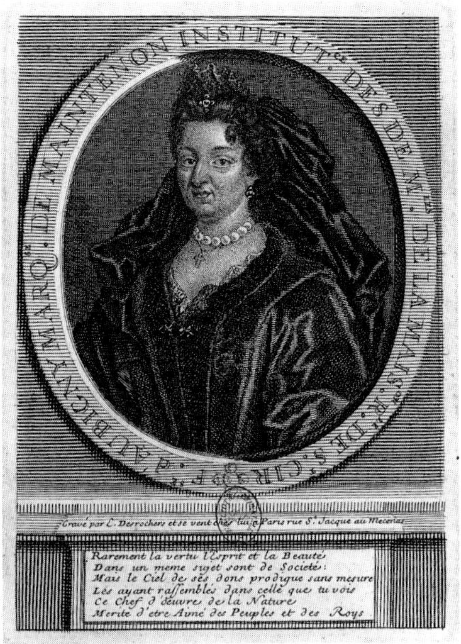

FIGURE 23.
Etienne-Jahandier Desrochers, *Portrait of Mme de Maintenon*, ca. 1726–54. Paris, Bibliothèque Nationale, Département des Estampes.

But if Pompadour fashioned herself as a new Montespan, it was not solely because she wished to emulate the grave comportment of Montespan as lady-in-waiting in her waning years. The compass of her imitation was broader than that. If we scan the complete mature lives of both favorites, some striking parallels emerge. Both royal companions were sparkling intellectuals, shining brightly in literary and philosophical salons prior to their appearance at court. Both were famous virtuosi at court, Montespan a talented dancer in fêtes and ballets, Pompadour, outstripping her predecessor and paragon, the most gifted royal companion France had ever seen—an accomplished actress, singer, and dancer, and the producer and director of operas and ballets. Both were fervent patrons of the most celebrated musicians and writers of their epochs; Montespan's steadfast protection of such Olympians as Lully, Molière, Racine, Corneille, and La Fontaine may have set an example for Pompadour's role as Maecenas to the editors of the *Encyclopédie*, Diderot

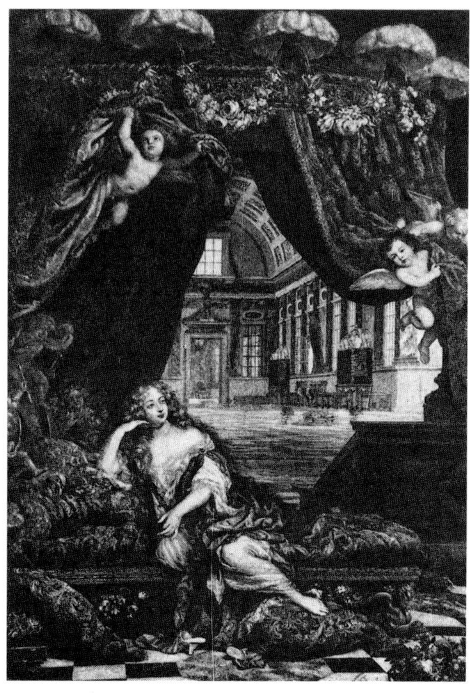

FIGURE 24.
Anonymous, *Portrait of Mme de Montespan*. Paris, Bibliothèque Nationale, Département des Estampes.

and d'Alembert; to the authors Montesquieu and Voltaire, as she is cast in La Tour's pastel; and to a host of other eminent writers and musicians, making her the most astute and generous patroness in France's history. Finally, Montespan's ardent interest in and patronage of architecture and gardens could have prompted Pompadour to consciously mimic her predecessor when she presided over the construction and decoration of her château and gardens at Bellevue and her "hermitages" and gardens at Versailles, Fontainebleau, and Compiègne. Montespan may also have influenced Pompadour when she remodeled and decorated her other residences, including the châteaux at Etioles, Crécy, Champs, Saint-Ouen, Ménars, and Choisy. Astonishingly, she still had the time and the energy to restore her Parisian *hôtels,* Pontchartrain and d'Evreux.[15]

Montespan's principal architectural creation was the opulent château de Clagny

(1674–75), designed by Jules Hardouin-Mansart, with gardens by André Le Nôtre. In an engraving after a canvas variously attributed to Pierre Mignard and Henri Gascars, Montespan reclines, on a daybed *en déshabillé*, in front of Clagny's most magnificent room, the *grand galerie*, thereby bestowing on it, and the château in general, her personal cachet (Fig. 24).[16] Even though Montespan's image as a sensual but cultivated Magdalene undeniably contrasts with Pompadour's more decorous savante persona in the Munich portrait (see Plate 4), a tableau emblematic of a royal mistress binds the two: draperies parted to reveal a self-possessed woman of culture and authority reclining languidly in front of accouterments of her intelligence and taste.

The intellectual emblems of Pompadour's portraits can be traced also to Caspar Netscher's likenesses of Montespan, signed and dated 1670 and 1671.[17] Here again the roots of Pompadour's iconography are embedded in the Grand Siècle. The first portrait of Montespan, which prefigures La Tour's pastel (Fig. 25; see Plate 3), features an ideally beautiful woman seated next to a desk bearing a book and a globe; the flowers she holds, signs of her feminine allure as mistress to the king, define her as the belle savante. In the second portrait (Fig. 26), which foreshadows Pompadour's roles as musician and reader, Montespan sits beside the same desk, which is now covered with a musical score and books. The seductive virtuosa strums the harp, a lute resting at her feet. Here is the genesis of some of La Tour's trappings nearly a century later: Pompadour has been perusing the musical score in her delicate hand; at the left, behind the marquise, a guitar, which replaces Montespan's lute, and another score lie on a couch; the books on the desk remain, and, as in Netscher's tableau, the talented favorite gazes off to the left at an unseen source of inspiration.

Pompadour had no less in common intellectually with Mme de Maintenon, dubbed "le bel esprit" (the sparkling wit) by her contemporaries, and with good reason. Like Pompadour, Maintenon in her early years was both the hostess and the stellar habituée of distinguished literary and philosophical salons, in which she dazzled her contemporaries with her conversation and impressed them with her epistolary skills. Like Pompadour, Maintenon surrounded herself with writers, enlisting Racine, Fénelon, and Bossuet to compose pieces for her school at Saint-Cyr. Like her eighteenth-century successor, she took pleasure in sponsoring concerts for the king. Her political prowess, like Pompadour's, was legendary: called "la machine qui conduisait tout" (the machine that drives the whole thing)—an appellation equivalent to the one that would be given to Pompadour, "le premier ministre" (the prime minister)—Maintenon entertained Louis XIV's envoys while embroidering and weaving tapestry.[18] This practice is reflected in Drouais's portrait of the dignified Pompadour seated at her tapestry frame (see Fig. 10), enthroned,

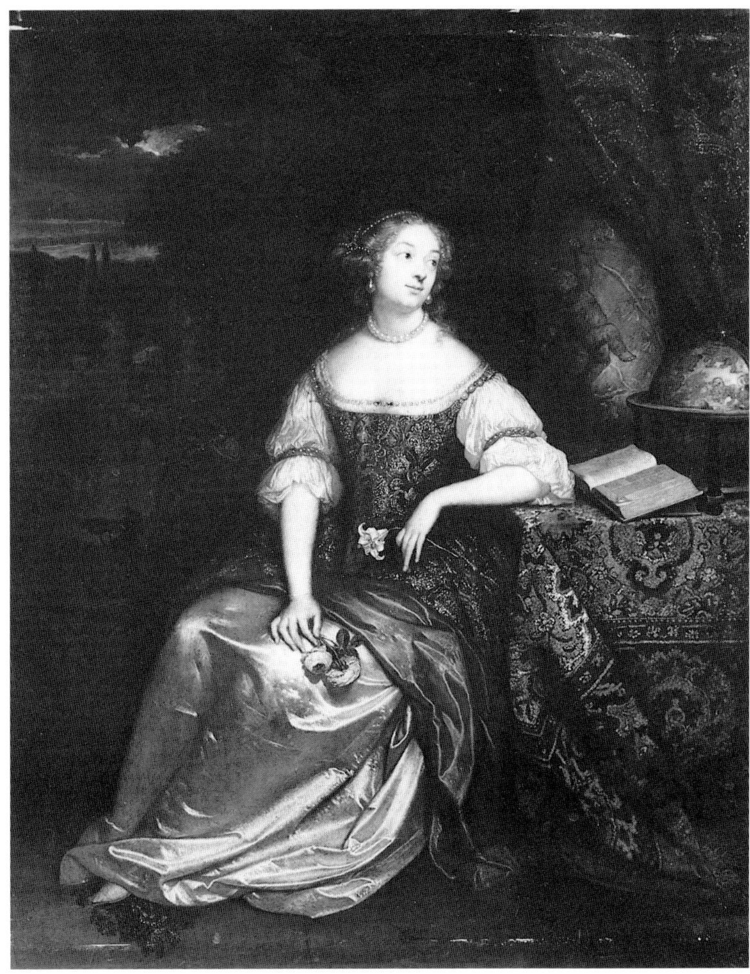

FIGURE 25.
Caspar Netscher, *Portrait of Mme de Montespan*, 1670. Dresden, Staatliche Kunstsammlungen, Gemäldegalerie Alte Meister.

as it were, in her room of state, to which Louis XV's emissaries flocked to solicit her favors.

Another source of the savante iconography of Pompadour's portraits Boucher himself provided. In 1734, long before undertaking Pompadour's portraits, he was com-

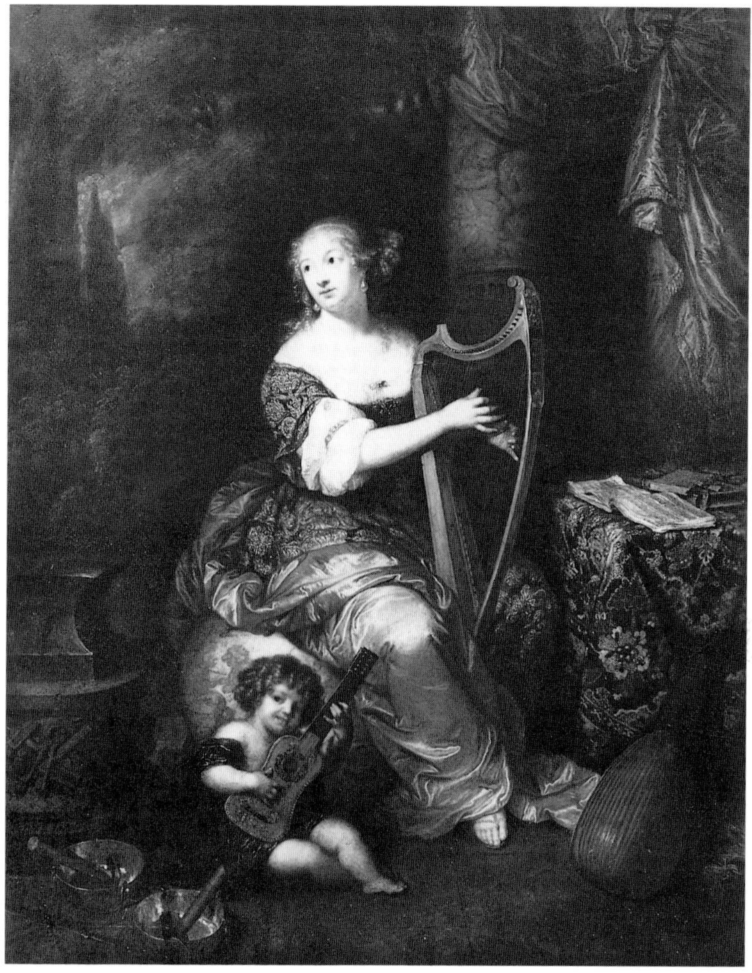

FIGURE 26.
Caspar Netscher, *Portrait of Mme de Montespan*, 1671. Dresden, Staatliche Kunstsammlungen, Gemäldegalerie Alte Meister.

missioned to illustrate a scene from Molière's play *Les Femmes sçavantes*, one of thirty-three engravings Boucher designed for the seventeenth-century playwright's complete dramatic oeuvre (Fig. 27).[19] Boucher's drawing, which was engraved by Laurent Cars, captures the moment in the play when its antifeminist protagonist, Chrysale, a man of limited abilities, admonishes his sister Bélise and her female

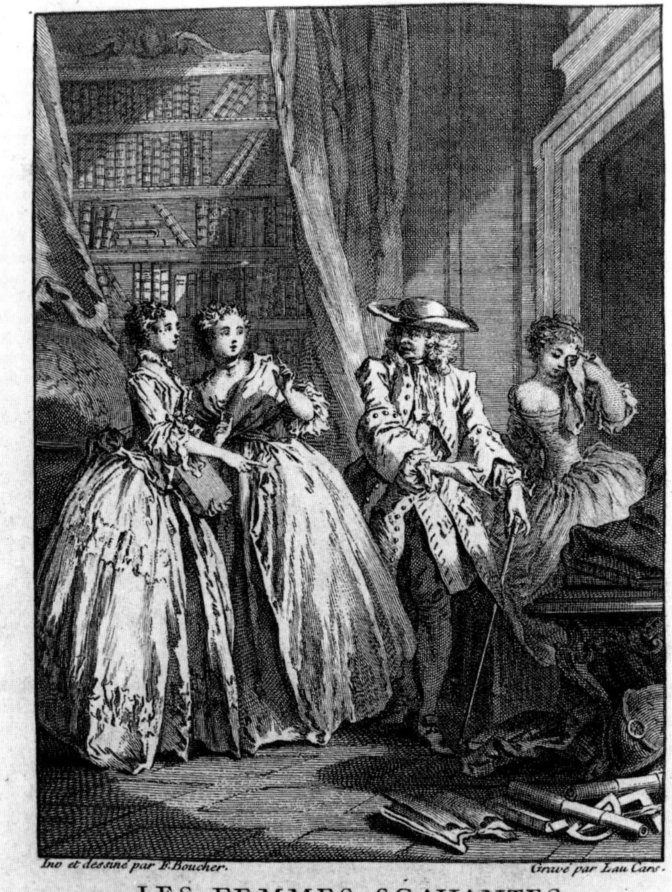

FIGURE 27.
Laurent Cars after François Boucher, *Scene from Molière, Les Femmes sçavantes*, 1734. Collection of the author (photo: University of Delaware Photographic Services).

companions for the intellectual obsessions that have distracted them from their household duties, the proper province of the virtuous bourgeoise:

> I'm sick of those eternal books you've got;
> In my opinion you should burn the lot,
> Save for that Plutarch where I press my collars,
> And leave the studious life to clerks and scholars;
> And do throw out, if I may be emphatic,
> That great long frightful spy glass in the attic,
> And all these other gadgets, and do it soon.[20]

Not only was Boucher faithful to Molière's lines by foregrounding the telescope, books, spyglass, and other "gadgets" of erudition, but, paradoxically, in adhering to a text that censures the noetic aspirations of women, he invented the ingredients of an iconography and setting that he subsequently reshaped to laud the most famous femme savante of the eighteenth century. Sixteen years later he drew upon his own design, varied by a different attitude and his unique subject, to construct his seminal Louvre portrait of Mme de Pompadour (see Plate 2). The cultural equipage situated in the right-hand corner of the engraving reappears in the same spot in the portrait, but Boucher's variations accommodate Pompadour's personal talents and interests: thus the telescope and the spyglass are recast as the rolled-up architectural plan and the tubular top of the furled literary or historical document, but the globe and the open book remain. Doubtless Pompadour instructed Boucher to include among her scholarly attributes the large leather-bound volume embossed with her coat of arms and her pencil holder to complete his tribute to her learning and accomplishments. In both the print and the portrait, the copious libraries of the women are placed behind them at the left. The open doorway at the right of the engraving metamorphoses into the gilt-framed mirror behind Pompadour's harpsichord, which supplants the rococo table at the right of the print. Finally, Boucher felicitously substitutes Pompadour's elegant period chair for the globe squeezed in behind Bélise at the left. Boucher was ingenious—he fashioned the rudiments of Pompadour's savante trappings in the earlier print—but we can surmise that artist and patron collaborated: it is likely that Pompadour knew not only the engraving but also the play, for there were two copies of it in her library.[21] While discounting the pretentiousness of Molière's femme savantes, she was probably inspired by their scholarly interests and used the accouterments of their learning for her own iconography.

The femme savante was an issue of burning topicality in the Women's Quarrel of the Enlightenment, but, as we have seen, it traces back at least to the time of Molière's play (1672). This fervent discourse engendered other engravings, either produced in individual sheets or collected in *recueil*, devoted to actual savantes who, through their achievements in art, music, literature, science, drama, and patronage, contributed notably to France's cultural legacy. These engravings provide a significant iconographic framework for Pompadour's learned likenesses; after all, she was acutely aware of these intellectuals and must have seen herself, in her portraits as in her life, as the descendant of a fertile lineage.

The most comprehensive compendium of engravings saluting learned women was the *Recueil de Portraits des personnes qui se sont distinguées tant dans les Armes que dans les belles Lettre[s] et les Arts (Suite of Portraits of Persons Who Have Distinguished Themselves As Much in Arms as in Belles-Lettres and the Arts*, Paris, ca. 1726–54), engraved and edited by Etienne-Jahandier Desrochers and completed after his death by Gilles-Edme Petit. This important collection, which evinces the Enlightenment's "recovery of nerve" to pay tribute to its citizens' spirit of intellectuality, industry, excellence, self-assurance, fame, and humanism, oddly enough is innocent of scholarly inquiry.[22] While the suite portrayed both men and women, women, in an age of growing feminist awareness, occupy much of it and were classified suitably in Petit's catalogue as "femmes sçavantes."[23] One of those learned women was "La Belle Laure," the identity conferred upon Pompadour by two critics of the Salon of 1755. Because the *Recueil* was published during Pompadour's lifetime, it will be highlighted here as comprising one of the most important iconographic contexts of her femme savante portraits.

The Desrochers prints, in addition to others outside the suite I will examine, are in turn inextricably entwined with the *éloges de savantes*, a strain of encomia praising France's most distinguished learned women.[24] Constituting a thread in the fabric of the Women's Quarrel, these *éloges* consisted of intellectual biographies augmented by catalogues of the savantes' oeuvres. All the rage throughout the eighteenth century, the encomia have a pedigree originating in the seventeenth century, when they were bred by the ferment of women's intellectual activity in Parisian salons and by their agitation for an education worthy of their abilities. Whether written during the Enlightenment or the Grand Siècle, the *éloges*, as well as the engravings that parallel them, asserted the increased visibility of the savante in French society and expressed a long-deserved recognition.

Both the *éloges* and the engravings highlight certain femmes savantes who achieved great renown; from queens down to gifted bourgeoises, like Pompadour, these women were lauded equally for their scholarly accomplishments. A brief chronological survey of some of these women will provide a sense of the company in which Pompadour was placed by her admirers, her portraitists, and herself.

Perhaps Pompadour saw herself following in the footsteps of Marguérite de Valois (1552–1615). It certainly appears that way, since she owned two copies of the *Mémoires de la Reine Marguérite* (1658, 1661). The two women had a great deal in

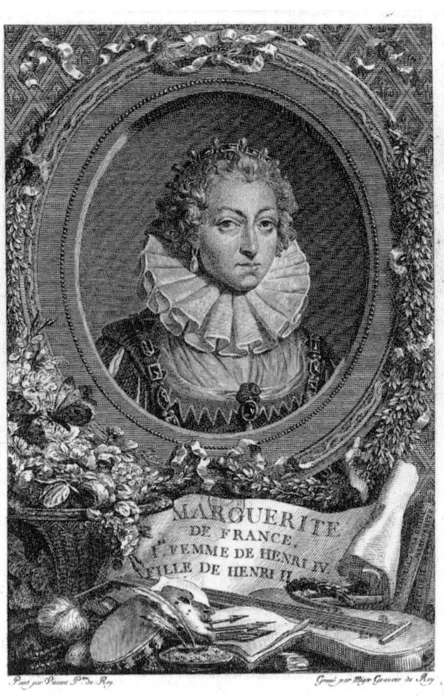

FIGURE 28.
Simon-Charles Miger after François-André Vincent, *Portrait of Marguérite de Valois*. Paris, Bibliothèque Nationale, Département des Estampes.

common: in Simon-Charles Miger's engraving after François-André Vincent's later eighteenth-century portrait (which is not in the *Recueil*, Fig. 28),[25] "La Reine Margot" was encoded as queen of the liberal arts, as Pompadour was to be in her own portraits. One of France's first *salonnières* and protectresses, Marguérite de Valois was lauded by Marguérite Buffet in *Nouvelles Observations sur la langue françoise, . . . avec les éloges des illustres sçavantes, tant anciennes que modernes* (*New Observations on the French Language . . . with Encomia of Illustrious Savantes, Whether Past or Modern*, Paris, 1668): "[She] was also very clever and one of the most learned and wisest of her time. This princess loved the sciences so ardently that her table was forever surrounded by the most erudite men."[26] In a similar tenor, the *Almanach des Dames sçavantes françoises* (Paris, ed. 1732), one of the most comprehensive *éloges* of this strain, honors Marguérite de Valois for her literary talents: "She had a marvelous facility for composing in prose and in verse, which can be judged by the *Poësies* and the *Mémoires* she has bequeathed to us."[27]

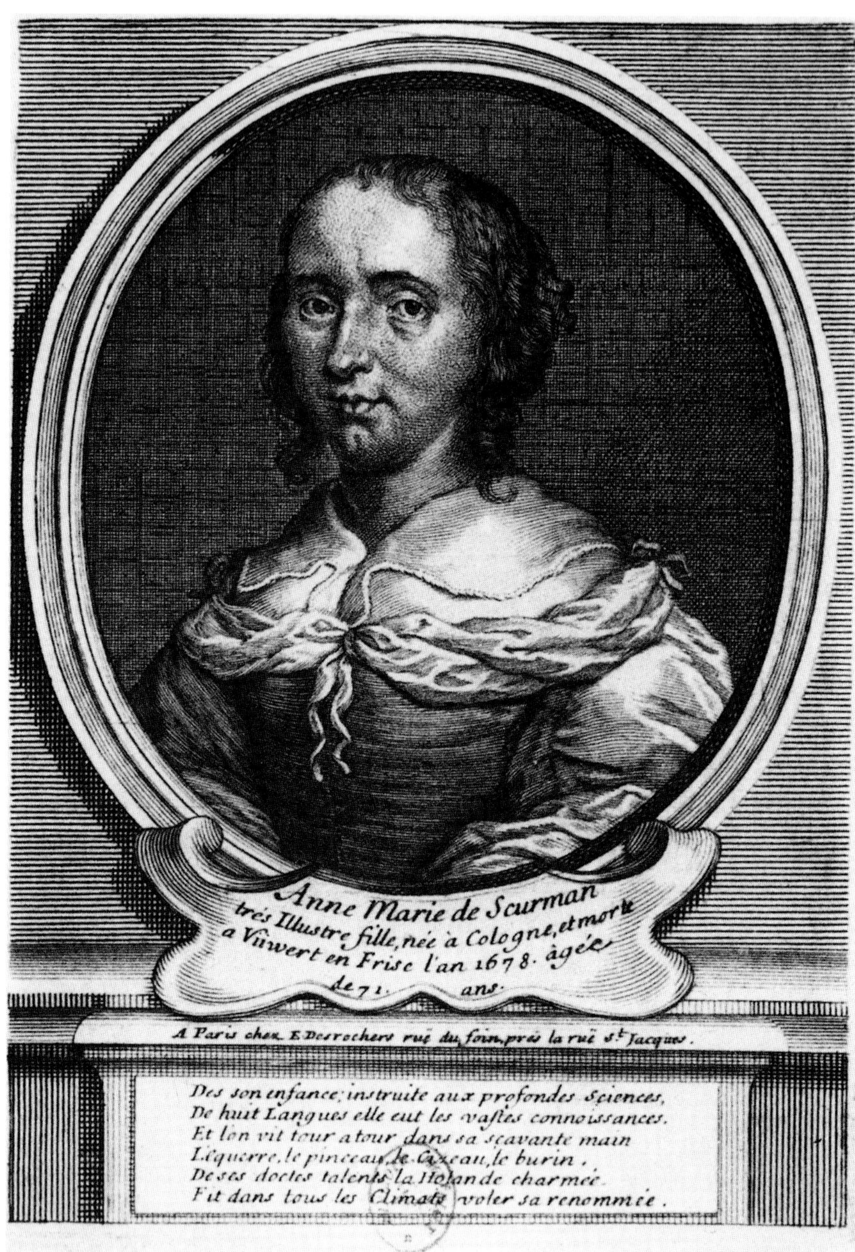

FIGURE 29.
Etienne-Jahandier Desrochers, *Portrait of Anne Marie van Schurman*, ca. 1726–54. Paris, Bibliothèque Nationale, Département des Estampes.

Anne Marie van Schurman (1607–1678), dubbed by her contemporaries "the Dutch Minerva," achieved international renown, especially in France, by triumphing in virtually every area of the sciences, thereby setting an example for all women who dedicated themselves to intellectual endeavors. Her intellectual acumen is evinced in Desrochers's engraved portrait, in which she stands in front of her library (faintly indicated in the print) and gazes steadfastly at the beholder (Fig. 29).[28] Significantly, Desrochers, here and in several other portraits of savantes, was not constrained by the current stereotypes of beauty, as were the engravers of fashion plates and Boucher himself, for he did not feel compelled to idealize the plain Schurman. The versifier of the print, François Gacon, also understanding that Schurman opted for the cerebral over the physical, pays homage to her lifelong instruction "in the profound Sciences": she was proficient in eight languages, painting, sculpture, and engraving, not to mention mathematics, philosophy, theology, music, and literature. She had no time to learn the art of makeup. In recognition of her vast erudition, she received honorary doctorates from the Universities of Bologna and Padua, an ironic comment on the policy that barred her and all other women from institutions of higher learning. She could not be ignored, nor did she wish her female contemporaries to shirk their responsibility to study. Thus she engaged in the Women's Quarrel by arguing that study is the duty and proper occupation of a woman of station and leisure, in spite of being prohibited from applying her knowledge in a profession.[29]

Four great French women writers of the second half of the seventeenth century, whose works Pompadour collected, were honored in Desrochers's suite. The first, Henriette de Coligny, the comtesse de La Suze (1618–1673; Fig. 30), was a renowned specialist in the lyric, most notably the elegy. La Suze's verses were collected in the popular *Recueil de pièces galantes, en prose et en vers*, which was printed in at least six four-volume editions from 1666 to 1745, the latter of which Pompadour owned. Also a famous beauty who lived independently in high society after divorcing her second husband, La Suze was praised by authors of encomia for combining in her elegies intelligence, tenderness, and noble sentiments with a simple, natural style. In this regard, Marguérite Buffet asserted that La Suze eclipsed even Horace himself. Writers of panegyrics, including the novelist Madeleine de Scudéry, were at a loss to say which quality of La Suze was more admirable: her beauty or her intelligence. The engraving shows us both qualities: her allure combined with a serious, unflinching gaze.[30]

The second is the brilliant novelist and chronicler of the history of the French court, the comtesse de Lafayette (1634–1693; Fig. 31). Her pensive and melancholy countenance conveys something of the essence of her psychological and tragic novels, *La Princesse de Montpensier* (1662) and *La Princesse de Clèves* (1678), which Pompadour possessed—three editions of the latter, in fact. Besides the novels, Pompadour,

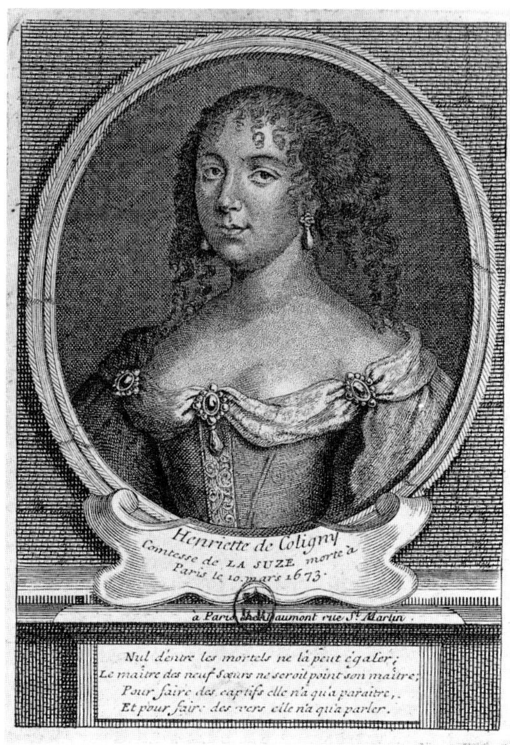

FIGURE 30.
Jean-François Daumont, *Portrait of the Comtesse de La Suze*. Paris, Bibliothèque Nationale, Département des Estampes.

as savante companion of the king, also steeped herself in Lafayette's histories of the court.[31] But Pompadour may also have empathized with Lafayette as a woman made cynical by the mean-spirited, self-serving machinators at court; the letters of both women reveal their disaffection and pessimism.

The third author, Mme Deshoulières (1634–1694; Fig. 32), whose two-volume *Poësies* Pompadour also included in her library, was one of the most celebrated femmes savantes of the seventeenth and eighteenth centuries. Very well educated, Deshoulières gained great renown for her lyric poetry, particularly her idylls; she was appointed to the Academies of the Ricovrati and Arles, and, despite the fact that the French Academy would not admit her because of her gender, her verses were read at its public sessions. A celebrated beauty, Deshoulières died of breast cancer

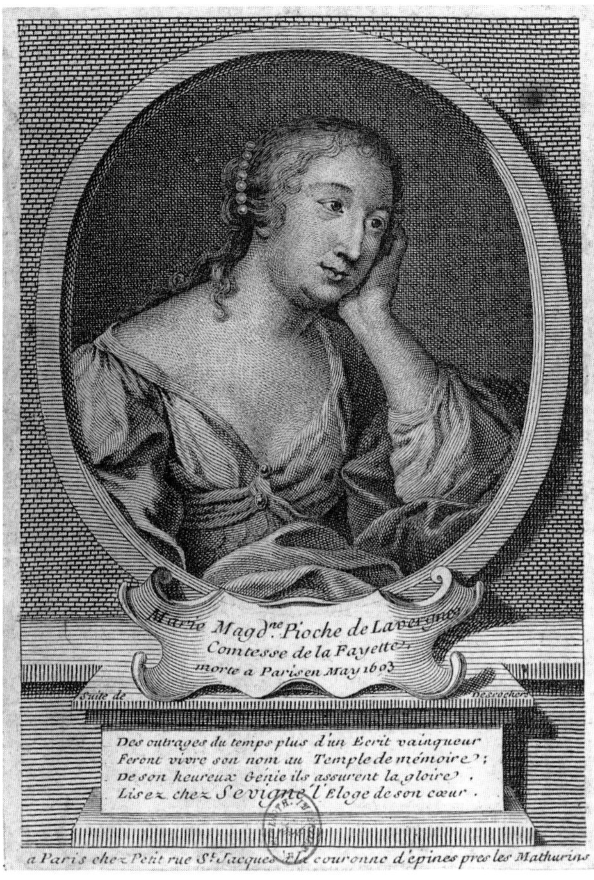

FIGURE 31.
Etienne-Jehandier Desrochers, *Portrait of the Comtesse de Lafayette*, ca. 1726–54. Paris, Bibliothèque Nationale, Département des Estampes.

just short of her sixtieth birthday, but her legacy lived on. Titon du Tillet commemorated her, along with La Suze and Madeleine de Scudéry, as one of the Three Graces on his sculpted monument to genius, the *Parnasse François* (1708–18); Voltaire saluted her in his *Temple du Goût*; and P.-A. Alletz, in his encomium *L'Esprit des femmes célèbres du siècle de Louis XIV, et de celui de Louis XV, jusqu'à présent* (*The Spirit of Celebrated Women from the Century of Louis XIV and That of Louis XV Up to the Present Day*, 1768) praised her thus: "Her works are regarded as a model of natural and tender Poetry: one admires in them the beauty of sense, the graces of expression, the harmony and the lovely disposition of the rhymes."[32]

Deshoulières's fame was also perpetuated in another suite of engravings dedicated to men: *Les Illustres Français, ou tableaux historiques des grands hommes de la*

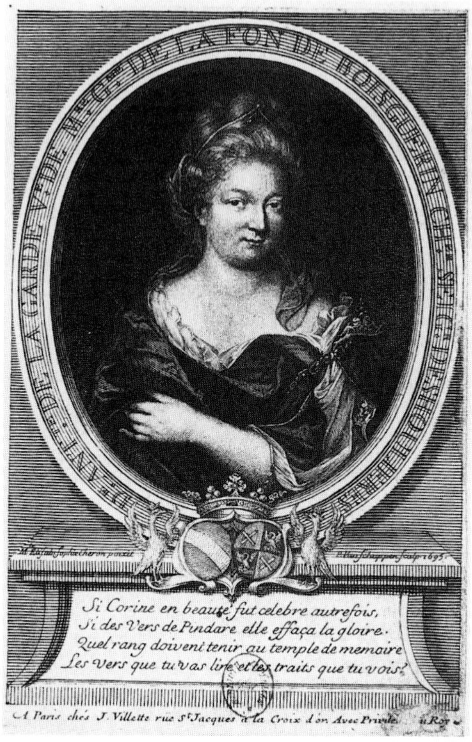

FIGURE 32.
Pierre van Schuppen after Elisabeth-Sophie Chéron, *Portrait of Mme Deshoulières*. Paris, Bibliothèque Nationale, Département des Estampes.

France, pris dans tous les genres de célébrité jusqu'en 1792 (*The Illustrious French, or Historical Pictures of the Great Men of France, Culled from All Genres of Celebrity up to 1792*), designed by Clément-Pierre Marillier and engraved by Nicolas Ponce. Here a medallion in the center of the print depicts Deshoulières in classical profile, with ovals picturing important events of her life flanking her image (Fig. 33). Below the medallion and the ovals is a bucolic landscape populated by animals and birds, signifying her legendary idylls.[33]

Desrochers depicts the fourth *femme-auteur,* Marie-Catherine Desjardins de Villedieu (1640?–1683; Fig. 34), as the professional author she was, seated at her desk with open book and inkwell and quill. Of humble origins, Mme de Villedieu lived by her pen; to support herself, she was obliged to write prolifically. A versatile poet,

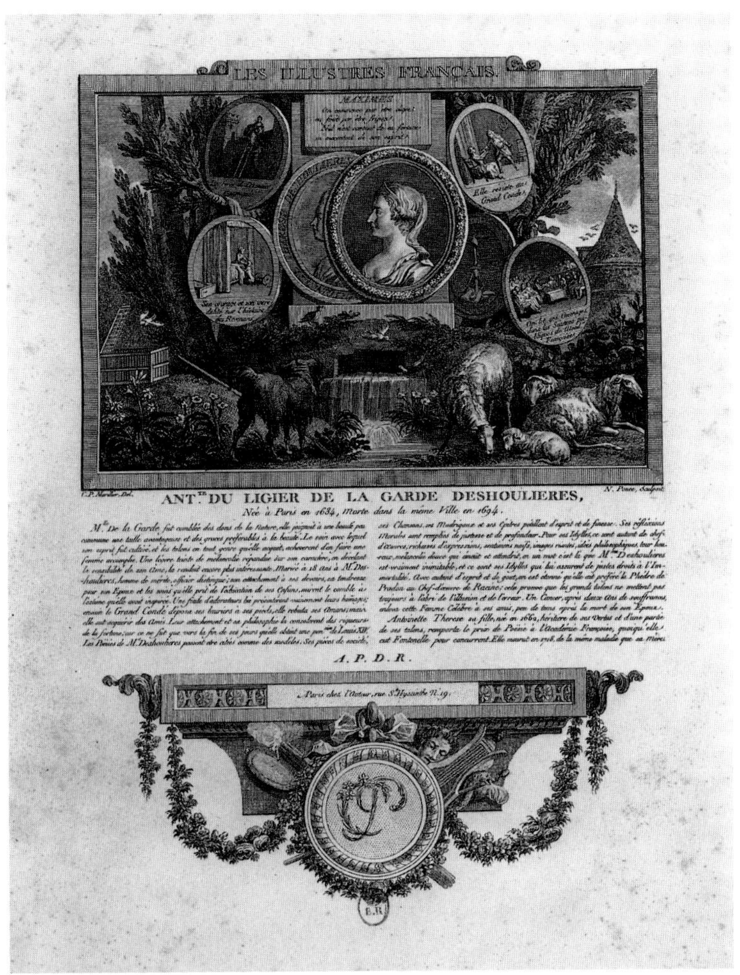

FIGURE 33.
Nicolas Ponce after Clément-Pierre Marillier, *Portrait of Mme Deshoulières*, 1816. Paris, Bibliothèque Nationale, Département des Estampes.

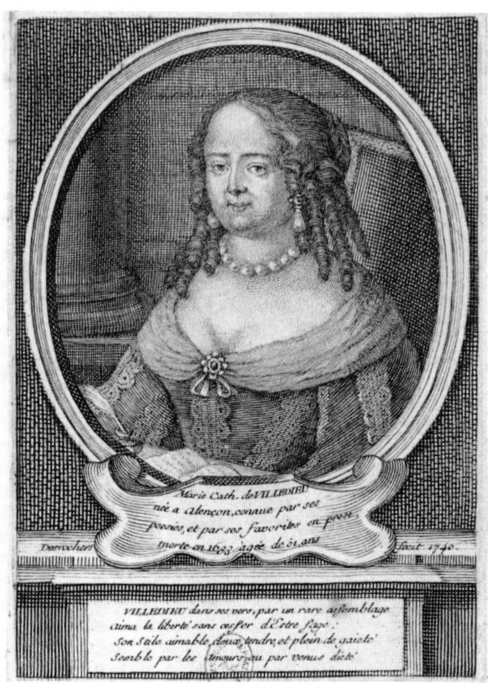

FIGURE 34.
Etienne-Jahandier Desrochers, *Portrait of Marie-Catherine Desjardins de Villedieu*, 1740. Paris, Bibliothèque Nationale, Département des Estampes.

playwright, letter writer, and novelist, Villedieu was immensely popular during her lifetime: her historical novels especially appealed to the tastes of a growing elite audience. As Alletz states, Villedieu "set out to celebrate [love's] power over the human heart. . . . In short, it was her obsession to employ all her talents to speak the language of the passions." By the time Pompadour acquired Villedieu's complete works, the *Oeuvres de Mme de Villedieu* (Paris, 1741) had been collected in twelve volumes. Little known today but greatly esteemed in the seventeenth and eighteenth centuries, Villedieu was a major woman novelist.[34]

Lauded as they were, these writers were no match in the eyes of the French for their illustrious "Sapho" and "Tenth Muse," the prolific historical novelist and *salonnière*, Madeleine de Scudéry (1606–1701; Fig. 35), generally regarded as the première savante of the seventeenth century. When fashioning her image, Desrochers departed from his customary candor by idealizing and bedecking this famously

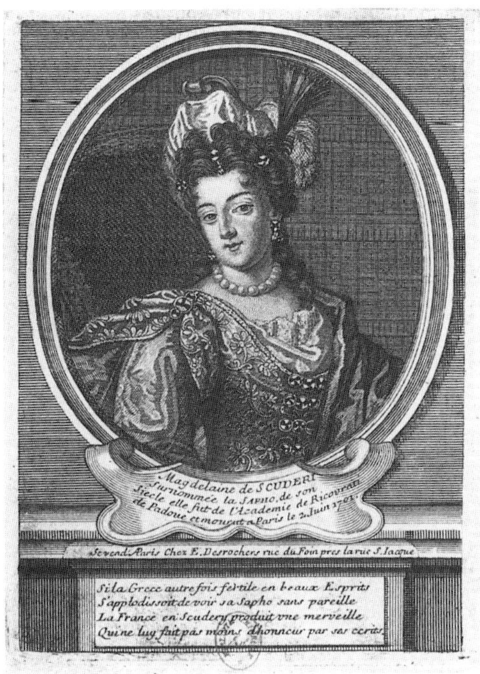

FIGURE 35.
Etienne-Jahandier Desrochers, *Portrait of Madeleine de Scudéry*, ca. 1726–54. Paris, Bibliothèque Nationale, Département des Estampes.

unglamorous spinster in conformity with the prevailing notion of the belle savante. Perhaps he did so because of Scudéry's *précieuse* novels, which glorify ideal, unapproachable heroines admired from afar by blindly smitten suitors. Pompadour was a devotee of this kind of literature: in her library were Scudéry's principal novels. Virtually every *éloge* written in the seventeenth and the eighteenth centuries recounts Scudéry's accolades, which for a woman were legion. She was awarded the coveted prize for eloquence by the all-male French Academy, which at the same time paradoxically barred her from membership because of her gender. She was also granted pensions by people in the highest places, including Cardinal Mazarin and Louis XIV himself.[35]

The multitalented Elisabeth-Sophie Chéron (1648–1711) may have served as a paragon of intellectual versatility for Mme de Pompadour: both women were artists, versifiers, and musicians. Desrochers returned to his usual vein in his engraved por-

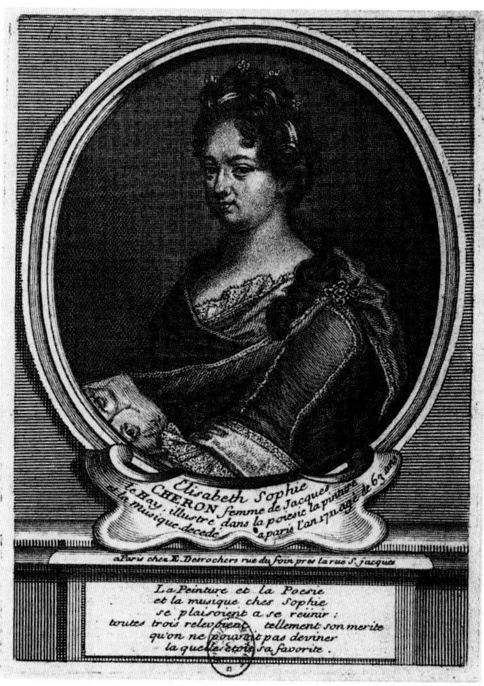

FIGURE 36.
Etienne-Jahandier Desrochers, *Portrait of Elisabeth-Sophie Chéron*, ca. 1726–54. Paris, Bibliothèque Nationale, Département des Estampes.

trait of Chéron (Fig. 36): she is corpulent, middle-aged, and focused, and she holds the wide-eyed mask of imitation, signifying her distinction in poetry and painting. Her skill in the latter earned her a unique place in the illustrious Royal Academy of Painting and Sculpture in 1676.[36]

Desrochers continued his realistic mode in the *Portrait of Anne le Fèvre, Mme Dacier* (1652–1720; Fig. 37), the most eminent woman classicist of her generation. In a fictive imitation of an antique medal, he evokes her profession and fame through her classical profile and belaureled chignon. Desrochers meticulously, almost ruthlessly, details her prominent, irregular nose and her elderly jowl: bulging features that he exaggerates to underscore her strong character. As Gacon's expository verses tell us, Dacier's character was marked by the rarest virtues. The sestet also states that she was taught by her husband and father. With the doors of colleges and universities closed to women, she was one of the fortunate few who could develop her tal-

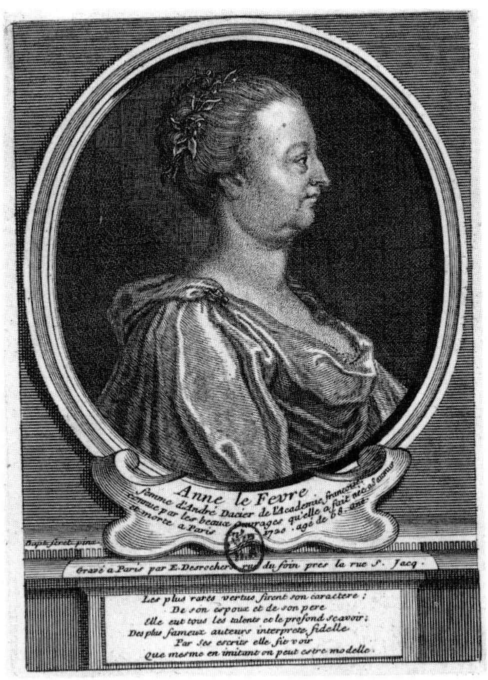

FIGURE 37.
Etienne-Jahandier Desrochers, *Portrait of Anne le Fèvre, Mme Dacier,* ca. 1726–54. Paris, Bibliothèque Nationale, Département des Estampes.

ent through familial tutoring and nurturing. When most of her female contemporaries could barely write a grammatical letter, Dacier scrupulously translated and wrote scholarly commentaries on the most daunting writers of antiquity: Homer, Anacreon, Sappho, Aristophanes, Plautus, and Terence, among them. Fond of the classics but not schooled in Greek and Latin, Pompadour acquired nearly all of Dacier's translations.[37] The *Almanach* extolled Dacier most eloquently: "No one has spoken with greater truth of the art of poetry, nor better knew the theater of the Ancients. . . . One finds in all of her writings a great erudition, much solidity of mind, with a noble eloquence."[38]

Along with just about every femme savante imaginable (Fig. 38)—at the left, Marguérite de Navarre and the comtesse de La Suze; in the center, the letter writer Mme de Sévigné; and at the right, Madeleine de Scudéry and the comtesse de Lafayette—Dacier was saluted in a multiple engraving in *Les Illustres Français.*[39] This

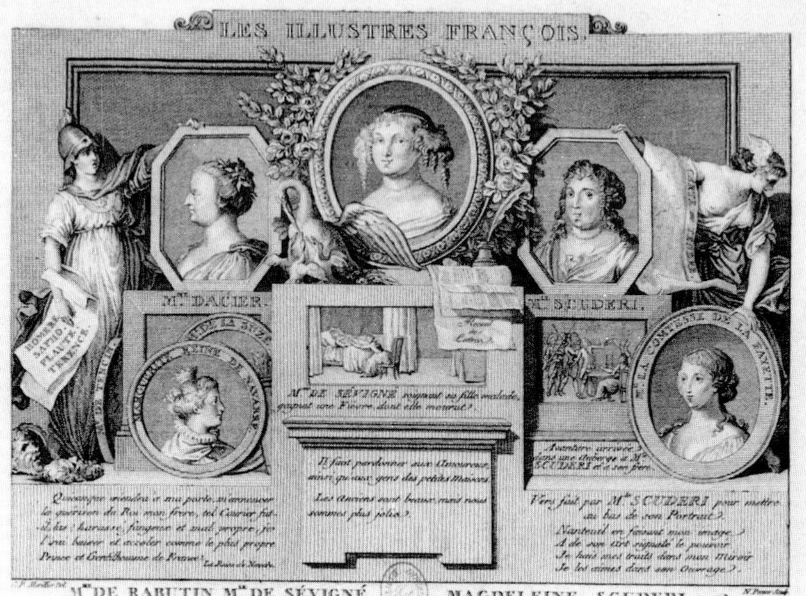

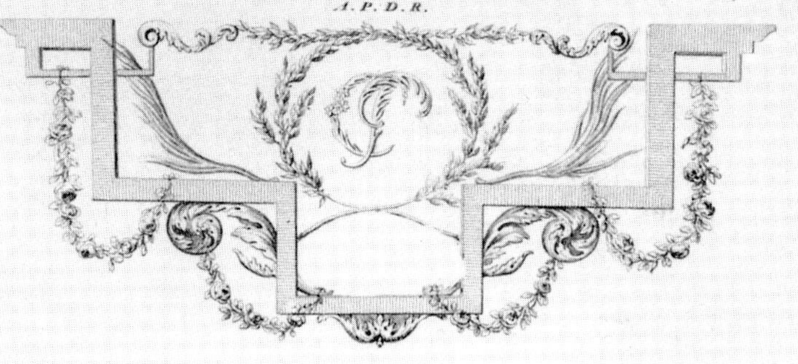

FIGURE 38.
Nicolas Ponce after Clément-Pierre Marillier, *Engravings of Femmes savantes from Les Illustres Français*, 1816. Paris, Bibliothèque Nationale, Département des Estampes.

constellation of learned women, engraved at the end of the eighteenth century, testifies to the enduring legacy of the femme savante well into the Revolutionary period.

For Pompadour, the lives of these and many other femmes savantes became standards to follow and patterns to refine and personalize, and their engraved likenesses defined the tradition in which Pompadour's own portraits are to be understood. The idea of the learned woman was in the air when Pompadour's portraits were painted, and prominent embodiments of this idea were historical presences. She fashioned her life after the accomplishments of these predecessors and coevals, the cultivated women celebrated in the engraved and literary encomia. Her portraitists represented the brilliant success of her emulation. And, as I will discuss further, her portraits were also embedded in a solid tradition of painted likenesses of eighteenth-century educated women. Acutely aware of this strain, she selected the inherited iconography that would place her among the elite femmes savantes.

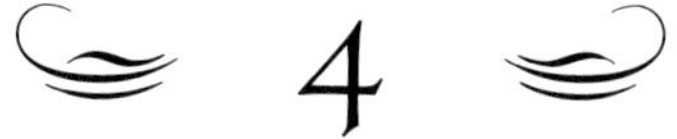

PICTURING ENLIGHTENED WOMEN

The portraits of Pompadour as learned woman are the most lavish examples of the "intellectual portrait," a type that flourished in France from the 1730s until the end of the century.[1] Fashioned by some of the greatest painters of the eighteenth century, these portraits, with their makers, have nonetheless been scanted, at times altogether ignored, in the literature, because of the general neglect of eighteenth-century French painting until recently. But they are among the most striking and compelling works of the period; they evoke the intellectual acumen and affirm the status of their sitters. At the same time, they evince the fervent commitment of the Enlightenment to pay homage to some of its most gifted and accomplished citizens.

Likenesses of both savants and savantes proliferated. Even though men were infinitely better educated than women, it is impossible to say with certainty that portraits of men set the standard for those of women. Both have iconographic sources in seventeenth-century Netherlandish painting and in French fashion plates, but these pictorial antecedents were also produced concurrently in the seventeenth century. Be that as it may, with her interest in art, Pompadour would have known both the Netherlandish portraits and their eighteenth-century French progeny.

Allied as they are with likenesses of savants by iconography and genus, Pompadour's images were most likely shaped with the intellectual pictorial tradition in mind. This strain was inaugurated by Jacques-André-Joseph Aved, who was trained in Amsterdam and dubbed the "French Batave" because of his stylistic affinities with seventeenth-century Netherlandish realism.[2] Pompadour may have known Aved's most famous savant portraits, among them the affecting likeness of the celebrated composer, music theorist, and musician Jean-Philippe Rameau (Dijon, Musée des Beaux-Arts, ca. 1728; Fig. 39), who is pictured in an inspired moment as he sings to the strains of his violin.[3] Aved's slightly later portraits of Count Carl Gustaf Tessin, the Swedish ambassador to France (Stockholm, Nationalmuseum, Salon of 1740;

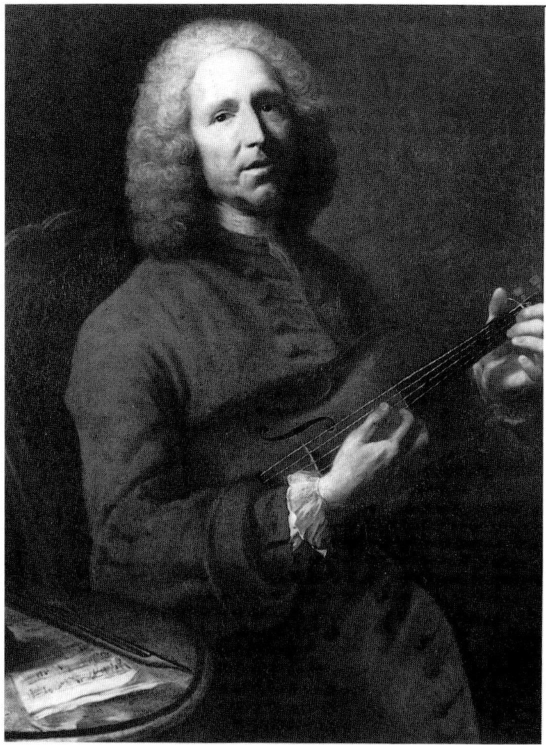

FIGURE 39.
Jacques-André-Joseph Aved, *Portrait of Jean-Philippe Rameau*, ca. 1728. Dijon, Musée des Beaux-Arts (photo: © Musée des Beaux-Arts de Dijon).

Fig. 40), and of the political economist Victor Riqueti, marquis de Mirabeau (Musée du Louvre, Salon of 1743; Fig. 41), are no less trenchant and contain iconography similar to that in Pompadour's likenesses. Aved pictures Tessin as the consummate *amateur* (lover of the arts). Portrayed in informal dress in his collector's cabinet and holding an engraving after Raphael's *Galatea*, he is flanked by a globe at the lower right and a desk with a book, inkwell, and quill, signs of his knowledge and erudition.[4] Book, globe, writing implements, and study—the whole panoply of scholarly attributes—are all staples of Pompadour's likenesses fashioned a decade later. The noetic accouterments in Mirabeau's great portrait resonate as well. Head sharply turned, face taut, the keenly intellectual Mirabeau stands in his study in front of a voluminous collection of books that foreshadows those shown in Pompadour's por-

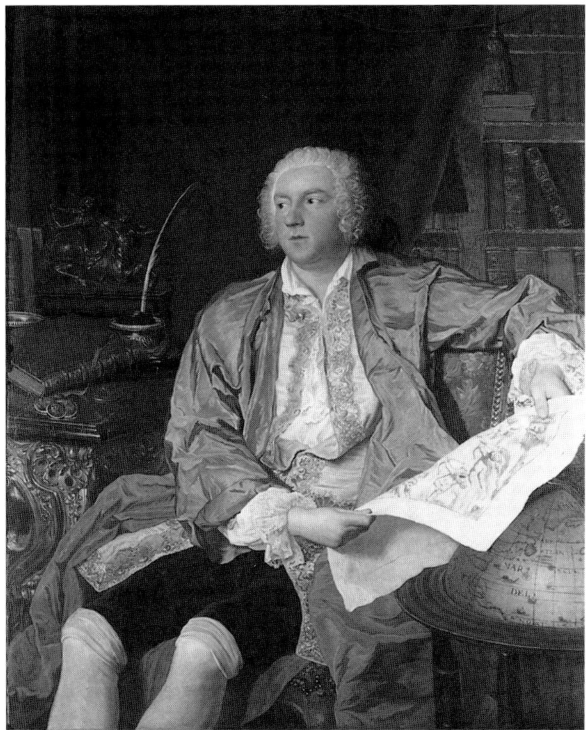

FIGURE 40.
Jacques-André-Joseph Aved, *Portrait of Count Carl Gustaf Tessin*, 1740. Stockholm, Nationalmuseum (photo: © Nationalmuseum).

traits. He steadies and points to the *Commentaries of Julius Caesar* on a desk that also holds the usual scholar's inkwell and quill.[5]

At about the same time, La Tour pictured the male professional in his study, surrounded by trappings of learning, in two works that presage his portrait of Pompadour. In a pastel of Gabriel-Bernard de Rieux, president of the Paris Parliament (Los Angeles, J. Paul Getty Museum, Salon of 1741; Fig. 42), the similarities to La Tour's pastel of Pompadour are obvious.[6] Both pastels feature imposing seated full-length subjects, whose feet rest on an Aubusson carpet and who delicately finger a supple page. Both sitters are flanked by a globe and a desk with books and papers. La Tour's *Duval de l'Epinoy* (Lisbon, Calouste Gulbenkian Foundation, Salon of 1745; Fig. 43), a likeness of the secretary to Louis XV, features the gallant and shrewd

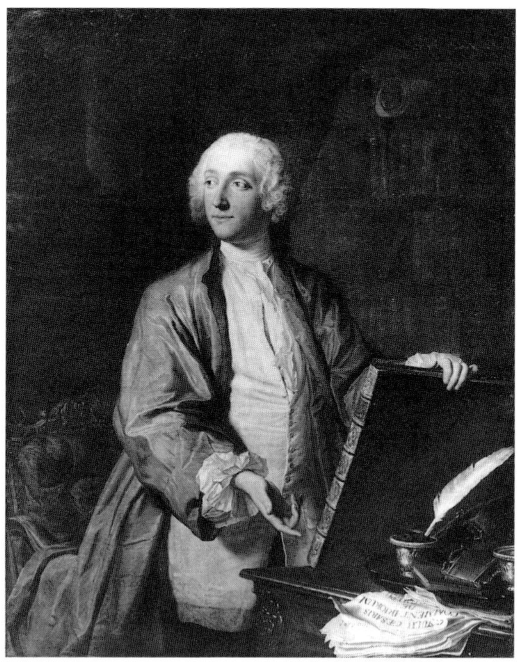

FIGURE 41.
Jacques-André-Joseph Aved, *Portrait of Victor Riqueti, Marquis de Mirabeau*, 1743. Paris, Musée du Louvre (photo: RMN).

Duval as a fashionably dressed intellectual seated in a luxurious period chair near a desk supporting a book and a globe.[7]

La Tour's pastel of Pompadour (see Plate 3) also has affinities with the lineage of "state-portraits" of artists, comparable to the French royal portrait.[8] The portrait of Pompadour is perhaps iconographically closest to Largillierre's *Portrait of Charles Le Brun* (Musée du Louvre, 1686; Fig. 44). Louis XIV's royal painter assumes here the mantle of the director of the Royal Academy of Painting and Sculpture.[9] Like Pompadour, Le Brun sits regally in an opulent period chair, surrounded by the paraphernalia of learning and accomplishment. Le Brun's portfolio, book, and globe, on the floor at the left, reappear in Pompadour's portfolio, globe, and books at the right. Le Brun's own oil study, on an easel behind him, finds its counterpart in the rustic

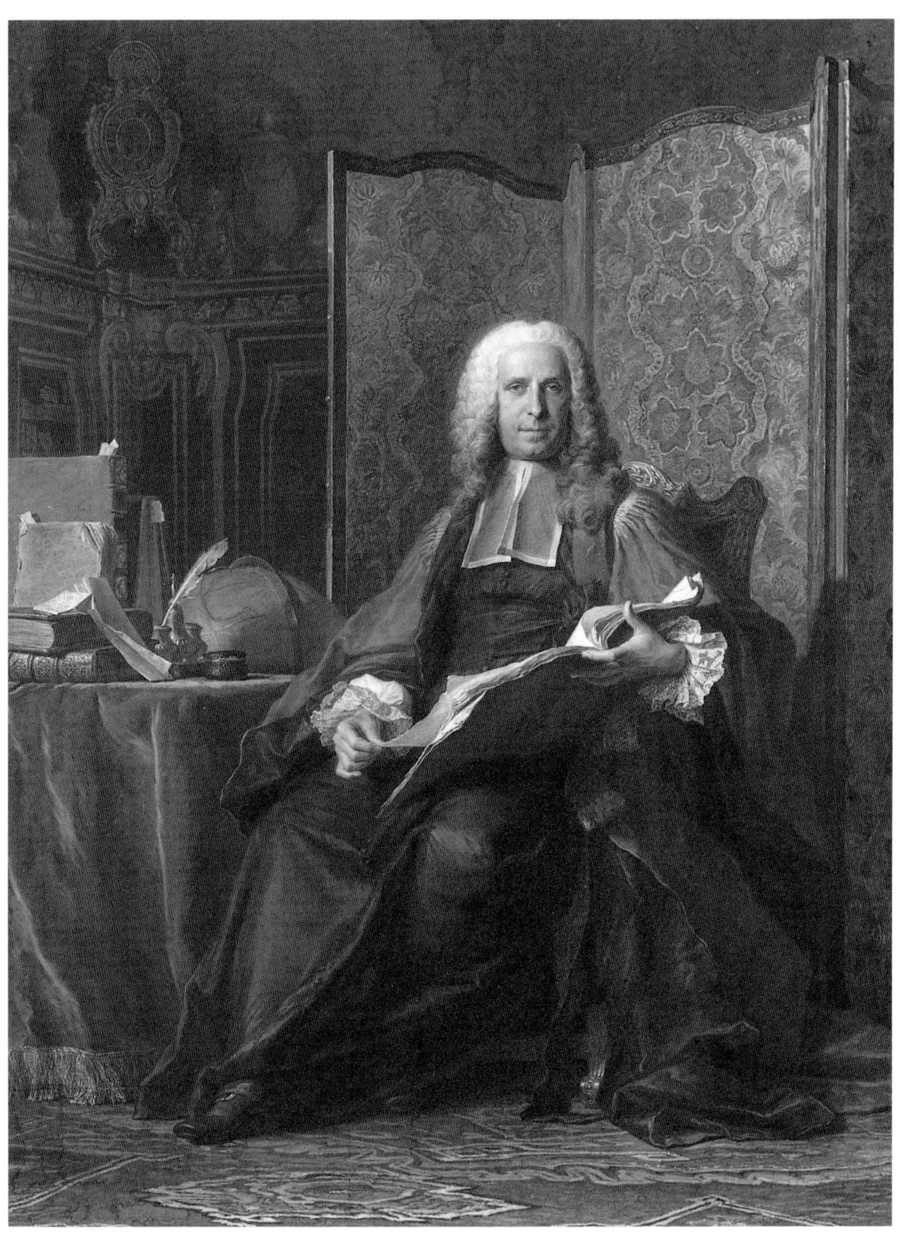

FIGURE 42.
Maurice-Quentin de La Tour, *Portrait of Gabriel-Bernard de Rieux*, 1741. Los Angeles, Collection of the J. Paul Getty Museum.

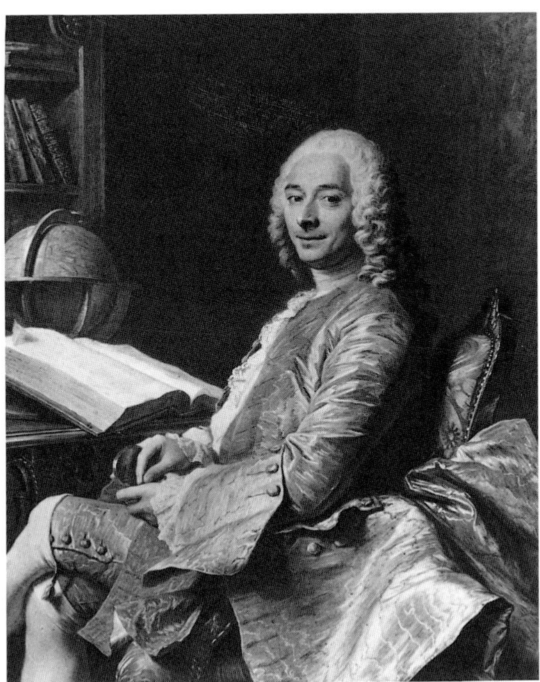

FIGURE 43.
Maurice-Quentin de La Tour, *Portrait of Duval de l'Epinoy*, 1745. Lisbon, Calouste Gulbenkian Foundation.

landscape behind Pompadour, a painting she collected and presumably patronized. The most striking common element of the two pictures is the engraving that spills over the table at the right: in the Le Brun, it is a print after one of his paintings; in the Pompadour, it is her signed engraving from Pierre-Jean Mariette's *Traité des pierres gravées* (1750). La Tour and Pompadour may have known either the Largillierre itself; its descendant, Mignard's *Self-Portrait* (Musée du Louvre), which Mignard's daughter presented to the Royal Academy in 1696; or the source of both portraits, Henri Testelin's *Portrait of Louis XIV as Protector of the Arts* (1666–68), which was at Versailles.

Pompadour surely saw the portrait of her brother, Abel Poisson, marquis de Vandières, fashioned by Jean-François de Troy in 1751 (Versailles, Musée National du Château; Fig. 45) during Vandières's sojourn in Rome. The young Vandières's earnest devotion to architecture is signified by his copy of Vignola and the plan of the French Academy of Rome on his *bureau plat* (flat table). Styled also as a connoisseur of impeccable taste and fashion, Vandières is clad in a sumptuous gold-

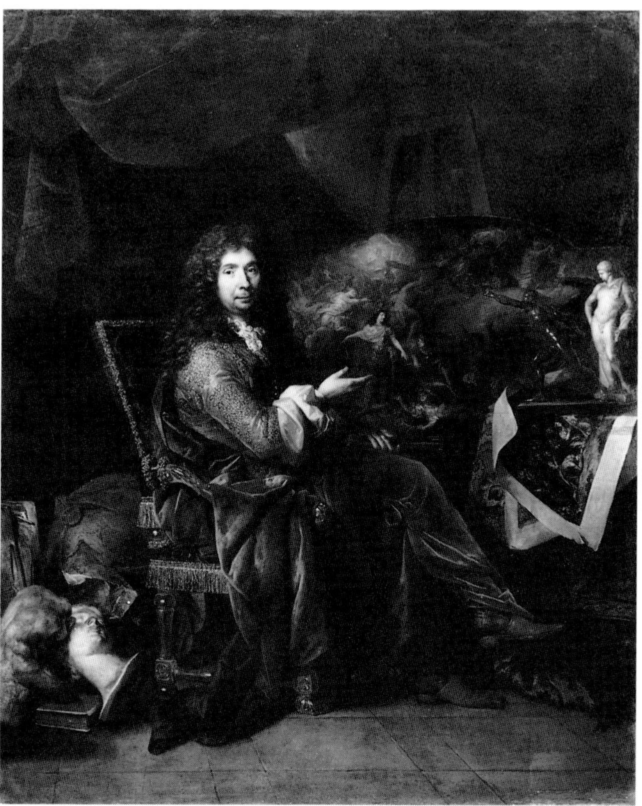

FIGURE 44.
Nicolas de Largillierre, *Portrait of Charles Le Brun*, 1686. Paris, Musée du Louvre (photo: RMN).

brocaded red velvet jacket and seated before an opulent porcelain vase mounted on a bronze stand at the right.[10]

The savant portrait strain gave impetus to Pompadour's intellectual images, but her likenesses are more deeply embedded in the tradition of portraits of accomplished and learned women. The remainder of this chapter will be devoted to a selection of these portraits—specifically, popular images of woman readers, scientists, and musicians—not only because they illuminate Pompadour's images but also because they are interesting in their own right.

Boucher's portraits of the marquise as reflective reader were foreshadowed by likenesses of bookish women produced from the 1730s through the end of the century. La Tour's *Mme Rouillé de l'Etang* and Aved's *Mme de Varennes as Reader*, both exhibited in the Salon of 1738, are two of the earliest representations of female readers, and they convey verisimilitude and psychological nuance.

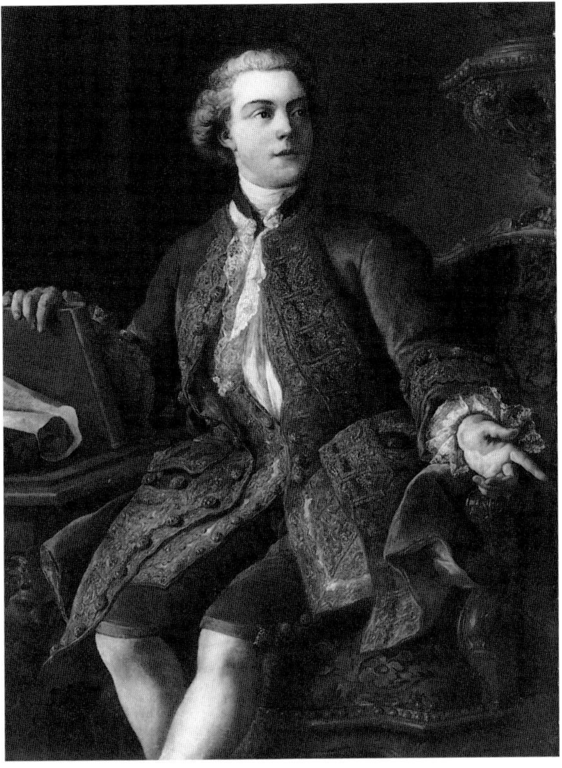

FIGURE 45.
Jean-François de Troy, *Portrait of Abel Poisson, Marquis de Vandières*, 1751. Versailles, Musée National du Château (photo: RMN).

The representation of Mme Rouillé de l'Etang (Fig. 46), "dressed in a Polish mantelet, reflecting, a book in her hand," according to the Salon *livret* (descriptive pamphlet),[11] conveys a sense of immediacy and conviction and illustrates La Tour's naturalistic theories and his physiognomic approach: "They suppose that my understanding is only skin deep, but I delve, without their knowing it, into the recesses of their personality and take possession of them in their entirety."[12] It was easy for La Tour to apply this theory to his portrait, for he knew his sitter and her husband well. He represents her devotion to literature in the profusion of volumes on her desk, and he seizes the moment of her poetic reverie, as she looks up from a

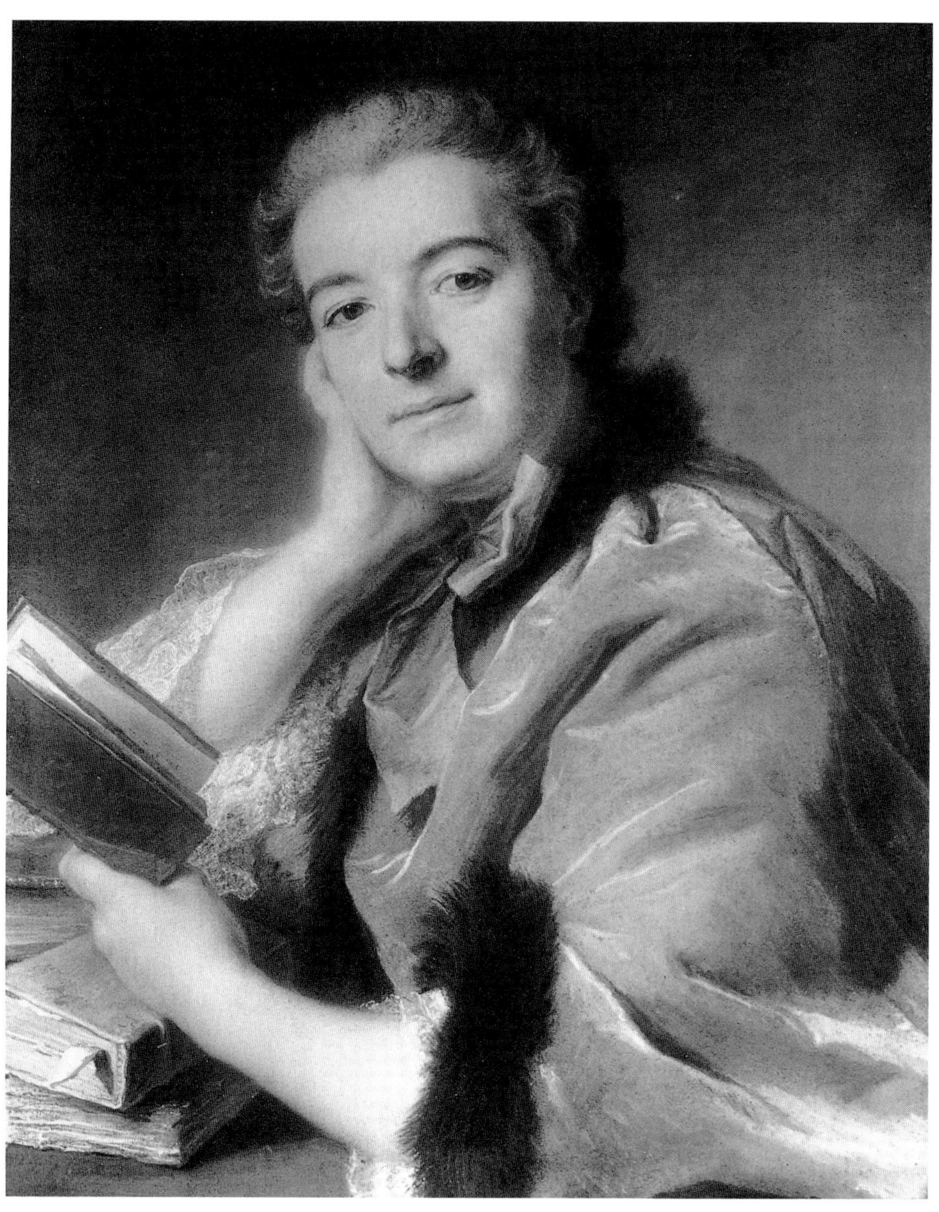

FIGURE 46.
Maurice-Quentin de La Tour, *Portrait of Mme Rouillé de l'Etang*, 1738. Private collection.

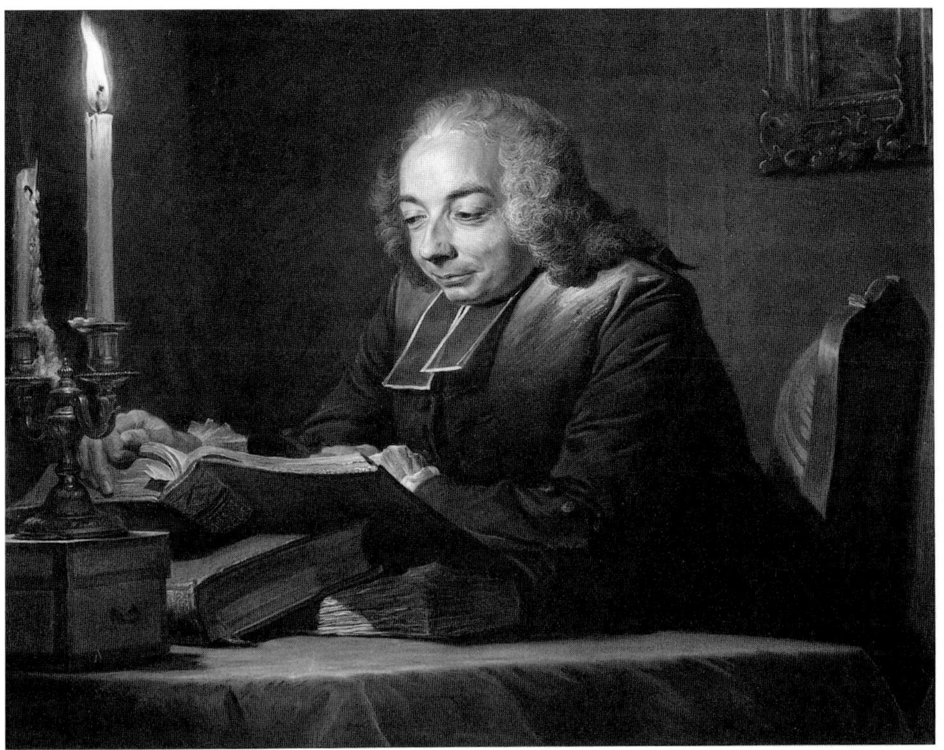

FIGURE 47.
Maurice-Quentin de La Tour, *Portrait of Abbé Huber, Reading*, 1742. Geneva, Musée d'Art et d'Histoire (photo: © Musée d'Art et d'Histoire).

book to muse. The sitter forms a monumental pyramid that reinforces her strong individualized features and her serious demeanor. Her domestic space is nebulous, so that La Tour can concentrate—and he does so sympathetically—on her corpulent middle-aged features as well as imply that she is interested not in externals but in the world of ideas and the imagination, the mark of a true femme savante. She uses the volumes about her for edification; Pompadour, imaged as the reflective reader in her portraits nearly twenty years later, used them for display.

La Tour's portrait of a bookish woman brings to mind his roughly contemporaneous pastel *Abbé Huber, Reading* (Geneva, Musée d'Art et d'Histoire, Salon of 1742; Fig. 47).[13] La Tour fashions the images of his friends with equal intimacy, individuality, and sympathy, depicting them with tomes, signs of their intellectual curiosity. But the differences between the two portraits illustrate La Tour's varying notions of gender: whereas the woman turns away from her book in order to meditate on its contents, Huber is actively absorbed in his reading, hunched over the book, grasping the other side of the volume. Male activity and female passivity parallel masculine specificity and feminine generalization. We know that the abbé is so riveted by his *Montaigne* that he disregards the late hour and remains oblivious to the recently guttered candle. The details of candle and printed spine are notably absent in the pastel of the woman, whose books elude us; the moment at which she muses on them is likewise unspecified. We must be content to see her posture and attitude as illustrative of timeless contemplation.

Aved, in his usual realistic fashion, imbues his *Portrait of Mme de Varennes as Reader* (location unknown; Fig. 48)[14] with elements from genre painting that enhance the naturalism of his portrait as well as gloss his sitter's appearance, character, and interests. The model of his portrait is the beautiful descendant of Molière, who, judging from her books and letter, has inherited from her forebear a love of literature and a penchant for writing. Mme de Varennes is also the worthy heiress in the artistic vein of seventeenth-century Dutch women readers, which her portraitist, "the French Batave," surely knew. Aved's likeness particularly recalls Vermeer's numerous paintings of absorbed readers. Like Vermeer's engrossed haute bourgeoises,[15] Mme de Varennes looms large in the composition, is luxuriously clad, and is situated near a window in the corner of a comfortable domestic space. The light that infuses his room, à la Vermeer, meticulously delineates the woman, her opulent fur-trimmed satin dress, the pearls that secure her chignon, and her accouterments of learning. But Aved eclipses his Netherlandish predecessor in his sensitive characterization of his sitter's alert, serene face. His singular deployment of the light symbolizes intellectual illumination and identifies him as an artist working in the Age of Enlightenment.

The *Portrait of Mme de Varennes* was exhibited in the same salon as Aved's portrait of the celebrated poet and writer Jean-Baptiste Rousseau (Fig. 49), whose image is available to us only in Jean Daullé's engraving after it. The two works were singled out from the others in the salon for special approbation—"generally applauded and esteemed by the connoisseurs."[16] The Age of Enlightenment appreciated its devotees of literature.

If as modern viewers we juxtapose these kindred portraits, we are struck by Aved's gendering of them. Physically, the artist beautifies and elegantly garbs Mme de Varennes according to the period construct of the belle savante, while he uncompromisingly exposes Rousseau's unvarnished corpulence, wrinkles, and jowls. The absorbed female reader is quiescently self-contained; but the active writer, the personification of poetry, turns outward at the moment of inspiration and creation with, as one of his contemporaries put it, "the fire of his works in his eyes." The reader holds her small, untitled volume with the utmost feminine delicacy and grace; he grasps his sheaf of papers and holds his quill with masculine gusto. Whereas Mme de Varennes's domestic interior is the epitome of stillness and tidiness, enhancing her serene beauty, Rousseau's is a whirlwind of disarray, the scholar's working study, replete with titled books identifying the sources that fueled his fiery creation. Even if Mme de Varennes had been a renowned author like Rousseau, Aved, his naturalism notwithstanding, doubtlessly would have idealized her portrait according to the period notion of the beautiful learned woman.

No painter better understood the knack of flattering a belle savante than Jean-Marc Nattier, "the Pupil of the Graces, the Painter of Beauty." With the rare exception of his humble image of Marie Leczinska, queen of France, whom he depicted attired in everyday "town" clothes, holding a Bible (Salon of 1748) or meditating on philosophical essays,[17] Nattier eschewed anything remotely connected with realism in order to pay an extravagant compliment. Such is the case in *The Princesse de Rohan Holding a Book* (Toledo, Ohio, Toledo Museum of Art, Salon of 1741; Plate 6), his most glamorous and inventive tribute to a woman reader. Wielding the heightened rhetoric of his celebrated mythological portraits, Nattier fashions the princess (née Marie-Sophie de Courcillon, 1713–1756) as a quasi-deity swathed in the timeless draperies of eternal beauty and youth.[18] Corresponding to this august persona, he exalts her with the tropes of contemporary literary encomia: her monumental form, pristine, porcelain-like complexion, and perfect oval face outstrip the beauty of her perfunctory natural environment—and even the heavens above.

Her book is equally lofty: the quarto *Histoire universel[l]e* (Fig. 50), the second word of its title perplexingly misspelled, perhaps because the artist did not know or care about his orthography, or because he miscalculated how much space he needed to fit the complete title on the page. But, as in Boucher's generalized portraits of Pompadour, in which titles, texts, and musical scores are vexingly nebulous, Nattier's slip is consonant with his characteristic irreality. He seduces the viewer into the delusion that what the princess holds is a real volume, open to an identifiable page 270. The book, with its unusually generous margins, sizable format, and handwritten paginated versos (pp. 268, 270), misleads us into assuming that it is an actual deluxe first printed, bound-proof yet still unpublished copy, which either has been specially printed for her or has been submitted to her for final corrections and approval.[19] But the volume does not correspond to any of the numerous universal histories from previous centuries or those published at that time.[20]

In his customary hyperbolic manner, the portraitist pays the highest possible compliment to his beautiful, inspired sitter, enshrining her in perhaps his most brilliant likeness as the most sublime and learned woman in the universe and all of its history. And he had reason to do so. Characterized by her friend the abbé de Bernis as "one of the most beautiful women at court," "whose soul was as noble as her

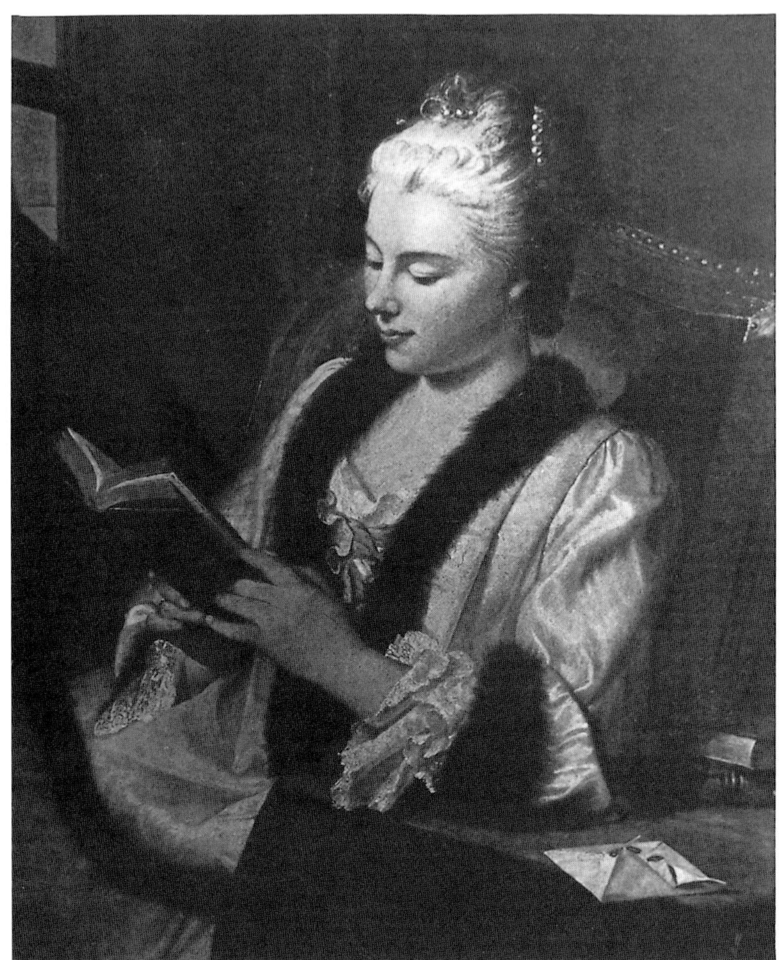

FIGURE 48.
Jacques-André-Joseph Aved, *Portrait of Mme de Varennes as Reader*, 1738. Location unknown (photo: *Gazette des Beaux-Arts* 13, 1935; University of Delaware Photographic Services).

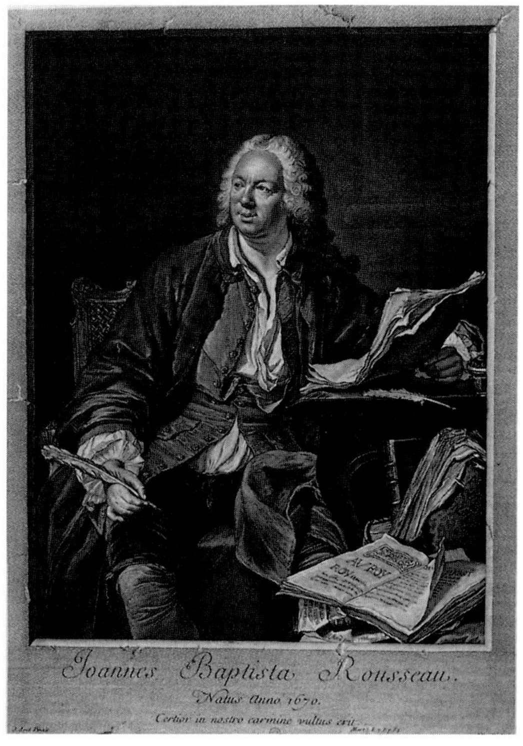

FIGURE 49.
Jean Daullé after Jacques-André-Joseph Aved, *Portrait of Jean-Baptiste Rousseau*, ca. 1738. Paris, Bibliothèque Nationale, Département des Estampes.

person,"[21] Marie-Sophie de Courcillon was an intellectual and a devotee of letters. In this regard, she was typical of the increasing numbers of French aristocratic savantes who consumed universal histories, signifying their thirst for unlimited knowledge. Among these educated women were Louis XV's daughters, who commissioned a universal history from their tutor Hardion, and Pompadour herself, who owned several volumes of this ilk. An entire rubric of her catalogued library is labeled "Histoire universelle."[22]

Nattier's gilded pictorial encomia were utterly outside the province of Jean-Etienne Liotard. His hauntingly pungent pastel of Mme d'Epinay (Geneva, Musée d'Art et d'Histoire, ca. 1757–59; Fig. 51), executed during the sitter's sojourn in Geneva (to which she traveled from Paris to consult Dr. Tronchin, the philosophe and Voltaire's

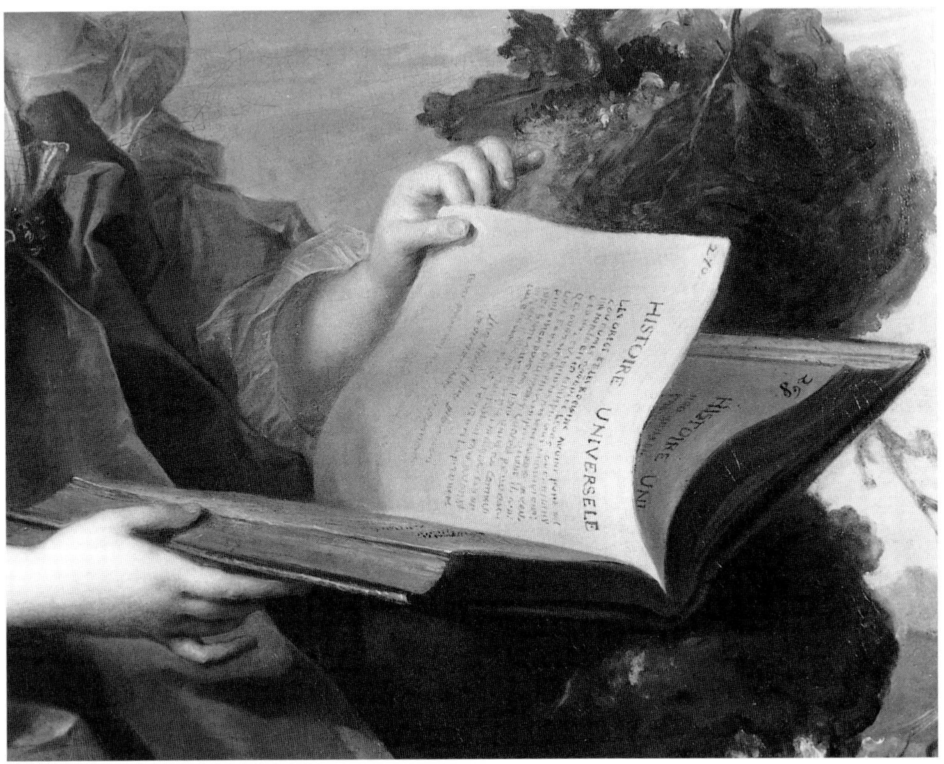

FIGURE 50.
Jean-Marc Nattier, *Portrait of the Princesse de Rohan Holding a Book* (detail), 1741. The Toledo Museum of Art, gift of Edward Drummond Libbey.

physician),[23] is the most candid and incisive likeness of a femme philosophe ever made. Liotard does not disguise the illness and infirmity that plagued Epinay throughout her life. In contrast, La Tour a few years earlier had presented the frail "philosophe" Pompadour as the paragon of self-confident health and Laura-like beauty.

One of the most distinguished and prolific *femmes-auteurs* of the Enlightenment, Epinay authored a progressive project on pedagogy for girls, a novel, plays, essays, and reviews, all of which earned her the admiration of her fellow philosophes, including her friend Voltaire, who, contemplating Liotard's likeness, wrote: "I humbly thank the philosophe who places her finger on her chin, and who has a bit of a tilted air, given to her by Liotard; her soul is as beautiful as her eyes."[24] Even more trenchant is Epinay's own literary self-portrait, which she wrote at age thirty in 1756, just a year or so prior to Liotard's pastel: "I am not the least bit pretty; yet I am not ugly. I am small, thin, very well put together. I have a youthful air, without freshness, and a noble, sweet, lively, witty, and interesting demeanor, without luster."[25] These characterizations were not lost on Liotard; but Liotard, like Voltaire and Epinay herself, pictures a diffident *woman* rather than a self-possessed philosophe concerned with noble ideas and the life of the mind.

Seated in a Louis XV chair in intimate half-length, almost disconcertingly close to the viewer, Epinay engages the beholder with her penetrating eye, encircled by sickly shadow, the nucleus of her emaciated countenance. This strangely beautiful face, still youthful, is enlivened by an inscrutable, even mischievous smile, which together with her tilted head and piquantly poised finger equivocates between the playful coquette and the pensive philosophe. Epinay's posture and attitude are analogous to her early writings, contemporaneous with her portrait, which oscillate between the wittily humorous and frivolous, and the timid, serious, and tender, bespeaking a fledgling author and young woman who has yet to find her true self.[26] This tentativeness is underscored by the reserved compactness of Epinay's triangular shape, which is relieved only by the decidedly feminine undulations of her lace bonnet and left sleeve. Her portrayal, then, contrasts notably with the conviction of portraits of her male philosophic colleagues, especially those of Diderot by Louis-Michel Van Loo (1767) and Fragonard (1769).

The index finger of Epinay's left hand marks a passage titled "DIALOGVEX" ("Dialogue number ten"; Fig. 52) in the small volume she cradles in her lap. On one level, we may read her dialogue as a signifier of the intimate conversation Epinay engages in with the beholder. While we cannot identify the book precisely, because its text was not meant to be read, Epinay's literary milieu and oeuvre provide some clues. A form favored by the philosophes because it facilitated the free exchange of ideas and established equality among the interlocutors, the dialogue abounded in Epinay's early canon, including her *Lettre à mon fils* and *Mes Moments heureux*, printed together in a small edition in Geneva in 1759 during the author's sojourn there.[27] Epinay may very well display to her interlocutor this her first publication. While number ten was fictive—she published the First, Second, and Third Dialogues in 1761 after her return to Paris[28]—Liotard, who obviously had a strong rapport with his sitter, may also have been paying her a supreme compliment by increasing the number of her works to an abundant and seamless ten.

We exit the library of the reader and enter the laboratory of the scientist to look at selected portraits of women passionately interested in advances in the natural, physical, and experimental sciences that were sweeping Europe and revolutionizing ideas about the universe.[29]

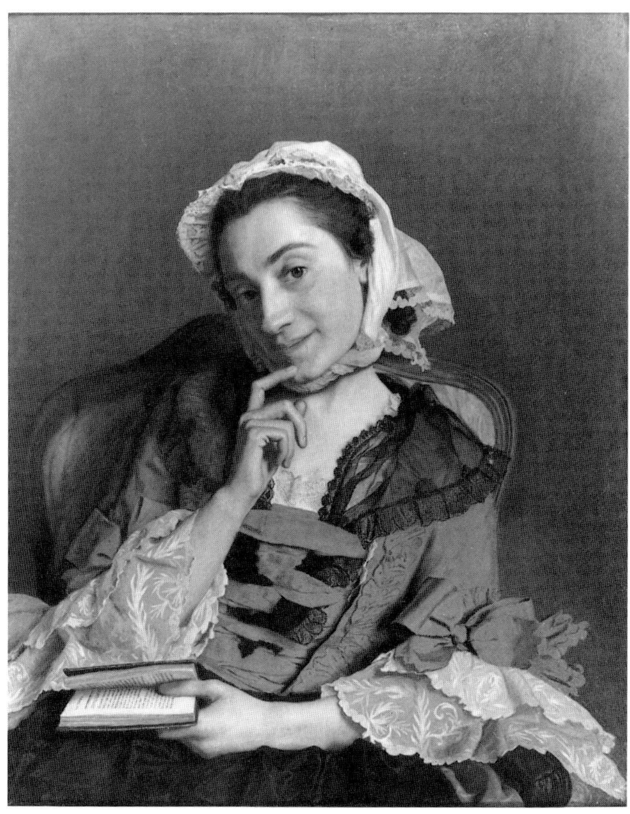

FIGURE 51.
Jean-Etienne Liotard, *Portrait of Mme d'Epinay*, ca. 1757–59. Geneva, Musée d'Art et d'Histoire (photo: © Musée d'Art et d'Histoire).

Exclusion from universities and the Royal Academy of Sciences, where one could have received proper systematic training, did not prevent women from studying, experimenting, and writing about science. In the seventeenth century, they already gathered in their salons and formed scientific coteries to educate themselves and to be tutored in the natural philosophy of Gassendi, the physics and cosmology of Descartes, and later the experimental physics of Newton, the greatest of them all. Seemingly insatiable, they witnessed and participated in dissections and swarmed to public lectures and courses geared to their interests. An entire industry of popularized scientific publications grew up to serve them; written in a conversational style

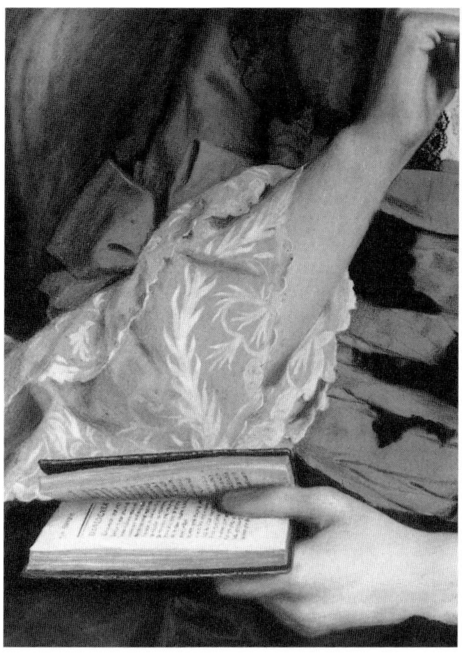

FIGURE 52.
Jean-Etienne Liotard, *Portrait of Mme d'Epinay* (detail), ca. 1757–59. Geneva, Musée d'Art et d'Histoire (photo: © Musée d'Art et d'Histoire).

and seasoned with the discourse of gallantry and love familiar to readers of novels and poetry, these books transmuted labyrinthine science into a palatable and intelligible form.[30] At times these books appear in portraits.

François de Troy ingeniously wedded portraiture to genre in the earliest painted encomium to a woman of science, *The Astronomy Lesson of the Duchesse du Maine* (Château de Sceaux, Musée de l'Ile-de-France, ca. 1702–5; Fig. 53).[31] One of the most visible women of learning during the later reign of Louis XIV and the dawn of the Regency, Anne-Louise-Bénédicte de Bourbon-Condé (1676–1753) was at the very summit of the French nobility and is best known as the spirited hostess of fêtes, theatrical performances, operas, and ballets, held at her château de Sceaux. Flamboyance aside, the duchess was also a serious savante steeped in classical languages—the busts of Socrates and Seneca on pedestals in her portrait encode her devotion to the ancients—and sufficiently trained in the sciences to use the microscope and the telescope, an ability that would have been applauded by her guiding genius, Descartes.

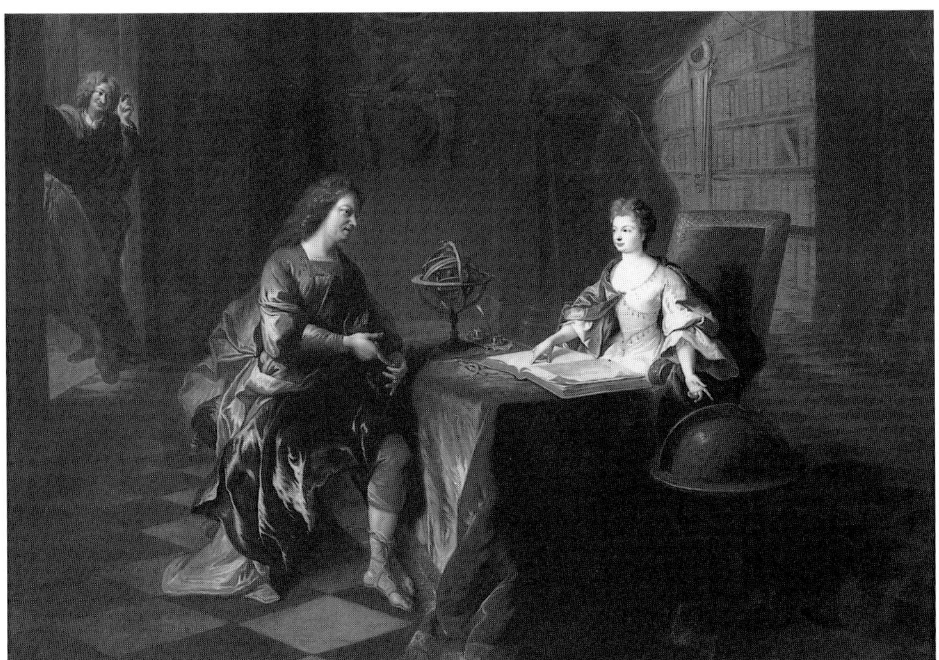

FIGURE 53.
François de Troy, *The Astronomy Lesson of the Duchesse du Maine*, ca. 1702–5. Château de Sceaux, Collection du Musée de l'Ile-de-France (photo: Pascal Lemaître).

She is represented in her apartment at Sceaux, surrounded by scientific paraphernalia: a barometer on a pier attached to ample bookshelves, behind her at the right, and a desk with a protractor, compass, inkstand, and astrolabe. Enthroned as the duchess of knowledge in a luxurious chair befitting her high rank, the diminutive scholar takes in the lesson of her tutor, the famous academician Nicolas de Malézieu who, seated on his humble tabouret, counts off on his fingers the planets of the universe known to the age. No passive learner, the duchess speaks confidently and keenly with him, indicating with her right hand a passage in the illustrated scientific volume and, with her left, a celestial globe on the floor.

Although the duchess was not physically beautiful, de Troy portrays her as the quintessential belle savante. When plain women of science wished for stellar beauty, they perforce resorted to artifice. The duchess applied to her features a florid maquillage, which is visible in her portrait. This dense red-and-white paint not only transforms her into the perfect period beauty but also augments her radiance: she becomes as effulgent as one of the astronomical bodies she studies in her scientific tome. The shadowy, unvarnished features of her tutor throw into relief her own whiteness and comeliness. Of lower rank and lesser physical endowment, at least in de Troy's fictive pictorial realm, the tutor Malézieu augments the duchess's knowledge and, by way of contrast, her beauty.

One of the most illustrious femmes savantes of the eighteenth century was Gabrielle-Emilie Le Tonnelier de Breteuil, marquise du Châtelet (1706–1749), an acquaintance of Pompadour and the duchesse du Maine, sharing their talent as thespians. Better known to her contemporaries as a Newton and a Leibniz in female guise, du Châtelet, the most eminent woman scientist of her generation, wore diamonds while doggedly deciphering the mysteries of the physical world—a consummate belle savante.[32]

Du Châtelet's persona as comely intellectual is pictured in two distinguished portraits: Nattier's characteristically eternalized icon, signed and dated 1743 (Salon of 1745, location unknown; Fig. 54),[33] and Marianne Loir's more forthright, quotidian image of a few years later (Bordeaux, Musée des Beaux-Arts, ca. 1745–49; Plate 7).[34] In both tableaux the erudite physicist is accompanied by scientific equipage—in the Nattier, books in the foreground and astrolabe and telescope in the niche at the right; in the Loir, a desk with a celestial globe, set square, and paper overwritten with calculations.

However, as in other period portraits of belles savantes, these intellectual trappings are counterbalanced by signs of the woman's beauty and grace. Nattier shapes a timeless poetic icon: perfect beauty and learning combine in the marquise's flawless oval face and impeccably white bust. Conceding to her more naturalistic idiom, Loir assimilates the approachable middle-aged scholar and the fashion plate: du Châtelet does her physics, mathematics, and geometry in a fur-trimmed frock of the dernier cri, a dress that plunges low enough to expose a skin of uncommon whiteness. Du Châtelet's legendary bijoux are insinuated into both portraits. Nattier decorates the marquise's chemise at the bust with a modest string of pearls, while Loir dangles another one from du Châtelet's papers at the right. Loir balances the marquise's brilliance and her graces by juxtaposing a geometrical compass in her right hand and a carnation in her left: the flower's pinkish white tint reiterates the delicate tincture of her perfect complexion.

In a rare departure from the tradition of picturing savantes with untitled books, Nattier depicts du Châtelet proudly displaying her *Institutions de physique*, first published anonymously in 1740, then revised in 1742; it is probably the latter edition that Nattier includes in her portrait dating one year later. In her book, the marquise took on the formidable task of synthesizing the materialism of Newton's physics with the metaphysics of Leibniz, adding historical background and information on the latest developments in physics. One of the promulgators of these developments, she worked all night long in the laboratory at her château de Cirey (doubtlessly sans jewelry) and entertained the most eminent scientists of the day, who came to Cirey to "Newtonize" with her and her companion, Voltaire.

The *Institutions* was not the only work produced by this largely autodidactic and informally tutored savante. Despite the fact that she was barred from membership because of her gender, the Royal Academy of Sciences published her *Dissertation on the Nature and the Propagation of Fire* (1738). Du Châtelet's chef d'oeuvre was her two-volume *Principes mathématiques de la philosophie naturelle* (1749), the definitive French translation of Newton's *Principia Mathematica*, which she augmented with commentary.

No wonder, then, that this passionate lover of learning engaged, albeit obliquely, in the Women's Quarrel. She expostulated:

> I feel the full weight of the prejudice which so universally excludes us from the sciences; it is one of the contradictions in life that has always amazed me, seeing that the law allows us to determine the fate of great nations, but that there is no place where we are trained to think. . . . Why [do] these creatures whose understanding appears in every way similar to that of men, seem to be stopped by some irresistible force, this side of a barrier. . . . Let people give a reason, but until they do, women will have reason to protest against their education. If I were king . . . I would redress an abuse which cuts back, as it were, one half of human kind. I would have women participate in all human rights, especially those of the mind. It would seem as if they were born only to deceive—this being the only intellectual exercise allowed them. The new education would greatly benefit the human race. Women would be worth more and men would gain something new to emulate. . . . I am convinced that many women are either unaware of their talents by reason of the fault in their education or that they bury them on account of prejudice for want of intellectual courage. My own experience confirms this. Chance made me acquainted with men of letters who extended the hand of friendship to me. . . . I then began to believe that I was a being with a mind.[35]

Like her painted portraits, literary encomia to the marquise equivocate between the belle and the savante. For instance, the expository verses of Etienne Fessard's engraving after a lost Nattier (Fig. 55) reconcile the notions of the marquise's scientific proficiency and the allure of her beauty by asserting: "It is thus that Truth / To better establish its sway, / Has taken the traits of beauty, / And the graces of Eloquence."[36] Similarly, Daquin's legend and sestet on a kindred engraving, published by Jean-

François Daumont after the same lost Nattier (Fig. 56), on the one hand salute the marquise's "love of the sciences" (not mastery of the sciences) and poeticize "the immortal Emilie" (her first name) who, while flying through the air next to Newton, measures the universe with him. Yet, despite her alleged parity with the great male physicist whose work she translated, she is inevitably relegated to his distaff side, for she remains "the ornament of her sex and of our century / The goal of [whose] work is to enlighten Mankind."[37]

Perhaps the closest literary analogue to Nattier's apotheosis of the mârquise du Châtelet was written by her longtime companion and intellectual partner, Voltaire, who knew her best. However, rather than saluting her and her work with the perspicacity one would expect from an intimate, Voltaire deifies his mistress with the tropes of contemporary society poetry and, like Nattier, generalizes the serious scientist into the ideal femme; this goddess tames and transforms barbarous, male physics into palatable, feminized cuisine:

> Reader, open this erudite work;
> Physics, for us, has left its savage air,
> And you will guess by its charming language
> That it is Venus who teaches us.
> Yes, Venus-Uranie, she has the bust of one,
> And of the other she has all the intellect.
> The true philosophe reads her;
> Who sees her, I know it, cannot be well behaved.[38]

The final couplet is enlightening: while the philosophe (presumably male) is edified by the goddess's work, he is propelled right out of the realm of the intellect into a sensual wilderness when he beholds her seductive person.

Nattier's *Portrait of the Marquise du Châtelet*, exhibited in the Salon of 1745 (see Fig. 54), begs comparison with his own *Portrait of Joseph Bonnier de la Mosson* (Washington, D.C., National Gallery of Art, 1745; Fig. 57), which was shown in the salon one year later. The most renowned of all natural-history and natural-science *amateurs* in eighteenth-century France, Bonnier is celebrated by Nattier in front of his lavish laboratory-pharmacy, called by a contemporary "one of the finest cabinets" in Paris. Here we are exposed to a remarkable array of scientific devices and specimens, including a hydraulic instrument and a multitude of "phials placed on shelves . . . containing an abundance of fetuses, serpents and other rare animals," as another witness puts it. Garbed in his sumptuous dressing gown, Bonnier dominates his setting, his right arm resting on the first volume of *Histoire naturelle*, his left steadying another formidable tome.[39]

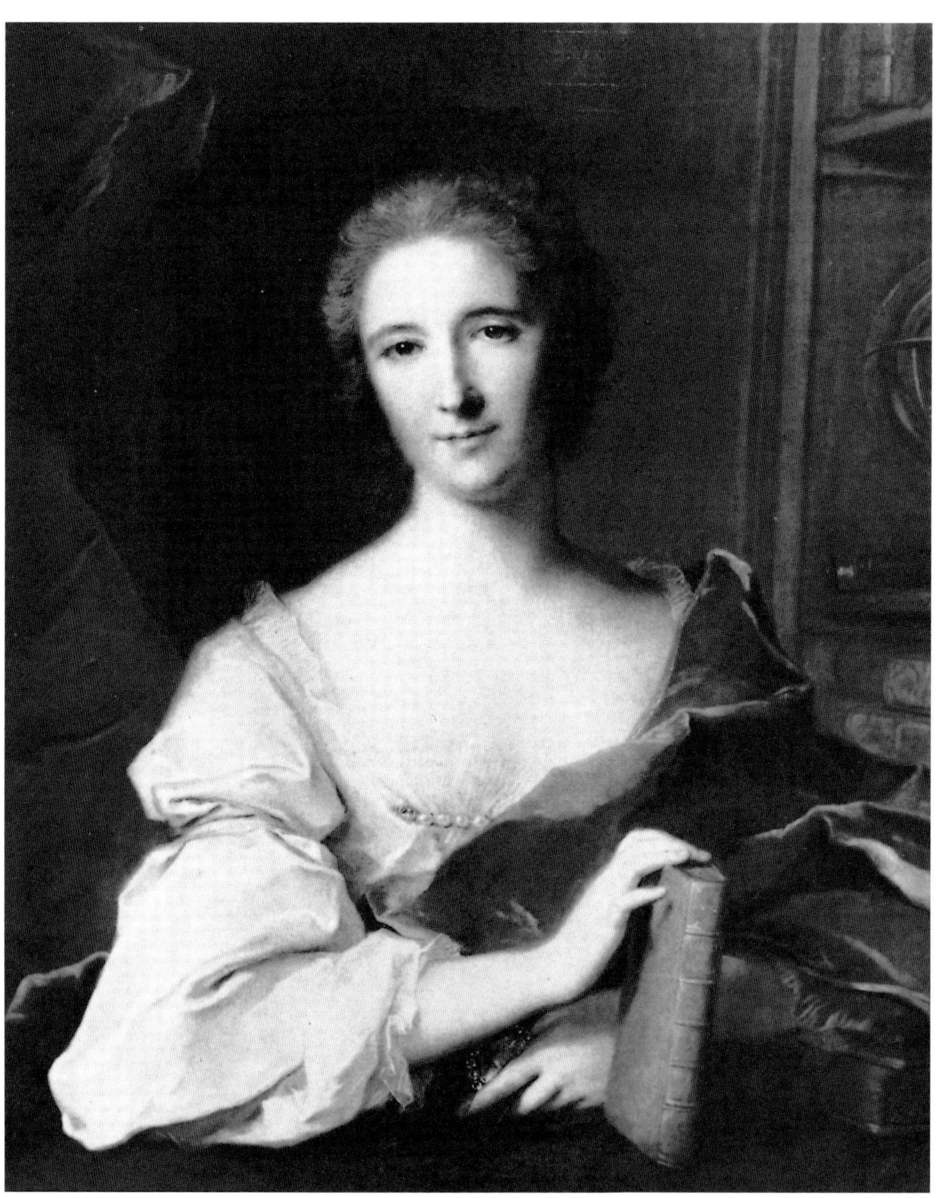

FIGURE 54.
Jean-Marc Nattier, *Portrait of the Marquise du Châtelet*, 1743. Location unknown (photo: Courtesy of the National Gallery of Art, Washington, D.C., Photographic Archives).

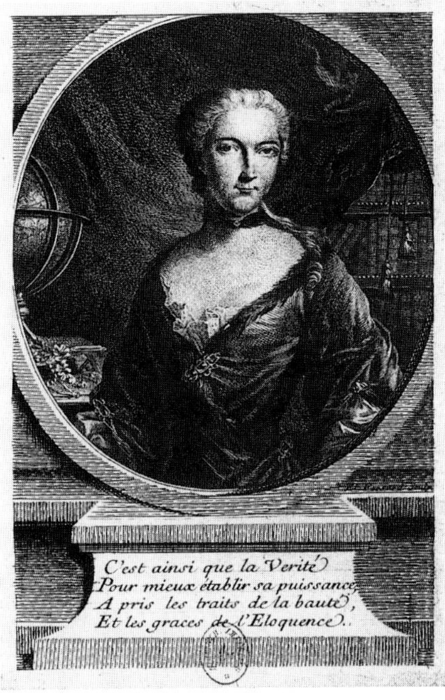

FIGURE 55.
Etienne Fessard after Jean-Marc Nattier, *Portrait of the Marquise du Châtelet.* Paris, Bibliothèque Nationale, Département des Estampes.

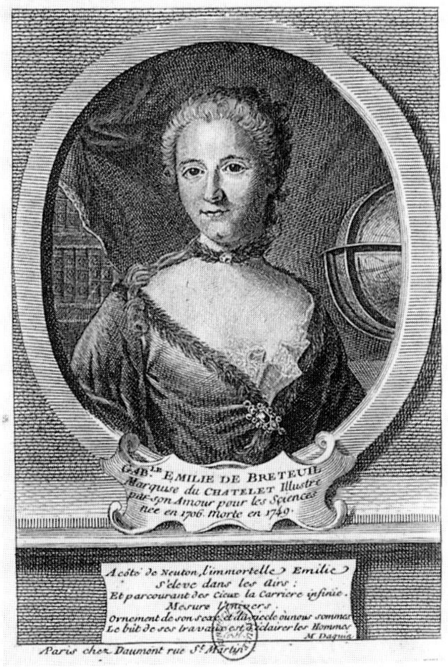

FIGURE 56.
Jean-François Daumont after Jean-Marc Nattier, *Portrait of the Marquise du Châtelet.* Paris, Bibliothèque Nationale, Département des Estampes.

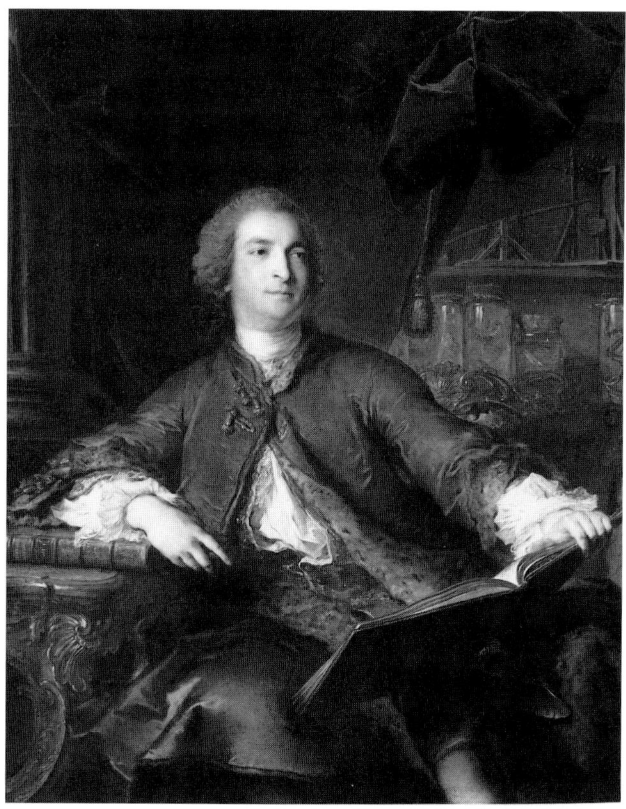

FIGURE 57.
Jean-Marc Nattier, *Portrait of Joseph Bonnier de la Mosson*, 1745. Washington, D.C., National Gallery of Art, Samuel H. Kress Collection (photo: © Board of Trustees, National Gallery of Art).

Nattier's aesthetic beautifies and imbues with grace both the male *amateur* and the female professional; yet in spite of this overriding sensibility, his portraits are gendered differently. Less proficient in the sciences than the female Newton and Leibniz, Bonnier is nonetheless fashioned more imposingly and authoritatively. The diagonal that sweeps through his person from lower right to upper left energizes him with a force, panache, and swagger with which the static pyramid and dominant vertical comprising the marquise cannot compete. His expansiveness overpowers her compactness. The delicate hand that fingers her small book of "charming language" and the "graces of eloquence" pales beside his vigorous grasp of an anonymous tome. Despite the fact that Nattier presents us with a Venus-Uranie for all time, this goddess of physics and astronomy is outstripped by the modish male Parisian, who is every inch of his time.

Newton's "philosophie naturelle," championed by du Châtelet and Voltaire, exercised the greatest single influence on science during the first half of the eighteenth century. As early as the 1720s, the salons were pulsating with it, and as the century progressed, increasing numbers of educated women wholeheartedly embraced it.[40]

One of those women was Mlle Ferrand, whom La Tour depicts meditating on her Newton in an incisive pastel exhibited in the Salon of 1753 (Munich, Alte Pinakothek; Fig. 58).[41] Pictured in three-quarter length in the intimacy of her study and clad in her *déshabillé du matin* to facilitate comfortable contemplation, Ferrand interrupts her reading to discourse with the spectator who has just entered her intellectual domain. La Tour honors Ferrand's intelligence. Her firm pyramidal form may ingeniously allude to the solid geometry employed by her English muse and undoubtedly concretizes the resoluteness of her active mind. Her wide-eyed acuity and firm mouth, as well as her upright attentiveness, signal to the beholder that Newton's physics is energizing her being. She clearly conveys that cerebral vigor. Her open hand and splayed fingers, directing the viewer to her ear and then on to her book, indicate that she wishes to hear what her interlocutor has to say about Newton's optics and gravitational theory.

Her tome, albeit magnified for expressive purposes—its monumentality signifies its importance—is Voltaire's *Eléments de la philosophie de Newton*, whose first edition is actually a rather modest though richly illustrated octavo of 399 pages. Nevertheless, like Ferrand's book, the actual *Eléments* is identified on its rectos with the words "DE NEUTON." First published in Amsterdam in 1738, the volume was dedicated by Voltaire to its principal catalyst, the marquise du Châtelet (this time the deified "Minerve de la France"), to enshrine her glory and that of her sex. In the preface, Voltaire elaborates on the importance of Newtonian physics for people of all classes and both genders, counseling women to apply themselves to science as assiduously as their Gallic Minerva applies herself.[42]

Mlle Ferrand, about whom we possess no biographical information, was a bourgeois beneficiary of Voltaire's attempt to disseminate to the French public in intelligible language Newton's opaque physics and its scientific method. This experimental method had displaced the outmoded but nonetheless entrenched a priori rationalism of Descartes and his principal French disciple, Fontenelle, whose *Entrétiens sur la pluralité des mondes* (1686) enjoyed a great vogue among women of the period. A sensational success in France, the *Eléments* was reissued in several editions throughout the eighteenth century—Mlle Ferrand may be reading the 1752 edition hot off the press—and caused one reviewer to gush: "Finally Voltaire appeared, and immedi-

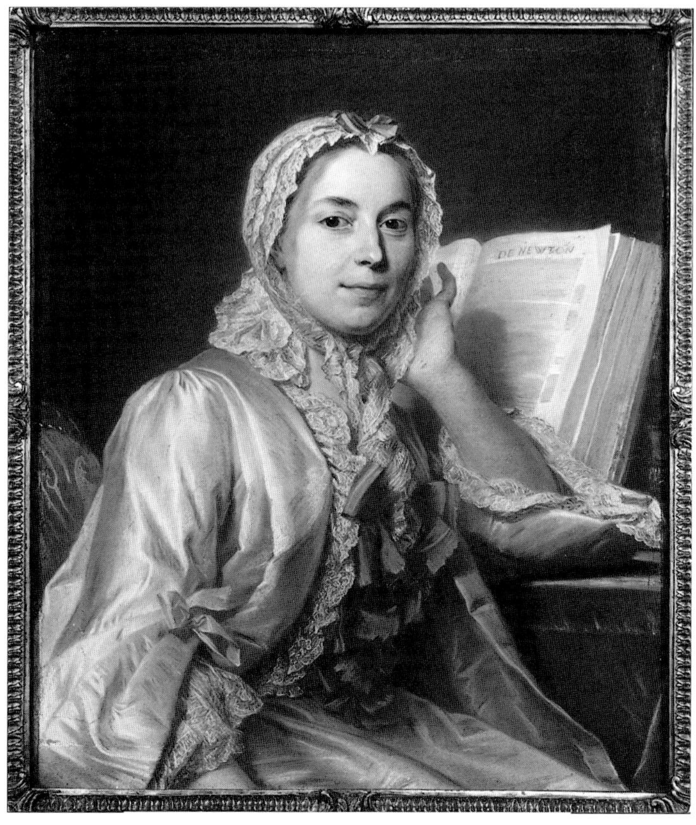

FIGURE 58.
Maurice-Quentin de La Tour, *Mlle Ferrand Meditating on Newton*, 1753. Munich, Alte Pinakothek (photo: Bayerische Staatsgemäldesammlungen).

ately Newton is understood or about to be; all Paris resounds with Newton, all Paris stutters Newton, all Paris studies and learns Newton."[43] One native Parisian, Mme de Pompadour, was apparently taken with Newton: in her library were Voltaire's *Oeuvres complettes* (1757), which contained the *Eléments*, and a copy of Francesco Algarotti's *Il Newtonianisme pour les dames* (1738),[44] one of the major popularizing scientific works geared to women, whose author "Newtonized" with du Châtelet and Voltaire.

The discussion here of musicians begins with La Tour's engagingly trenchant pastels of his patroness and friend, Françoise-Thérèse Butinon des Hayes (1714–1756), better known to her contemporaries and to posterity as Mme de La Pouplinière. Descended from the famous theatrical and musical Dancourt family, La Pouplinière was a gifted harpsichordist and music theorist, trained by Rameau, and a generous patroness of artists, writers, philosophers, and musicians (including Rameau), whom she and her Maecenas-husband entertained at their enlightened salon at Passy.[45]

La Tour pictures several aspects of La Pouplinière's personality in the pastels. In his *préparation* for a now-lost portrait (Saint-Quentin, Musée Antoine Lécuyer, ca. 1740–45; Fig. 59),[46] the comely performer regards us shrewdly and circumspectly while elegantly turning a page of her musical score. The delicate way in which she lifts her pinky finger and with the others taps the base of her music stand evokes the graceful pose of the harpsichordist touching her keys. Her riveting eyes glow with the legendary acumen that prompted Marmontel (whose play she critiqued) to extol her "happy facility of memory and intelligence . . . this spirit of eloquence which owes to inspiration . . . this harmony of mind and taste."[47] Those fiery eyes also betray her ebullience: "My heart, my blood is still most passionately tumultuous. I have a sensibility and an ardor that throw me out of the window. . . . My imagination is always in motion."[48]

Yet La Tour's image of La Pouplinière also conjures up the coquette, whose music stand could very well substitute for her mirror, from which she looks up to flirt with the beholder. This gendered image contrasts sharply, for example, with Aved's impassioned *Portrait of Rameau* (see Fig. 39), in which the male musical genius exudes inspiration as he tunes his violin.

In the second, imposing pastel of La Pouplinière, attributed to La Tour and dating from about the same time as the first (location unknown; Fig. 60),[49] the artist reinvents her as the serious intellectual and music critic admired by Voltaire as the "musician" and the "philosophe." Seated nearly full-length in a luxurious armchair and dressed in the sumptuous clothing one would expect of the wife of an immensely wealthy tax farmer, Mme de La Pouplinière poses sedately with a musical score. In manuscript, it is a piece of what appears to be accompanied vocal music, perhaps one of Rameau's chamber cantatas, which were often performed at Passy. The score also intimates Mme de La Pouplinière's critically acclaimed reviews. In her most celebrated critique, "Excerpt from the Book by M. Rameau entitled *Génération harmonique*" (1737), the student perspicaciously analyzed the complex arithmetical and geometrical harmonics of the teacher. The critique received rave notices in the musical camp known as the "ésprits" and received the approbation of the editor of the musical review *Le Pour et Contre*, in which it was published, and of Voltaire, who hailed it as a work of "uncommon merit."[50]

La Tour's homage to this serious female musician and steadfast patroness, seated with her musical score, foreshadows by nearly a decade—its personal and penetrating

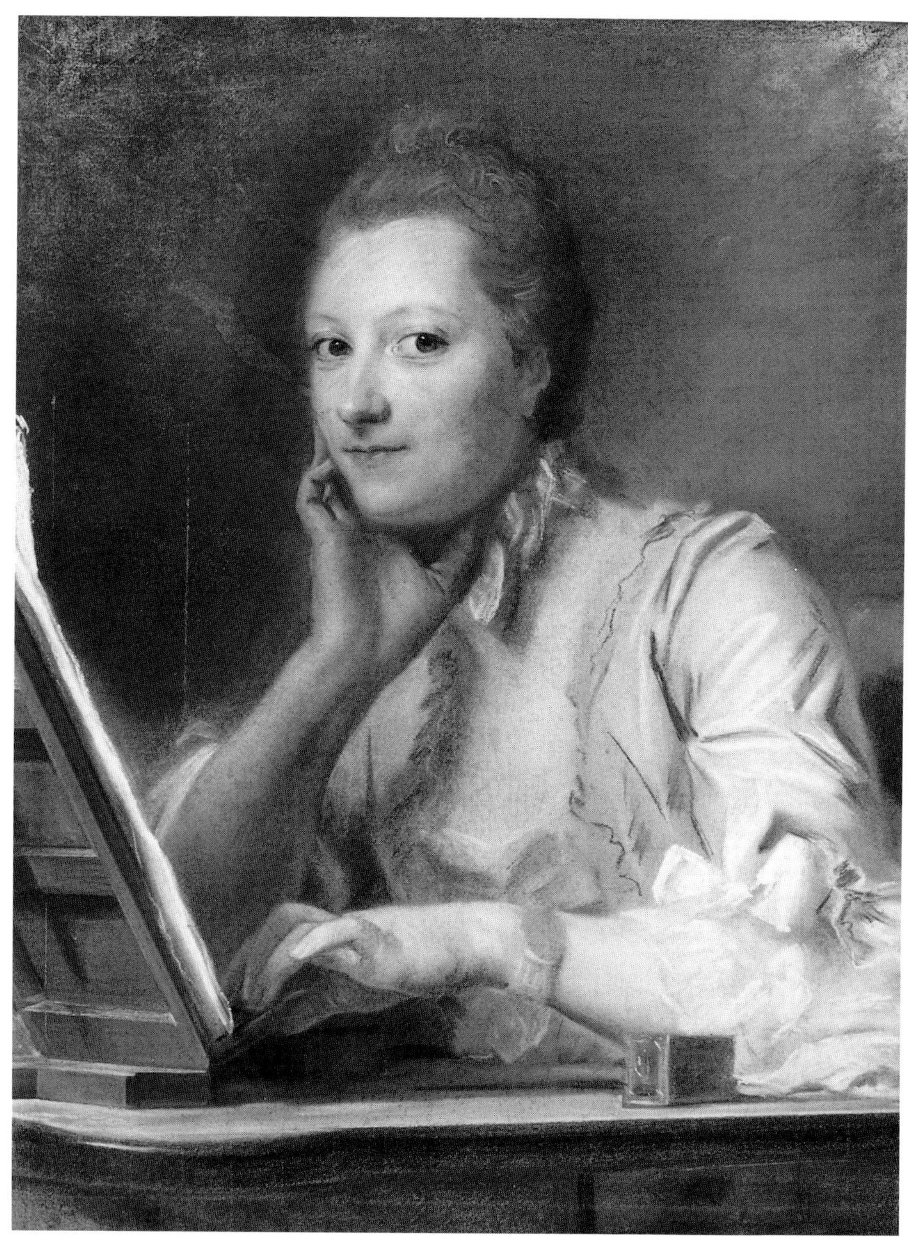

FIGURE 59.
Maurice-Quentin de La Tour, *Portrait of Mme de La Pouplinière*, ca. 1740–45. Saint-Quentin, Musée Antoine Lécuyer (photo: Bulloz).

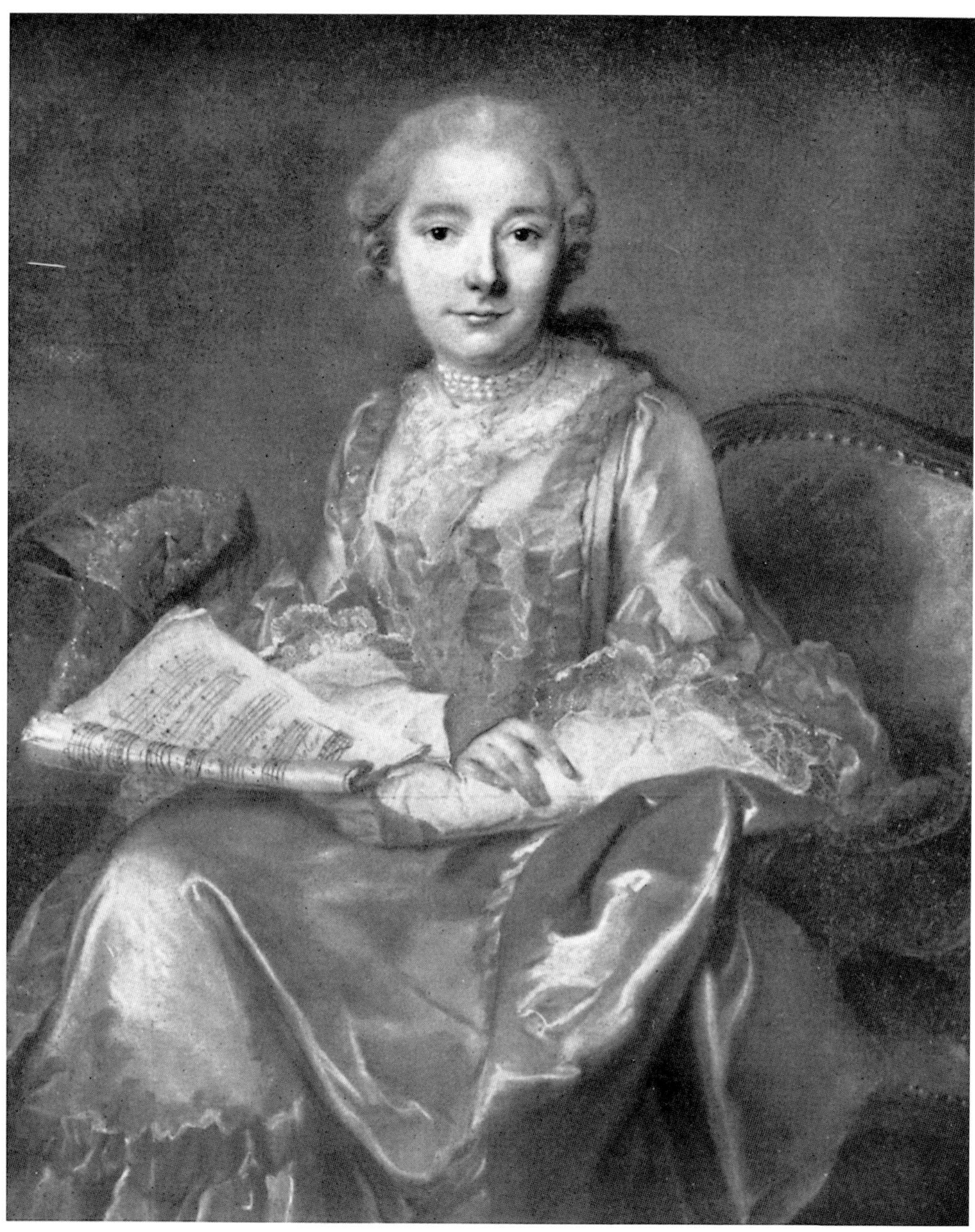

FIGURE 60.
Attributed to Maurice-Quentin de La Tour, *Portrait of Mme de La Pouplinière*, ca. 1740–45. Location unknown (photo: Courtesy of the National Gallery of Art, Washington, D.C., Photographic Archives).

cast notwithstanding—his more famous pictorial tribute to Mme de Pompadour: the seeds of his 1755 pastel lay in his own oeuvre.

A member of Mme de La Pouplinière's circle and a fellow student of Rameau was the gifted harpsichordist, composer, and amateur painter Anne-Jeanne Boucon (1707–1780), who in 1747 married her kindred musician, the celebrated violinist, composer, and Master of the King's Music, Jean-Joseph Cassanéa de Mondonville. Boucon was the daughter of the connoisseur Etienne Boucon. The pastellist Rosalba Carriera, in her *Mémoires,* mentions her participation in concerts given by the great *amateur* Pierre Crozat in the 1720s. No doubt Mme de Mondonville was acquainted with Mme de Pompadour. They shared an interest in the harpsichord, and Pompadour supported Mondonville's husband, a champion of French music over Italian, in the debate called "la Querelle des Buffons."[51]

A habitué of Mme de Mondonville's salon and a good friend of both husband and wife, La Tour made pastels of each of them. Jean-Joseph Cassanéa, in the year of his marriage (Saint-Quentin, Musée Antoine Lécuyer; Fig. 61), convivially engages the viewer as he tunes and listens to his violin. The more restrained likeness of Anne-Jeanne (Saint Louis Art Museum; Plate 8) was commissioned as a pendant later and exhibited in the Salon of 1753. The pastel of Mme de Mondonville was hailed by the critics for its verisimilitude.[52]

In this confidential half-length, Mme de Mondonville elegantly leans on her *clavesin ordinaire.* On this single-manual harpsichord rests her chef d'oeuvre in manuscript, *Pièces de Clavesin de Madame de Mondonville,* which, like many period compositions for the harpsichord, begins with thirty-second notes marking the baroque flourish known as a "tirade." But Mme de Mondonville displays rather than performs her musical piece; in this regard, her portrait is gendered. At the same time, her studied casualness, together with her aristocratic refinement and self-possessed half smile, conforms to the period comportment of *honnêteté.* In addition to privileging conspicuous leisure and luxurious repose, ideals that inform Boucher's Munich portrait of Pompadour, *honnêteté,* a class ideal of the aristocracy and the upper bourgeoisie, also connoted civil, polished, and agreeable behavior—in short, sophistication and style.[53] But La Tour indicates that Mme de Mondonville's sophistication is merely one component of her multifaceted personality. Her soulful, almost melancholy eyes bespeak a sensibility that also resonates in the elegiac *pièce de concert,* composed by her teacher Rameau and named, in her honor, "La Boucon."[54]

Although posterity has obscured the achievements of this remarkable woman, Mme de Mondonville was esteemed during her lifetime. Before her marriage she performed for the Regent, Philippe d'Orléans, as well as for Pierre Crozat. She was regarded as one of the best harpsichordists of the early eighteenth century. Further, as a composer she was saluted by the critic La Font de Saint-Yenne as one "of our

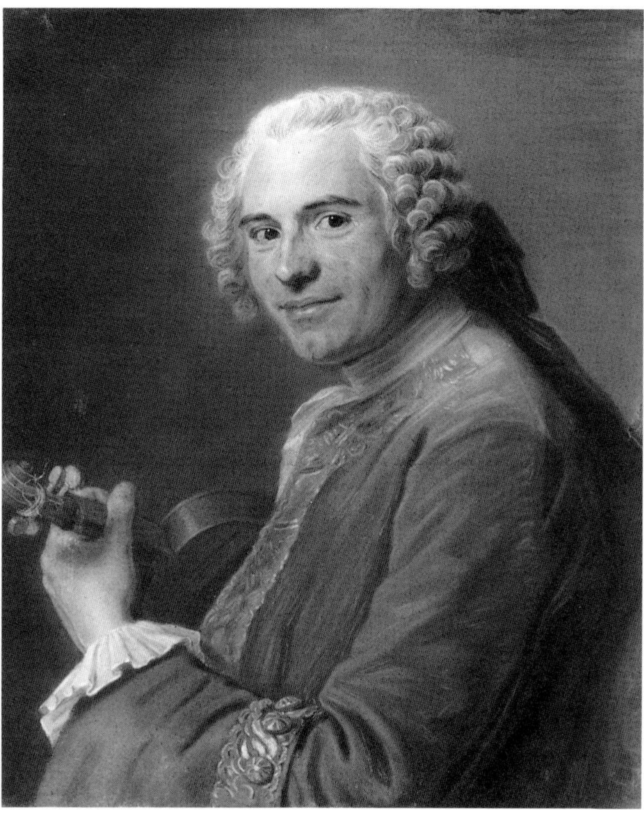

FIGURE 61.
Maurice-Quentin de La Tour, *Portrait of Jean-Joseph Cassanéa de Mondonville*, 1747. Saint-Quentin, Musée Antoine Lécuyer (photo: Bulloz).

illustrious authors" who honored the nation and whom La Tour honored in his pastels.[55]

Among the most famous portraits of Enlightenment women musicians are Nattier's full-length likenesses of "Mesdames," two of Louis XV and Marie Leczinska's daughters. The first is *Mme Henriette Playing the Bass Viol* (Versailles, 1754, Musée National du Château; see Fig. 11), which I have described as an "intellectual partner" to La Tour's pastel of the musician Mme de Pompadour at the Salon of 1755. The second, *Mme Adélaïde with a Musical Score* (Versailles, Musée National du Château, 1758; Fig. 62), was commissioned as a pendant to her sister's image and

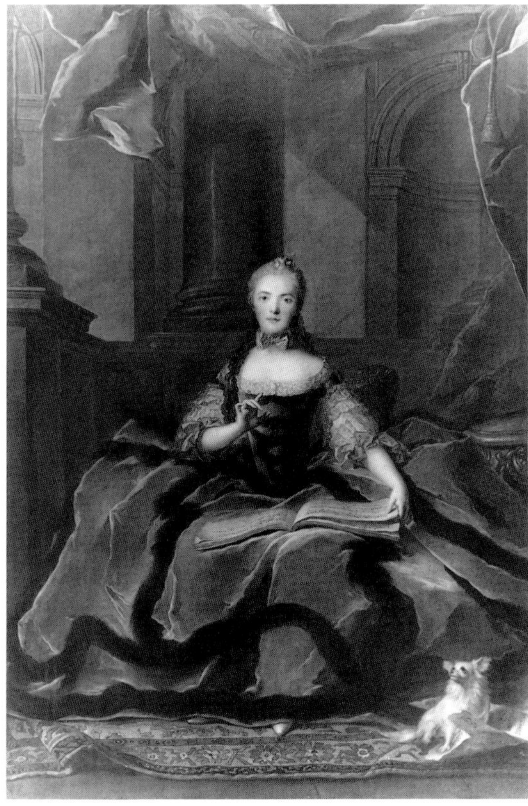

FIGURE 62.
Jean-Marc Nattier, *Mme Adélaïde with a Musical Score*, 1758. Versailles, Musée National du Château (photo: RMN).

was on view at the Salon of 1759. They incandesce with the staffage of the royal ceremonial portrait, one of Nattier's fortes.[56]

And why shouldn't they? The daughters of the king of France, Mesdames were expert, versatile musicians who played several instruments and performed with their masters and other professionals. The font of their musical devotion and proficiency was their mother, who was much more than a matronly devotee of the Bible, as she is pictured by Nattier in her portrait of 1748. The queen played several instruments and, upon her marriage to Louis XV in 1725, sponsored a multitude of operas and concerts—the "Concerts chez la Reine"—which over many years featured the most famous composers and performers of the day.[57] These concerts may have been the impetus for the performances Pompadour orchestrated in her Théâtre des Petits-Appartements.

Thus music was central to the princesses' education. Mme Henriette's penchant for the bass viol was unusual at the time, since women generally eschewed such unwieldy, masculine-gendered instruments, which detracted from their femininity.[58] Nattier deftly camouflaged Henriette's ungainly posture by swathing her legs in ample folds of drapery. She thus plays this cumbersome seven-stringed bass viol with the elegance and *sprezzatura* of a princess. To Henriette's left is her two-manual harpsichord, which she learned to play under the tutelage of Mlle Couperin, the composer's daughter. The harpsichord, on which is a sheet scripting a short cantata, suggests Henriette's versatility as well as the basso continuo that a partner would have played in duet with her.

Nattier's portrait constructs Mme Adélaïde as the conductor of a performance. She holds a score while beating the measure of the "presto" movement with her elegantly raised hand. On the console at the right is the fine, signed violin that she played, according to one source, "superlatively." More versatile than her sister, Adélaïde also touched the harpsichord, strummed the guitar, and bowed the cello.[59]

The *Portrait of Mme Adélaïde with a Musical Score* could almost be said to have taken its cue from La Tour's pastel of Pompadour, exhibited at the salon four years earlier (see Plate 3). Some of the pastel's features resonate in Nattier's canvas. Both musicians are seated full-length in a Louis XV chair, musical scores in hand. A stringed instrument with an additional score rests at their sides, a carpet cushions their feet, and a flourish of drapery heightens them. While Adélaïde's dog, which impudently feasts on the musical sheet on the floor at the right, finds no counterpart in the pastel, it echoes Pompadour's spaniel brushing up against her papers in Boucher's Munich portrait, exhibited in the salon just two years previously.

Leaving the aristocratic court and entering the bourgeois realm of the Paris theater, let us now examine the portraits of Marie-Justine-Benoîte Duronceray, Mme Favart (1727–1772), one of the most celebrated and versatile actresses of her time, widely acclaimed for her stirring declamation, graceful dancing, droll comedy, and masterful imitations of foreign accents. Nourished in childhood by her musician parents, these talents bloomed in her maturity during her performances at the Paris fairs, Italian Comedy, and the Opéra-Comique, where she triumphed again and again. A composer and a playwright, Mme Favart also collaborated with her husband, the renowned dramatist Charles-Simon, on numerous plays. Mme de Pompadour must have known her fellow thespian personally, since the marquise appointed Charles-Simon director of the Opéra-Comique.[60]

But it was Favart's melodious playing and silvery singing that François-Hubert Drouais and Liotard enshrined in two great portraits dating from 1757 and located,

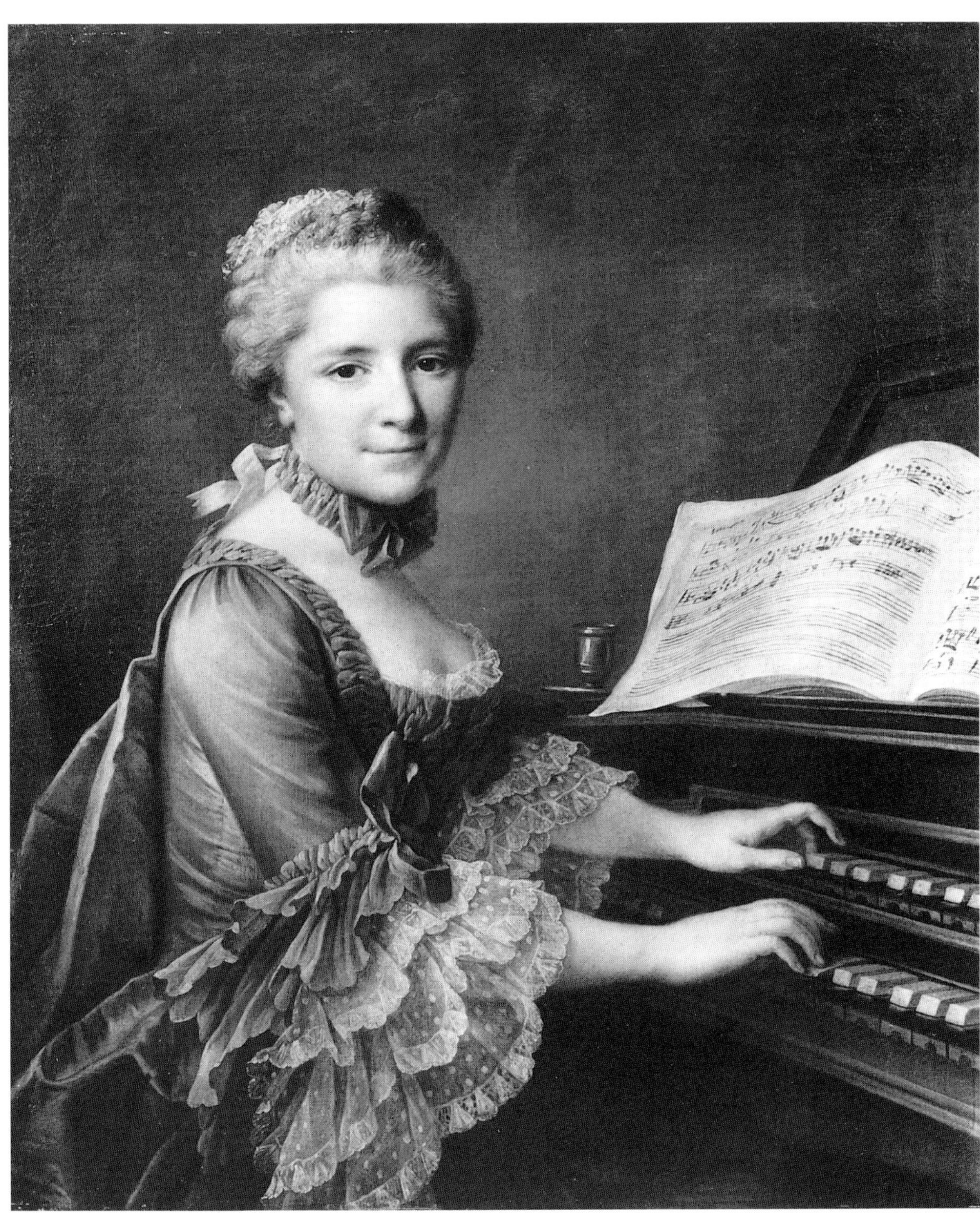

FIGURE 63.
François-Hubert Drouais, *Portrait of Mme Favart*, 1757, New York, The Metropolitan Museum of Art, Mr. and Mrs. Isaac D. Fletcher Collection, bequest of Isaac D. Fletcher, 1917.

respectively, in the Metropolitan Museum and the Oskar Reinhart Museum (Figs. 63, 64).[61] Drouais privileges her proficiency as a harpsichordist in a refreshingly vivid and psychologically penetrating likeness, which departs from his usually vacuous portraits of learned women, such as *La Marquise d'Aiguirandes Holding a Book* (Cleveland Museum of Art, 1759).[62] Its incisive cast notwithstanding, the portrait of Favart remains well within the canon of beauty that we have come to know as the province of the belle savante. Posing at the queen of feminine-gendered instruments, Mme Favart is every inch the fashion plate. Her modish wide-necked sack dress adheres to her bodice, enhancing her feminine form, and her silk sleeves flow into triple lace *engageants* (hanging undersleeves with lace cuffs), counterpointing her smooth arms and hands. Pretty and sympathetic, with a "sensitive soul, an inalterably blithe heart, and a gentle philosophy," as one of her eulogists put it,[63] Mme Favart at her two-stave harpsichord plays the treble and bass lines of a composition in manuscript, perhaps a piece of music she composed to accompany the Italian airs, *ariettes* (little airs), or *couplets choisis* (selected couplets) she chanted on stage.

Liotard's portrait, even more singular than Drouais's, is an ebullient likeness of a now dark-haired, broad-featured beauty in the throes of playing her guitar and singing. This likeness is exceptional among savante portraits, for it depicts a woman not as a static icon of beauty but as an actual performer. The pastel effervesces with Favart's famous theatrical verve, which in turn is accented by the Pompadour pompon in her cadently wavy hair and her animated shadow on the wall. In fact, the portrait consciously evokes the theater; its actress sports semifanciful stage dress and sings while accompanying herself, as Favart often did on stage. Liotard may even represent her in a specific role. In the play *The Harvesters*, Favart chanted, "Sportively singing a song / And wearing picturesquely a bunch of flowers on her head."[64]

Mme Favart's portrait is a pendant; its companion (location unknown; Fig. 65) pictures her husband seated at a table marking a passage in his book—perhaps the fifth volume of the *Théâtre complet* the couple coedited—which he lets drop upon hearing his wife sing and play.[65] In these pendants Liotard has styled perhaps the most imaginative and poignant tributes to conjugal love, a marriage of talent, collaboration, and mutual admiration. In doing so, he reverses the customary gender roles in marriage portraiture: cast not as the usual passive muse of her husband's creativity,[66] here the wife is the active performer, whose gifts mesmerize her admiring, passive spouse.

Like most of her female contemporaries in their portraits, Pompadour is styled in her likenesses as the quintessential belle savante, in accord with the period construct of a beautiful woman. She is thus pictured as idealized, passive, and remote, in contrast to the particularized, active, authoritative, and psychologically penetrating images of her male counterparts. Boucher and La Tour fashion Pompadour as an

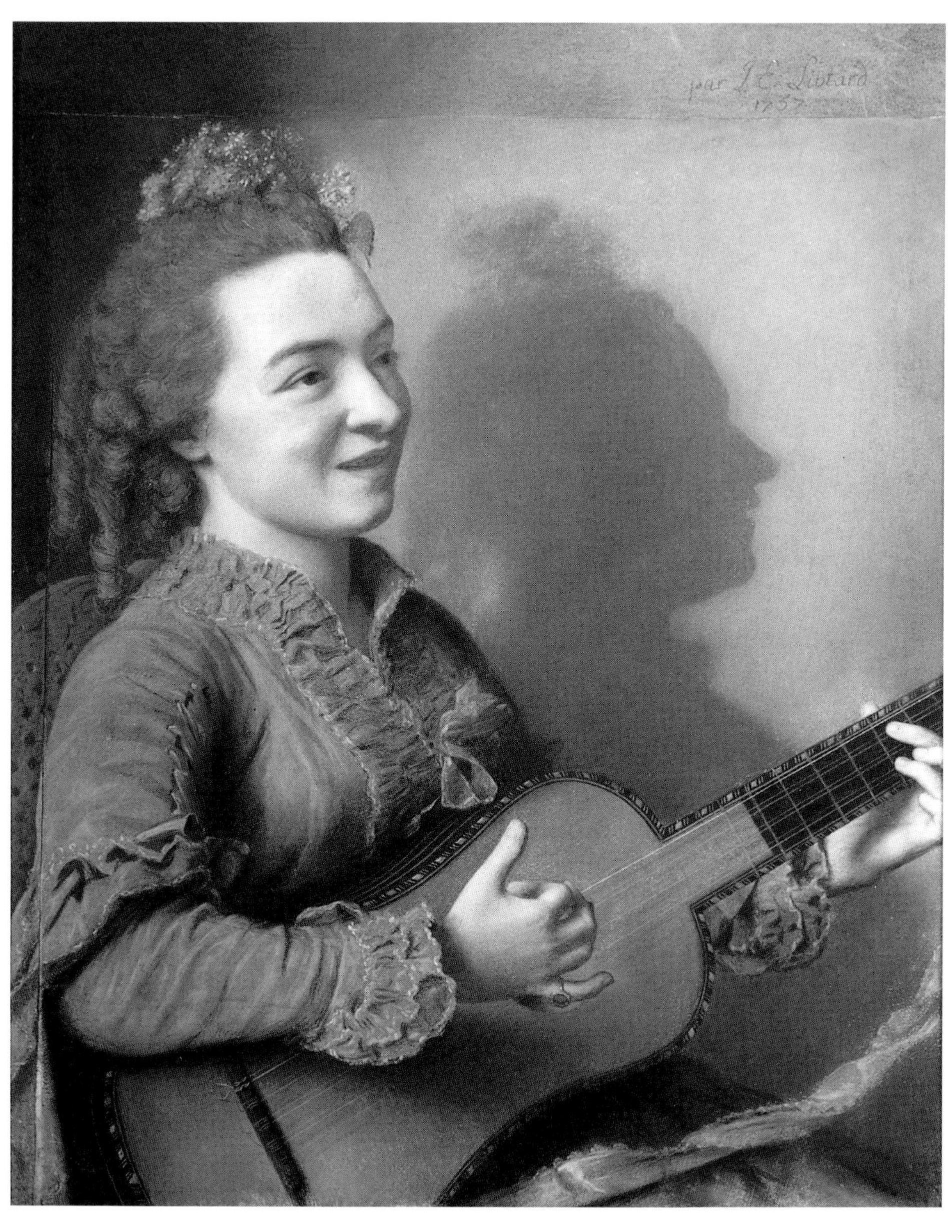

FIGURE 64.
Jean-Etienne Liotard, *Portrait of Mme Favart*, 1757. Winterthur, Oskar Reinhart Museum.

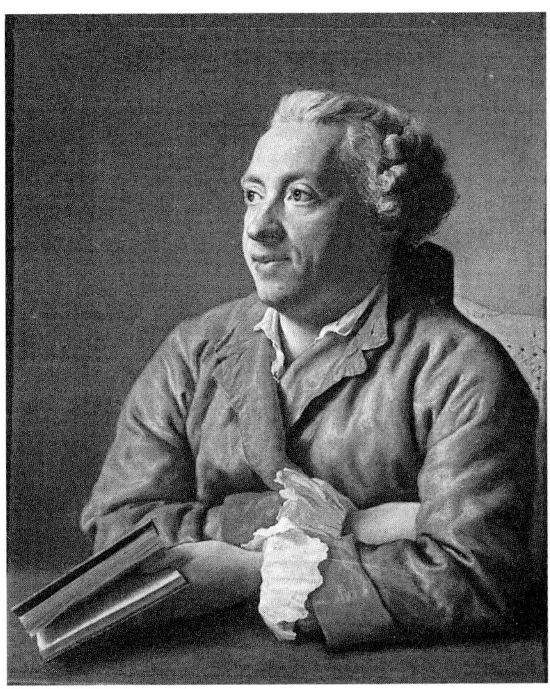

FIGURE 65.
Jean-Etienne Liotard, *Portrait of Charles-Simon Favart*, 1757. Location unknown (photo: Marcel Roethlisberger).

icon of physical and intellectual perfection—the beautiful Laura and the Venus-like philosophe. They assert her eternal beauty and her stature as the noble femme savante, assuring her indispensability to the crown for the remainder of her tenure as royal mistress. Nor would she have it any other way. It behooves us, the beholders of her portraits, to see beyond them, to recognize her true sensibility as a woman who was avidly devoted to ideas in life as well as art. In this regard, let us scrutinize La Tour's portrait, in which she manifests her intellectual commitment as a *salonnière*.

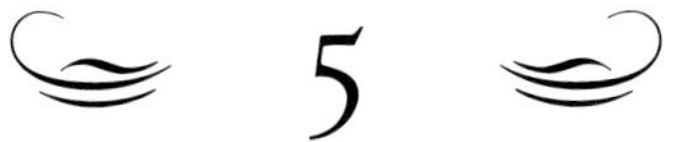

STYLING THE *SALONNIÈRE* AND THE PHILOSOPHE: MAURICE-QUENTIN DE LA TOUR'S PASTEL

In seventeenth- and eighteenth-century France, the social life of the educated classes was dominated by salons, gatherings devoted to reading and to discussing intellectual and cultural topics. Women traditionally presided over these coteries, thereby serving as the arbiters of taste in arts and letters during the period. They zealously promoted the great political philosopher Montesquieu, a habitué of the salons. His *Lettres persanes* (*Persian Letters*, 1721) remarked on the power of these cultural sovereigns:

> These women . . . form a kind of republic, whose members, always active, aid and serve one another: it is like a new State within a State; and whoever is at Court, in Paris, in the provinces, who observes the actions of ministers, magistrates, and prelates, if he does not know the women who govern them, he is like a man who can easily tell that a machine works, but does not know its inner springs.[1]

Pompadour was a *salonnière*, attending salons of others and presiding over her own, both before she became titular mistress of Louis XV and during her tenure as his cultivated companion and counselor. In Maurice-Quentin de La Tour's 1755 pastel, as I will suggest, she fashioned for herself the image of the consummate *salonnière* and arbiter of French arts and letters, as well as the image of a veritable philosophe, an equal to the Enlightenment intellectuals she patronized. The philosophes were French writers, philosophers, and scientists who believed in the supremacy and efficacy of reason. They belonged to an elite of education, intelligence, and talent irrespective of birth and took culture as their privilege and sign.[2]

Although women were barred from positions of power in society because of their feeble education and training, *salonnières*, in particular, nonetheless exercised significant social and economic influence within the circumscribed cadre of their intellectual coteries. In fact, this influence was considerable: they often determined the academic fortunes of many men in the arts and letters. Acutely aware of the *salonnières'* crucial social and financial clout, and hoping to receive the women's approbation of their work, savants eagerly sought entrée into these circles. This connection could be a crucial step toward the ultimate prize, acceptance into the French Academy, the pinnacle of French cultural institutions.[3]

But the *salonnières* were not mere catalysts of savants' academic careers or passive, ornamental hostesses; they created their coteries in order to fulfill their self-determined educational needs.[4] Since conventual curricula and private tutoring provided merely smatterings of knowledge, the most intelligent, ambitious, and tenacious women, such as Pompadour, participated in the discourse of the salon in order to complete their education. There they read and discussed the latest scholarship and availed themselves of the most erudite men of the time. Exhibiting and testing their own learning in the salon arena, the *salonnières* became active participants in this intellectual matrix, not only creating the spaces in which the Enlightenment was conceived and developed but in a significant way forging the ideas of the movement. The *salonnière* governed the discourse of the Enlightenment Republic of Letters,[5] a notion realized in La Tour's pastel.

The first notable salon of the eighteenth century was presided over by the marquise de Lambert (1647–1733), the brilliant hostess, author of essays on girls' education and champion of women's rights. Pompadour owned the 1748 edition of Lambert's *Oeuvres*, in which these essays appear. Her coterie, which attracted some of the most fecund minds of the period, flourished from 1710 to 1733. Nourished on the aristocratic culture of the Grand Siècle, Lambert governed a circle that, like Janus glancing back and forward, at once prolonged the romantic ideals and ludic gallantry of seventeenth-century *précieuse* salons and prefigured the liberal, philosophical bent of the Enlightenment. Dubbed the Antechamber of the French Academy, Lambert's salon was frequented by Fontenelle, the prolific popularizer of science and man of letters, a member of both the French Academy and the Royal Academy of Sciences, and by Charles-Jean François Hénault, then the president of the French Academy. The support of these habitués, along with Lambert's steadfast sponsorship, catapulted the budding Montesquieu into the French Academy.[6] The marquise herself was honored as the perfect *salonnière* and a remarkable savante in Etienne-Jahandier Desrochers's *Recueil de Portraits* (Fig. 66). Below her effigy are panegyrical verses that extol her patronage of intellectuals and her "profound knowledge," both of which make her a reincarnation of "Athenais":[7] perhaps Athena, the goddess of wisdom and patroness of the arts and sciences.

Another Janus-like coterie at once perpetuating the conservative manners and taste of the seventeenth century and spawning progressive Enlightenment ideals was

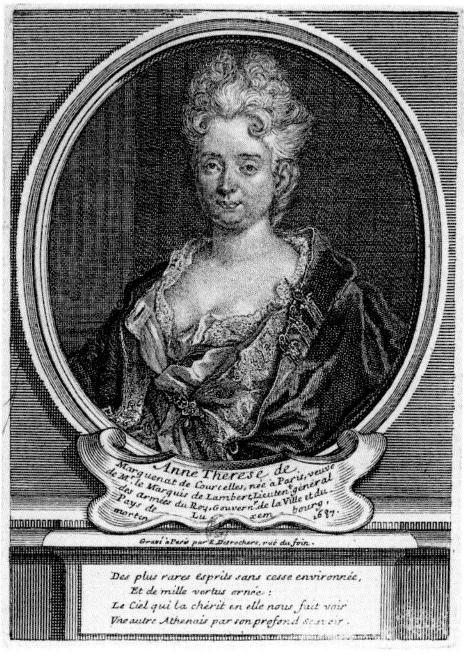

FIGURE 66.
Etienne-Jahandier Desrochers, *Portrait of Mme de Lambert*, ca. 1726–54. Paris, Bibliothèque Nationale, Département des Estampes.

directed by Mme du Deffand (1697–1780), a longtime friend of Louis XV and Pompadour, whom she visited in 1764 as Pompadour lay dying.[8] Having "interned" at the salons of Mme de Lambert and the spirited duchesse du Maine, Deffand fell prey to "ennui," which troubled her like a chronic fever and compelled her to lure to her aristocratic salon some of the most brilliant thinkers and distinguished men of the epoch: how could she be bored by her lover, the scintillating Président Hénault, or by her younger favorite, Jean Le Rond d'Alembert, the renowned scientist, philosopher, and future coeditor of the *Encyclopédie*, whose cause she successfully championed to the French Academy, or by the ever-witty Montesquieu?[9]

Although we have no evidence of Pompadour's attendance at Deffand's salon, it is likely that she knew about Deffand's proficient epistolary and epigrammatic skills, signs of a salon education.[10] Women of the salons perfected the art of correspondence, an indispensable accomplishment for a woman of education, breeding, and intelligence. Participants composed, read aloud, and discussed letters. Attending the

Parisian salons, Pompadour amplified and refined the slight epistolary training she had received in the Ursuline convent at Poissy. She became a polished letter writer—her letters are laced with wit and literary allusions—and we are fortunate that many of her missives have survived. The abbé de Bernis attested to Pompadour's epistolary skill: "With regard to the letters Mme. de Pompadour had written for the improvement of public affairs, I should never have supposed her capable of telling the truth to the king with such energy, and . . . eloquence. I loved her the better, and esteemed her the more for them."[11] This salon-nurtured proficiency is signified in Boucher's Munich portrait (see Plate 4) by a seal, a candle, sealing wax, and an envelope presumably encasing a letter, all resting on the rosewood writing table prominently displayed at the right of the canvas. The open drawer reveals an inkwell and a quill.

More important, Pompadour's participation in the salon facilitated her rise in status from bourgeoise to learned aristocrat. The seventeenth- and eighteenth-century salon was the primary locus of social mobility and class assimilation. Here, where nobles and non-nobles interacted intellectually, without regard to rank, distinctions of birth were superseded by intelligence, talent, and refined comportment.[12] This blurring of rank doubtlessly appealed to Pompadour, bourgeois by birth, titled through a royal liaison. But distinct from her acquired nobility as marquise, her status as learned woman, noble savante, forcefully asserted in her portraits, was earned by her own mental and artistic abilities and her assiduous application, as well as by her probable mimicry of the seasoned deportment of her aristocratic friends and fellow *salonnières*, Mme du Deffand and Mme de Tencin.

Mme de Tencin and the wealthy bourgeoise Mme Geoffrin served as her mentors when Pompadour embarked on her career as a governess of a learned coterie, a vocation that required a judicious apprenticeship. Pompadour's gatherings at Etioles and Versailles, attended by leading littérateurs and philosophes, were doubtlessly modeled on the coteries of learning held by these two women.

An inveterate intriguer and sexual adventuress, Mme de Tencin (1682–1749), who "studied" at Lambert's salon, inherited Lambert's habitués upon her death in 1733. Characterized by one of her guests, the poet, dramatist, novelist, and critic Jean-François Marmontel, as an extraordinary woman with an acute, supple, and alacritous mind,[13] Tencin, an accomplished novelist herself, presided over an assembly that was the hub of Parisian intellectual life from 1733 to 1749. It was the most comprehensive salon yet established in Paris, and it attracted the most distinguished savants of the era, including Montesquieu, whose *De l'Esprit des Lois* Tencin promoted, and the revolutionary materialist Helvétius, who later frequented Pompadour's coterie at Versailles. The topics of conversation—fine arts, science, politics, and principally literature—laid the foundations of Enlightenment thought.[14]

One of the salon's charming habituées was the younger, eager, and intellectually ambitious Mlle Poisson, Tencin's goddaughter and longtime student. Jeanne-Antoinette Poisson learned the art of governing a salon from her mentor, who guided her in intellectual and social matters from her youth through her marriage, when she established her own cultural assembly at Etioles, to her tenure as marquise at Versailles.[15] Virtually all of Tencin's guests flocked to her student's coteries.

The second of Pompadour's principal mentors was the tactful, kind, and conciliatory Mme Geoffrin (1699–1777), who had studied her role and inherited many of her mentor's regulars from Tencin's "Tuesdays." Despite her inadequate education—limited to readings supervised by her grandmother—the largely autodidactic Geoffrin founded and presided over the citadel of the Enlightenment philosophes and fostered their chef d'oeuvre, the *Encyclopédie*, as did her mentor, Tencin. Geoffrin was also a devoted and discriminating collector of art. Her Monday dinners lured the most renowned painters: Boucher, Nattier, La Tour, and Drouais—Pompadour's portraitists—among them. Joining the painters were the most accomplished sculptors of the period and the engravers Charles-Nicolas Cochin and Pierre-Jean Mariette—a veritable academy of artists, who socialized at the salon with *amateurs*, including the marquis de Marigny, Pompadour's brother.[16]

Among the group of writers and philosophers who gathered at Geoffrin's Wednesdays was the recently married Mme Lenormant d'Etioles, who met at Geoffrin's hôtel nearly all of the men of letters who later became her habitués. The scintillating young woman was a hit with Geoffrin's guests. Geoffrin's daughter, the marquise de La Ferté-Imbault, described Mme d'Etioles's triumph at the salon: "Pretty, well turned-out, natural, perfectly good, a wonderful singer; endowed with all of the talents to captivate, she was a great success with the old philosophes at the Wednesday gatherings."[17] True, the young *salonnière* emanated charm, but she did not attend merely to please and to parade her gifts; surely she was there to educate and cultivate herself, to forge her role as a femme savante and a femme philosophe.

It seems that her victories in Parisian salons were legion. One of her most famous conquests, when she was still Mlle Poisson, was her legendary performance chez Mme d'Angervilliers, wife of the minister of war: she sang the grand air from Lully and Quinault's opera *Armide* (1686) and played the harpsichord with such fervor that she beguiled the entire assembly. She moved in particular the comtesse de Mailly (a member of the queen's entourage and then the lover of Louis XV) to embrace her in a gush of gratitude.[18] Little did Pompadour's admirer know that in a few years her royal lover would even more passionately embrace the irresistible keyboardist. In 1742–43, following her advantageous marriage, she was fêted at suppers by no less than Président Hénault, who praised her in a letter to Mme d'Etioles's fellow *salonnière*, Deffand: "She knows music perfectly, she sings with all the blitheness and taste possible, knows hundreds of songs, performs comedy at Étioles in a theater as beautiful as that of the Opera."[19]

At her estate at Etioles, Pompadour perpetuated the Parisian salon tradition with the deliberate intention of nourishing her mind. In 1741–42, she invited many of the greatest intellects of the day: Montesquieu; the scientist and mathematician Maupertuis; her former teacher Crébillon, whose plays she later promoted through publication and performance at Versailles and on whom she conferred a pension; Fontenelle, the luminous link between her coteries and those of her Parisian mentors; and Voltaire, who unabashedly lauded her. Under her aegis at Versailles, Voltaire was appointed to the posts of historiographer to the king and Gentleman of the King's Chamber, and ultimately received membership in the Académie Française.[20] Pompadour thrived on adulation, but she also knew genius when she saw it.

In 1745, the abbé de Bernis gave her advice that she judiciously followed: "I counseled her to protect men of letters: it was they who gave the name of Great to Louis XIV."[21] After she became marquise de Pompadour in 1745, she used her position and power to promote savants on a scale never seen before or since. She became the *salonnière* par excellence, an enlightened Maecenas: "I am very glad to have contributed to the satisfaction of the Gentlemen of the Society of Sciences of Toulouse and to have given them proof of my esteem and of the regard I have for the sciences and the fine arts."[22] Needing continually to amplify her intellect, she was host to a reunion at her château de Choisy of many famous writers, including Bernis and Voltaire, as well as the celebrated historian Charles Pinot Duclos, whom she later named historiographer to the king after Voltaire's departure in 1750. Her Sunday toilette at Versailles was, moreover, the venue for intellectual discussions with Bernis, Duclos, and Marmontel, for whom she secured (via her brother, Marigny) the position of secretary of royal buildings.[23] After also obtaining for Marmontel a part in the privilege of the journal *Mercure François*, she wrote: "I love talent and literature, and it will always be a great pleasure for me to contribute to the happiness of those who cultivate them."[24] Her largesse knew no bounds: she promoted Tencin's friend, the poet and playwright Alexis Piron, to the French Academy, performed the plays of her habitués, and procured the position of usher of the ambassadors at court for her friend, the enlightened *amateur* La Live de Jully.[25]

If that were not enough, she sanctioned, however obliquely, the anticlerical—and potentially incendiary—gatherings of philosophes and physiocrats hosted by her doctor, the physiocratic economist François Quesnay,[26] who, under her sponsorship was appointed consulting physician to the king in 1749. She was a woman committed to learning, from time to time joining her colleagues at communal meals in Quesnay's entresol beneath her apartments.[27]

All of the portraits of Pompadour encode in various ways her role as Maecenas of the arts and sciences, recalling that several critics of La Tour's pastel and Boucher's

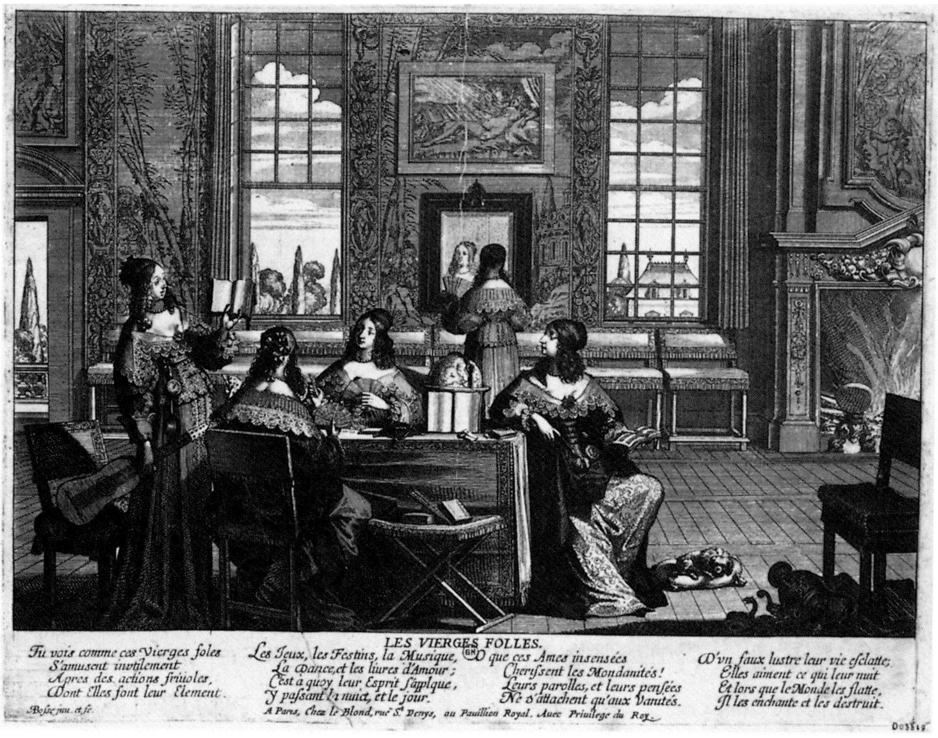

FIGURE 67.
Abraham Bosse, *The Foolish Virgins.*
Paris, Bibliothèque Nationale,
Département des Estampes.

Munich portrait recognized her as the consummate protectress. With the scope of Pompadour's patronage in mind, we can understand why at her death, when he had nothing more to gain from her, Voltaire gratefully and genuinely asserted, "In her heart she was one of us."[28]

Surely, when Pompadour commissioned La Tour to create his pastel, she saw herself and was seen as one of them, that is, as a philosophe and the quintessential femme savante (see Plate 3). The author of the *Second Letter to a Partisan of Good Taste* recognized the persona in his critique of the pastel in 1755. According to Furetière, the compiler of the *Dictionnaire universel*, a "philosophe" was a sage or scholar "with a resolute mind, elevated above the others." Bonneval saw philosophes as "more occupied than other men with augmenting the enlightenment of their mind."[29] Writing this definition in 1743, Bonneval had neither encountered a femme philosophe nor imagined that one could even exist. La Tour's pastel portrays imaginatively the philosophe and the savante presiding over her salon. Notwithstanding the dearth of salon images, which generally are confined to prints or pedestrian paintings, a glance at the tradition provides an appreciation of La Tour's striking innovations.

The earliest example is Abraham Bosse's seventeenth-century engraving *The Foolish Virgins* (Fig. 67), whose moralizing title and expository verses censure the secular pastimes of these worldly women, who in the versifier's Calvanist view would do better to devote themselves to God.[30] But the care with which Bosse lovingly details the women's elaborate costumes, the elegant appointments of their apartment, and their accouterments of earthly learning invites a different—and more positive—gloss, that of the decidedly serious cultural occupations of haute bourgeoises, who may very well correspond to contemporary *Précieuses.* During Bosse's time, these *Précieuses* assembled in large numbers to educate themselves in largely female spaces. As the principal chronicler of fashionable society during the first half of the seventeenth century, Bosse would have known these coteries. Thus his cultivated women gather around a table to play and sing music, a topic signified by the guitar held by the woman standing at the left and by the musical score displayed by the woman seated opposite her at the end of the table at the right. These learned ladies also study geography, an interest emblematized by the globe peeking out from behind the open book on the table; in fact, they are curious about all the knowledge contained in the profusion of volumes scattered about them.

Another variation of the female-directed coterie occurs in François Chauveau's *Exaltation de la Ruelle* (Fig. 68).[31] In the seventeenth century, the salon assembled in the *ruelle,* the space between the wall and the bed, from which the hostess directed the conversation.

Both the Chauveau and the Bosse privilege exclusively female gatherings, conforming in large part to historical fact: *Précieuse* circles were composed of self-educating women, sprinkled with a few male poets and gallants, who attended to entertain and to flatter. But in the Age of Enlightenment, Pompadour's era, these largely single-gender coteries were reconfigured into mixed-gender assemblies devoted to the business of shaping the Republic of Letters.[32]

This development is reflected in Jean-François de Troy's *Reading from Molière* (private collection, U.K., ca. 1728; Fig. 69). While probably not a literal pictorial record of an actual contemporary salon, the painting re-creates something of the tone of fashionable gatherings of the time. One of de Troy's justly popular *tableaux de mode* (pictures of fashionable life), the *Reading* depicts a sumptuously appointed rococo interior inhabited by well-bred and exquisitely garbed members of high society. The elegant women predominate and set the tone, but the gentleman seated in the right center holds the book and reads from it. He is the intellectual fulcrum of the group, mesmerizing his female audience.

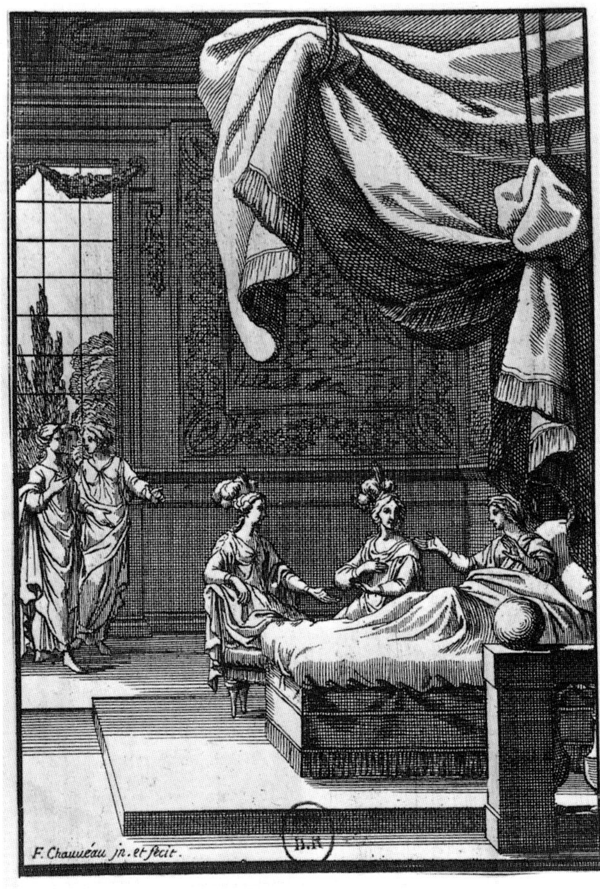

FIGURE 68.
François Chauveau, *Exaltation de la Ruelle.* Paris, Bibliothèque Nationale, Département des Estampes.

From the poetic de Troy I descend to the prosaic and literal re-creations of Mme Geoffrin's salon. The first, A. C. G. Lemonnier's *Une Soirée chez Mme Geoffrin en 1755* (Malmaison, Musée National du Château, 1812; Fig. 70), pictures a reading of Voltaire's tragedy *The Orphan from China.*[33] The playwright's genius presides in the bust elevated on a pedestal above the participants at left center. The hostess who organized and sponsored the event, one of only four women amid a multitude of

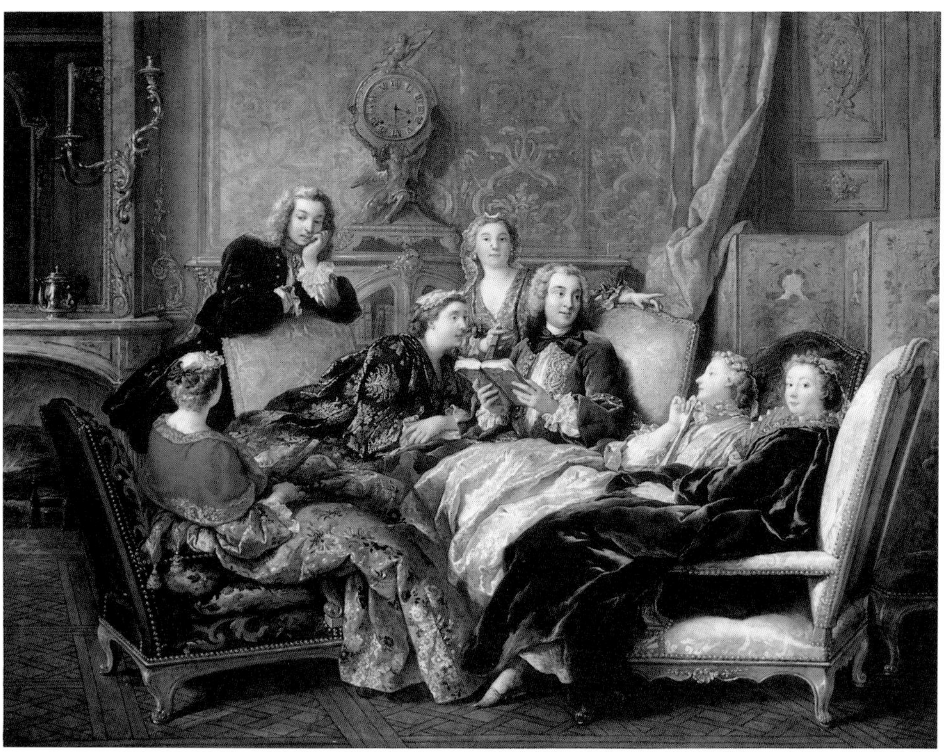

FIGURE 69.
Jean-François de Troy, *The Reading from Molière*, ca. 1728. Private collection, U.K.

men, is insinuated unobtrusively into the group, sitting on a chair third from right, gazing at the beholder. Her paintings, highlighted on the walls, actually overshadow the woman who collected them.

The second, decidedly awkward evocation of Geoffrin's salon is an engraving illustrating Jacques Delille's poem *La Conversation* (Paris, 1812; Fig. 71). Like the Lemonnier, it privileges the savant over the *salonnière*: Delille stands at the right reciting his poem, while the matronly Geoffrin sits among her habitués, in front of her pictures, gesticulating with delight. Again, the male luminary eclipses the ruling star of the Republic of Letters.

La Tour's pastel is singular among pictorial evocations of the salon, enthroning the quintessential *salonnière*—the governess of Enlightenment discourse—amid the men under her hegemony. The male guests in Pompadour's circle of learning are

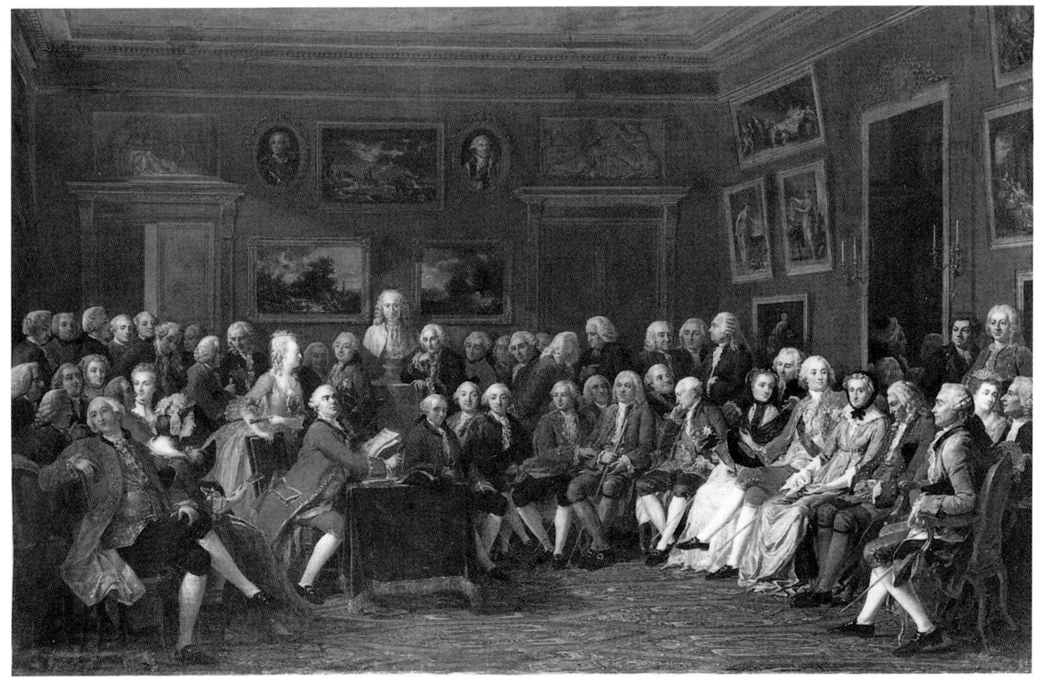

FIGURE 70.
A. C. G. Lemonnier, *Une Soirée chez Mme Geoffrin en 1755*, 1812. Malmaison, Musée National du Château (photo: RMN).

represented not by their persons, as they are in literal, prosaic images of Geoffrin's clique, but by their books, which she patronized. But in Pompadour's view, their contributions to Enlightenment thought are no more important than hers, and her shrewd iconographic program emphasizes her talents and accomplishments. This is a woman's intellectual coterie, a space in which Pompadour, following her *salonnière* mentors, proudly exhibits her own learning as much as she benefits from that of her male guests. Thus her talents as a gifted musician predominate. On the sofa at the left (Fig. 72), her guitar rests against a substantial book of music, and she displays a musical score.

La Tour also highlights the art that made Pompadour an able amateur engraver. Leaning against the ornate leg of her console table at the right is her portfolio, emblazoned with her coat of arms and full of engraved sheets. An engraved leaf bearing the stamp "Pompadour Sculpsit," followed by the inscription "Répresentation

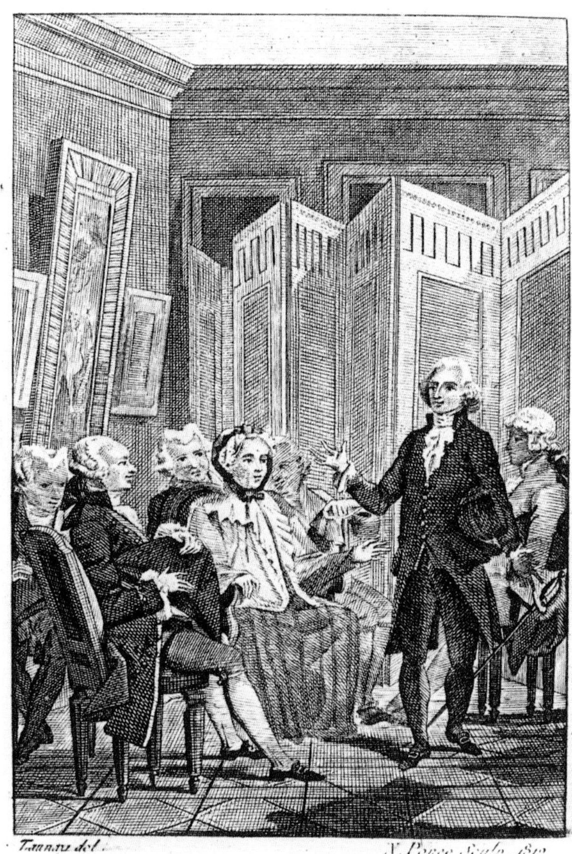

Il m'en souvient, j'ai vu l'Europe entière
D'un triple cercle entourant son fauteuil.

FIGURE 71.
Nicolas Ponce, *Jacques Delille Reciting His Poem, La Conversation, in the Salon of Mme Geoffrin*, from Delille, *La Conversation*, 1812. Baltimore, The Milton S. Eisenhower Library of the Johns Hopkins University.

de la situation dans laquelle est le Graveur en pierres fines, lorsqu'il opere et des divers Instruments qu'il employe" (Representation of the Situation of the Engraver of Gem Stones, When He Works, and of the Diverse Tools that He Uses; Fig. 73), cascades over the edge of the table. An abbreviated and slightly altered reproduction of an illustration explicating the art of engraving precious gems—Pompadour's interest—

FIGURE 72.
Maurice-Quentin de La Tour, *Portrait of Mme de Pompadour* (detail), 1755.
Paris, Musée du Louvre
(photo: RMN).

it is anchored by the volume from whence it comes: Pierre-Jean Mariette's tract on engraving, the *Traité des Pierres Gravées* (1750), which Pompadour owned.[34]

Her productivity in graphics also is saluted in Boucher's Munich portrait of 1756 (see Plate 4). Here Boucher foregrounds a portecrayon (for preliminary sketches) and an engraver's tool in front of their user's feet. At the left periphery, although certainly not marginalized, two of Pompadour's engravings spill out of her voluminous portfolio (see Fig. 13): a print after Boucher's etching of *Le petit Savoyard* (1751), signed "Boucher del . . . Pompadour sc," and an engraving from her corpus of fifty-two prints, plus title page, fashioned after Jacques Guay's intaglios and cameos, titled *Suite d'Estampes gravées par Madame la Marquise de Pompadour d'après les Pierres gravées de Guay, Graveur du Roy* (1755). In 1758 she augmented the original corpus with an additional eleven plates. This is quite an achievement for a woman who took up engraving as a hobby, and its presence in the portrait highlights Pompadour's

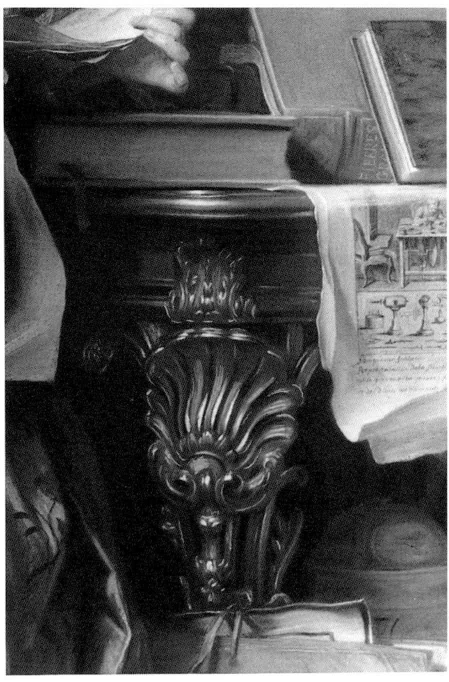

FIGURE 73.
Maurice-Quentin de La Tour, *Portrait of Mme de Pompadour* (detail), 1755. Paris, Musée du Louvre (photo: RMN).

role not only as an engraver but also as a patroness: as Donald Posner has shown, she was Guay's protector, champion, and historian.[35]

As a femme savante and philosophe, Pompadour was seriously interested in geography, a science amply represented in her library by many maps and books ranging from general studies of geography and cosmography to geographical grammars and dictionaries.[36] As Boucher does in his seminal Louvre sketch, La Tour includes Pompadour's globe in his pastel, perhaps one of the globes made by her cosmographer, Robert de Vaugondy. Pompadour, the *salonnière*, protected both men of letters and men of science, including Vaugondy and the royal cartographer César-François Cassini, who in 1750, about the time of Boucher's first Pompadour portrait, undertook a comprehensive topographic survey of France.[37]

The prominent rustic landscape with peasants (Fig. 74) on the wall behind the globe and the volumes on the desk seems incongruous in La Tour's pastel, a work

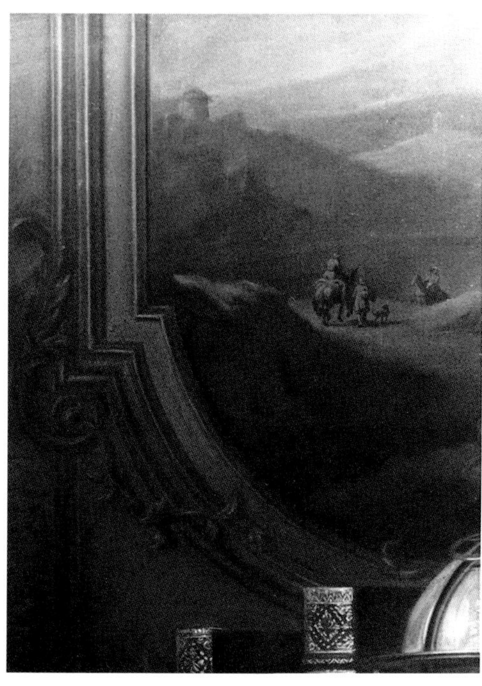

FIGURE 74.
Maurice-Quentin de La Tour, *Portrait of Mme de Pompadour* (detail), 1755. Paris, Musée du Louvre (photo: RMN).

that privileges high culture; but the landscape is appropriate, signifying Pompadour's artistic protection and taste. Like her mentor, Geoffrin, whose collection of pictures may have stimulated her own patronage, Pompadour protected some of the most important artists of the period, her portraitists above all. While the identity of the painter of the inset landscape is uncertain, Alden Gordon's research allows one to venture a guess. The Italianate ruins and round tower on the left suggest that the painting may be an Italian-inspired landscape by Joseph Vernet, similar to tableaux that Pompadour's brother Marigny purchased for her in Italy. If that is the case, the modern, Italianate landscape testifies to her cosmopolitan taste and her support of a great painter.[38]

The volumes on Pompadour's desk are most intriguing (Fig. 75). Specialists have

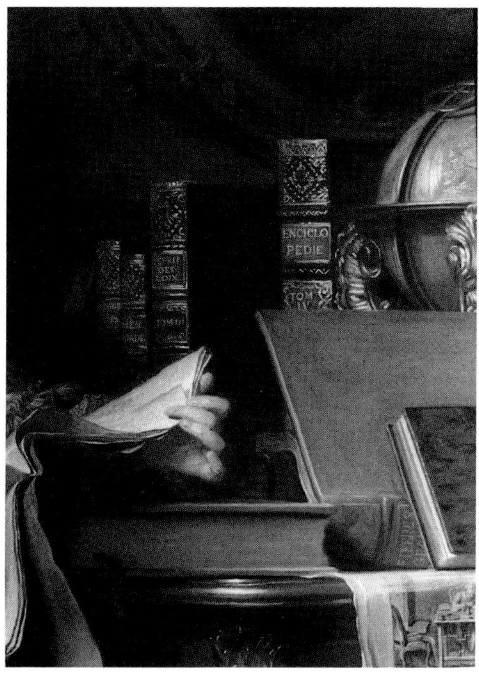

FIGURE 75.
Maurice-Quentin de La Tour, *Portrait of Mme de Pompadour* (detail), 1755. Paris, Musée du Louvre (photo: RMN).

identified them but have not probed why out of her library of 3,525 books, Pompadour chose to highlight these four in her official portrait. One assumes that they must have carried special significance for her.

Pompadour prized *Il Pastor Fido* (1590), Battista Guarini's famous and influential pastoral tragicomedy. Although we have no evidence that she could read Italian, she owned two Italian editions, one published by Leiden's Elzevir Press in 1659, the other in London by T. Wood in 1728, in addition to the four French translations (*Le Berger fidèle*, 1664, 1667, 1686, 1731) in her library.[39] Presumably she included this play—at the left, in the original Italian—because it inspired her professional and personal activities.

Pompadour doubtless identified with Guarini's character Amarillis, who personified beauty, nobility, and erudition.[40] In the theater from 1745 to 1750 Pompadour became a pastoral heroine. She organized, orchestrated, and starred in operatic pastorals and ballets, which were performed in her theaters at Versailles and Bellevue. Like *Il Pastor Fido*, her pastoral "Interludes"—*Tancrède, Sylvie, le Retour d'Astrée*, and *Ismène*, to name only a few—wedded dramatic text, music, dance, and spectacle.[41] In her bucolic element, Pompadour the singer, the dancer, the musician, transfigured as Amarillis and mesmerized everyone at court, especially Louis XV.

The parallel between Amarillis and Pompadour extended to the larger stage. Amarillis was the icon of the golden age, a halcyon epoch of chaste and faithful love.[42] At court, Pompadour ushered in a new era of intellectual pursuit and patronage, best documented in her portraits, and typical of the Enlightenment, which was characterized by d'Alembert in the *Encyclopédie* as a new golden age of ideas. Pompadour's new golden age in arts and letters coincided around 1750, when her portraits were in embryo, with the metamorphosis of her liaison with the king into a friendship characterized not by passion but by chastity and fidelity. This *amitié* and the excellence of her mind launched her as counselor of arts and letters to the king and inaugurated one of the greatest eras of cultural patronage in history. As Amarillis was the arbiter of the golden age in the pastoral realm, Pompadour was the sovereign of the golden age at court and in the Enlightenment Republic of Letters. In La Tour's pastel, she is enthroned.

Not fortuitously perhaps, Voltaire, a fervent admirer of Guarini, was the author of the book next to *Il Pastor Fido*. His *La Henriade* (1723), the first national epic poem in the French language, was generally regarded as "the greatest work of this century," devoted to the "glory of our nation."[43] Steeping herself in the history of France to fortify her role as learned titular mistress and counselor to the king, Pompadour collected twenty-six volumes on the reign of Henri IV. Among them were three editions of *La Henriade*, including the 1746 edition containing a preface by Marmontel, one of her most loyal salon habitués.[44]

In his prefatory remarks, Marmontel lauds Henri IV, founder of modern France, for his valor, generosity, humanity, and virtue, and he enjoins all kings—Louis XV among them—to follow Henri's example. In another part of his foreword, Marmontel praises Voltaire's genius and mastery of the "sciences" and exhorts the readers of *La Henriade* to cultivate learning and use it for the benefit and happiness of humanity.[45] Taking Marmontel's counsel to heart, Pompadour in her portrait presented herself, *La Henriade* at her side, as the mistress of erudition.

La Henriade is accented in the pastel also because Voltaire and the age in general saw a new Henri IV in Louis XV, who was present, though invisible, in everything connected with Pompadour. Certainly no Henri IV, Louis XV was nonetheless likened to his ancestor by some of the most proficient—and ambitious—flatterers of the day. The first edition of *La Henriade*, published in 1723, the year Louis XV reached his majority, was dedicated to the thirteen-year-old Bourbon. Voltaire urged

Louis to emulate his forefather, Henri le Grand, the "best prince, the gentlest master, the most intrepid captain, the wisest statesman of his century."[46] Pompadour would have known the frontispiece commissioned by Voltaire to accompany the epic, an engraving depicting Henri embracing his worthy successor, Louis. Inscribed at the bottom of the print is the sagacious advice of the seasoned monarch to his unripe heir: "Learn, child, courage from me, and real industry."[47]

In other works, too, Voltaire sees Louis XV as a reincarnated Henri IV. In his epigram "A Madame la marquise de Pompadour, à Etioles, juillet 1745," which he wrote to celebrate both Louis's victory at the Battle of Fontenoy and Louis's brevet making Pompadour a marquise, Voltaire likens the king's alleged dual prowess in combat and in love to Henri's and proclaims that the royal brevet was worthy of his illustrious ancestor. On another occasion, in a poem, Voltaire declares unabashedly that Louis, whose nickname was "Le Bien-Aimé" (Well Beloved), was more cherished than Henri, and again, this time in an epigram, he addresses Louis as "Mon Henri quatre" and Pompadour as "Zaïre" and "Alzire," the titular heroines of his plays that she promoted at Versailles.[48]

Voltaire was not alone in linking the two sovereigns. In 1743 Louis's enterprising minister of state, the marquis d'Argenson, asserted with great optimism that the king's mounting reputation would soon have the éclat of Henri's unassailable renown.[49] More significantly, Louis himself identified with his illustrious ancestor, albeit on a quite lugubrious note: in 1749, while enduring political travails and after reading the pamphlet *Awake, You Ghosts of Ravillac* (Ravillac was the assassin of Henri IV), Louis sadly predicted, "I see indeed that I will die like Henri IV."[50]

Pompadour herself was convinced that her king was a *nouveau Henri IV*. She owned Guay's matching cameos of the two men, the one of Louis inset into the pearl bracelet she wears in Boucher's portrait of 1758 (see Plate 1).[51] Subscribing to the legend casting her sovereign as the reincarnated Henri IV, Pompadour, who immersed herself in the histories of her predecessors, could very well have seen herself as a new Gabrielle d'Estrées, the most dazzling and intelligent of Henri IV's mistresses, who also was made a duchess and a marquise. Pompadour would have been moved by the passages in canto 9 of *La Henriade* that poeticize the love and devotion of the inseparable pair. As I have suggested, Boucher's 1758 portrait of Pompadour at her toilette descends from sixteenth-century depictions of royal mistresses at their toilettes, including Gabrielle d'Estrées.[52] Well versed in self-adulation, Pompadour had the iconographic connection clearly in mind in the 1750s.

The prominent penultimate volume on Pompadour's console table in La Tour's pastel is Montesquieu's *De l'Esprit des Lois*, the first systematic treatise on politics since Aristotle and one of the great contributions to Western thought. A rationalist, empiricist, humanist, and relativist, Montesquieu based his study of society on a profound understanding of the individual human being. A philosophe and frequenter of Parisian salons, he also enjoyed Pompadour's protection, as she demonstrates to the world in her portrait.

She owned two copies of *De l'Esprit:* an undated two-volume edition, probably the first edition of 1748, and the four-volume edition published in Amsterdam in 1749.[53] It is the third volume of the latter edition that is represented in the portrait. But why this volume? If she read the treatise, Pompadour knew that its first book, Book XIX, is one of the most important of *De l'Esprit,* containing the clearest and final definition of the *esprit général* . . . behind the laws, the very kernel of the work: "Of Laws in Relation to the Principles which form the General Spirit, the Morals, and Customs of a Nation," which asserts that "Mankind are influenced . . . by the climate, by the religion, by the laws, by the maxims of government, by precedents, morals, and customs; whence is formed a general spirit of nations."[54]

Book XIX also presents Montesquieu's feminist position, supporting the argument in the Women's Quarrel that women are the intellectual equals of men, entitled to enjoy a social and political status commensurate with their abilities. Pompadour would have appreciated Montesquieu's argument that women enjoy their greatest freedom under the monarchy; and when allowed to extend their activities outside the domestic sphere, they make a significant contribution to the development of sociability, manners, and politeness. More important, as far as Pompadour was concerned, women promote the refinement of taste and the progress of the arts. In short, when free, women advance civilization.[55] This is the essential idea informing the portrayal of Pompadour in La Tour's pastel.

Of the four books with readable titles, the remaining book on Pompadour's desk, the fourth volume of the *Encyclopédie,* appeared in 1754, just as her portrait was nearing completion. Presumably, she had not yet acquired the fifth volume, published in 1755, the year the pastel was exhibited in the salon. What more illustrious book could Pompadour the philosophe display in her study? The most serious and ambitious of all philosophic enterprises, the *Encyclopédie,* coedited by Diderot and d'Alembert in twenty-eight folio volumes from 1751 to 1772, was the great compendium of scientific, technical, and historical knowledge, epitomizing the skeptical, rational, and scientific spirit of the Enlightenment.[56] The subtitle of the *Encyclopédie—Dictionnaire raisonné des sciences, des arts et des métiers, par une société de gens de lettres*—reflects Pompadour's persona in the pastel, that is, the protectress of the sciences, arts, and crafts, and the men of letters who fashioned them. After all, her presence lent some support to Diderot and d'Alembert, whom she joined at Quesnay's gatherings at Versailles. Furthermore, because the *Encyclopédie* was compiled by the foremost philosophes of the time, its presence in her portrait underscores her own status as femme philosophe.

Assuming that the fourth volume was the last volume of the *Encyclopédie* that Pompadour acquired before La Tour undertook her portrait, I believe there is another reason for its inclusion in her portrait. Is it merely fortuitous that the first entries in it are *Conseil* (advice), *Conseiller* (counselor), and *Conseiller du Roi* (counselor to the king)?[57] These words describe the essence of Pompadour's role in life after 1750, when she counseled the king in matters of the arts and sciences (and much else) and in doing so firmly established her role as femme savante.

APPENDIX

Extant Eighteenth-Century Portraits of Mme de Pompadour

PAINTINGS

1. François Boucher, *Sketch for a Portrait of Mme de Pompadour at Her Toilette*, 1750. Private collection, England
2. François Boucher, *Sketch for a Portrait of Mme de Pompadour Touching the Harpsichord*, 1750. Paris, Musée du Louvre
3. François Boucher, *Portrait of Mme de Pompadour*, 1756. Munich, Alte Pinakothek
4. François Boucher, *Portrait of Mme de Pompadour*, Replica of the Munich Portrait, 1758. Private collection, Switzerland
5. François Boucher, *Portrait of Mme de Pompadour at Her Toilette*, 1758. Cambridge, Fogg Art Museum
6. François Boucher, *Portrait of Mme de Pompadour*, 1758. London, Victoria and Albert Museum
7. François Boucher, *Portrait of Mme de Pompadour*, 1759. London, Wallace Collection
8. François-Hubert Drouais, *Portrait of Mme de Pompadour*, 1763–64. London, National Gallery
9. François-Hubert Drouais, *Preparatory Study for the Portrait of Mme de Pompadour*, 1763. Orléans, Musée des Beaux-Arts
10. François-Hubert Drouais, *Preparatory Study for the Portrait of Mme de Pompadour*, ca. 1763. Private collection, Paris
11. François Guérin, *Portrait of Mme de Pompadour and Her Daughter, Alexandrine*. Private collection
12. Jean-Marc Nattier, *Portrait of Mme de Pompadour as Diana*, 1748. Saint-Omer, Musée de l'Hôtel Sandelin
13. Jean-Marc Nattier, *Portrait of Mme de Pompadour as Diana, Replica of the Saint-Omer Portrait*, ca. 1748. Versailles, Musée National du Château
14. Carle Van Loo, *Portrait of Mme de Pompadour as Sultana Taking Coffee*, ca. 1750–54. Saint Petersburg, Hermitage Museum
15. Carle Van Loo, *Portrait of Mme de Pompadour as Shepherdess*, ca. 1760. Versailles, Musée National du Château

DRAWINGS

1. François Boucher, *Bust of Mme de Pompadour Enframed by a Garland and Accompanied by Attributes of the Arts*, 1754. Private collection
2. Maurice-Quentin de La Tour, *Portrait of Mme de Pompadour*, 1755. Paris, Musée du Louvre
3. Maurice-Quentin de La Tour, *Préparations for the Portrait of Mme de Pompadour*, ca. 1752 or 1753. Saint-Quentin, Musée Antoine Lécuyer
4. Jean-Etienne Liotard, *Half-Length Profile Portrait of Mme de Pompadour*, ca. 1750. Paris, Fondation Custodia (coll. F. Lugt), Institut Néerlandais

NOTES

INTRODUCTION

1. The Enlightenment, with its hub in Paris, was the most important intellectual movement of the eighteenth century. It was committed to "the ardent and unshackled spirit of inquiry," the freedom to realize one's talents, "the revival of letters, the regeneration of ideas, [and the] return to reason and good taste." For these definitions, see Peter Gay's magisterial work *The Enlightenment: An Interpretation,* vol. 1, *The Rise of Modern Paganism* (New York and London, 1966), 36; *The Enlightenment: An Interpretation,* vol. 2, *The Science of Freedom* (New York and London, 1969), 11.

2. See Pierre de Nolhac, "François Boucher: Portraitiste de Mme de Pompadour," *La Revue de l'Art Ancien et Moderne* 41 (1922): 193–202; and Alfred Leroy, "The Portraits of Madame de Pompadour," *Connoisseur* 103 (1939): 301–6, who describe and locate the portraits but do little more. Johann Georg Prinz von Hohenzollern, "Die Porträts der Marquise de Baglion und der Marquise de Pompadour," *Pantheon* 4 (1972): 300–11, limits his discussion, largely based on secondary sources, of Boucher's Munich portrait to the marquise as stateswoman and fashion pacesetter; while Bernhard Rupprecht's analysis of the same painting, "Bouchers Pompadour-Porträt von 1756," in *Festschrift für Hermann Bauer zum 60. Geburtstag,* ed. Karl Möseneder and Andreas Prater (Hildesheim, 1991), 274–83, loses itself in metaphysical musings on Pompadour as a dilettantish dabbler and a mythological Venus and Flora.

3. Donald Posner, "Mme. de Pompadour as a Patron of the Visual Arts," *Art Bulletin* 72 (1990): 74–105.

4. For example, Posner conjectures that card playing and gambling had a higher priority for Pompadour than the visual arts (ibid., 104), but the duc de Croÿ, a habitué of the court, remarked on one occasion: " . . . petit jeu que le Roi aimait, mais Mme de Pompadour le haïssait et paraissait chercher à l'en éloigner." And on another occasion: "Elle n'aimait aucun jeu, et jouait plûtot pour polissonner et être assise que par goût." Whereas Posner pictures Louis XV studying architectural plans "with her at his side" (ibid., 83), Croÿ entered Pompadour's study and observed her alone: "Elle était, avec la plume à la main, à se promener sur ses plans du château de Crécy, et elle avait beau bâtir." See *Journal inédit du duc de Croÿ, 1718–1784,* ed. Vicomte de Grouchy and Paul Cottin (Paris, 1906), 1:73, 87, 152.

5. See Joseph Leo Koerner, *The Moment of Self-Portraiture in German Renaissance Art* (Chicago and

London, 1993); Marcia Pointon, *Hanging the Head: Portraiture and Social Formation in Eighteenth-Century England* (New Haven, Conn., and London, 1993); and Patricia Crown's review of Pointon and others, "Eighteenth-Century Visual Culture and Current British Art History," *Eighteenth-Century Studies* 28 (1994): 137–40.

6. See Donald Posner, "The 'Duchesse de Velours' and Her Daughter: A Masterpiece by Nattier and Its Historical Context," *Metropolitan Museum of Art Journal* 31 (1996): 134.

7. Richard Brilliant, *Portraiture* (London, 1991), 11.

8. See David R. Smith's numerous publications on self-fashioning and social masking, including: *Masks of Wedlock: Seventeenth-Century Dutch Marriage Portraiture* (Ann Arbor, Mich., 1982); "Rembrandt's Early Double-Portraits and the Dutch Conversation Piece," *Art Bulletin* 64 (1982): 259–88; and "Courtesy and Its Discontents: Frans Hals's *Portrait of Isaac Massa and Beatrix van der Laen*," *Oud Holland* 100 (1986): 2–34. Smith and others draw on Stephen Greenblatt's now-classic study, *Renaissance Self-Fashioning from More to Shakespeare* (Chicago and London, 1980).

9. See Pointon's chapter on Lady Mary Wortley Montagu in *Hanging the Head,* 141–57; and Kathleen Nicholson, "The Ideology of Feminine 'Virtue': The Vestal Virgin in French Eighteenth-Century Allegorical Portraiture," in *Portraiture: Facing the Subject*, ed. Joanna Woodall (Manchester and New York, 1997), 52–72.

10. Pointon, *Hanging the Head,* 141, 144; and Nicholson, "Ideology of Feminine 'Virtue,'" 54, 57.

11. See the following works by William L. Pressly: *The Life and Art of James Barry* (New Haven, Conn., and London, 1981), 113–19; *James Barry: The Artist as Hero*, exhib. cat., London, 1983, 66–67, no. 15, 67–68, no. 16, 69, no. 18, and 84–85, no. 28F; and "Genius Unveiled: The Self-Portraits of Johan Zoffany," *Art Bulletin* 69 (1987): 88–101; as well as Desmond Shawe-Taylor, *Genial Company: The Theme of Genius in Eighteenth-Century British Portraiture*, exhib. cat., London, 1987. On the theme in France, see Judith Colton, *The Parnasse François: Titon du Tillet and the Origins of the Monument to Genius* (New Haven, Conn., and London, 1979); and Joseph Baillio, *Elizabeth Louise Vigée Le Brun (1755–1842),* exhib. cat., Fort Worth, Tex., 1982, 95, no. 133.

12. See Mary D. Sheriff, "On Fragonard's Enthusiasm," *The Eighteenth Century: Theory and Interpretation* 28 (1987): 29–46.

13. See Mary D. Sheriff, *Fragonard: Art and Eroticism* (Chicago and London, 1990), 157–58, 164, 167.

14. The reader is referred to the author's archives for documentation of the corpus of Pompadour's other portraits.

15. "Femme Auteur. On dit, cette *femme* est Auteur, est Poëte, est Philosophe, est Medecin, est peintre" (Antoine Furetière, *Dictionnaire universel, contenant généralement tous les mots françois, tant vieux que modernes, & les termes des sciences & des arts*, 4th ed. [Paris, 1727; reprint, Hildesheim and New York, 1972], 2:n.p.).

16. "Sçavant, ou Savant. . . . Docte; qui a beaucoup lû, et étudié; qui a beaucoup de science, & d'érudition." "Sçavant. . . . Qui est bien instruit, bien informé de quelque chose" (ibid., 4:n.p.).

17. "Ce nouveau marié a trouvé sa femme plus *sçavante* qu'il n'eût souhaitté. . . . Les femmes qui affectent le titre de *sçavantes* ne sont pas sur un bon pied dans le monde" (ibid., n.p.).

18. M. Barthés, "Femme," *Encyclopédie, ou Dictionnaire raisonné des sciences, des arts et des métiers, par une société de gens de lettres. Mis en order & publié par M. Diderot . . . & quant à la partie mathématique, par M. d'Alembert . . .* (Paris, 1756), 6:469.

19. M. Desmahis, "Femme," ibid., 472.

20. "Ie veux donc bien qu'on puisse dire d'vne Personne de mon Sexe, qu'elle sçait cent choses dont elle ne se vante pas; qu'elle a l'esprit fort esclairé; qu'elle connoist finement les beaux Ouurages; qu'elle parle bien; qu'elle escrit iuste; & qu'elle sçait le monde; mais ie ne veux pas qu'on puisse dire d'elle, c'est vne Femme sçauante" (Madeleine de Scudéry, *Artamene, ov le Grand Cyrus* [Paris, 1656; reprint, Geneva, 1972], 10:401; translated by Erica Harth, *Cartesian Women: Versions and Subversions of Rational Discourse in the Old Regime* [Ithaca, N.Y., and London, 1992], 87).

21. Harth, *Cartesian Women,* 80.

22. See Katherine K. Gordon, "Madame de Pompadour, Pigalle, and the Iconography of Friendship," *Art Bulletin* 50 (1968): 249–62; Alastair Laing et al., *François Boucher, 1703–1770*, exhib. cat., New York, Detroit, and Paris, 1986–87, 252–55, no. 59, 267–71, no. 64; Nicholson, "Ideology of Feminine 'Virtue,'" 57; Posner, "Mme. de Pompadour," 77; Donald Posner, "People on File: Picturing the King and Others in Eighteenth-Century France" (unpublished paper read at the meeting of the Northeast American Society for Eighteenth-Century Studies, New York, Metropolitan Museum of Art, 1994), n.p. (I am grateful to Professor Posner for providing me with a copy of his paper); Perrin Stein, "Madame de Pompadour and the Harem Imagery at Bellevue," *Gazette des Beaux-Arts* 123 (1994): 29.

23. See, for the most pointed examples, Gordon, "Madame de Pompadour," 249: " . . . the Marquise undertook an artistic program designed to show the world that her relationship had been altered . . ."; Laing, *François Boucher,* 269: " . . . the idea of portraying Madame de Pompadour in this fashion was first tried out by [Boucher], though it no doubt originated with the sitter"; Posner, "People on File," 1994, n.p.: "Exaggerating somewhat, she made a claim to distinction, and importance, by choosing for herself the identity of an enlightened supporter of contemporary intellectual and artistic activity in France"; and Stein, "Madame de Pompadour," 29: " . . . Pompadour . . . saw in [Bellevue's] decoration an opportunity not only to demonstrate her taste, but also, through a purposeful and explicit program, to extol her virtues, talents and status."

CHAPTER 1

1. The most recent and reliable biographies of Pompadour are Jean Nicolle, *Madame de Pompadour et la société de son temps* (Paris, 1980); and Danielle Gallet, *Madame de Pompadour, ou le pouvoir féminin* (Paris, 1985), which together with *Correspondance de Mme de Pompadour avec son père, M. Poisson, et son frère, M. de Vandières,* ed. M. A. P. Malassis (Paris, 1878) (henceforth cited as Malassis); *Memoirs and Letters of Cardinal de Bernis,* 2 vols., trans. Katharine Prescott Wormeley (New York, 1901); Jacques Levron, *Pompadour,* trans. Claire Eliane Engel (London, 1963); *Mémoires du cardinal de Bernis,* ed.

Jean-Marie Rouart and Philippe Bonnet (Paris, 1980); Alden R. Gordon, *Masterpieces from Versailles: Three Centuries of French Portraiture*, exhib. cat., Washington, D.C., 1983, 74, no. 20; and Danielle Rice, "Women and the Visual Arts," in *French Women and the Age of Enlightenment*, ed. Samia I. Spencer (Bloomington, Ind., 1984), 244–45, are the bases for my biographical sketch.

2. "Madame d'Étioles avait toutes les grâces, toute la fraîcheur et toute la gaieté de la jeunesse: elle dansait, chantait, jouait la comédie à merveille; il ne lui manquait aucun des talents agréables. Elle aimait les lettres et les arts" (*Mémoires du cardinal de Bernis*, 87).

3. See Ann Plogsterth, "The Institution of the Royal Mistress and the Iconography of Nude Portraiture in Sixteenth-Century France" (Ph.D. diss., Columbia University, 1991), 17–18.

4. *Memoirs and Letters of Cardinal de Bernis*, 1:196.

5. "Moi qui donnerois ma vie pour elle, et dont les bontés me sont tous les jours plus précieuses. . . . Tout ce que je désire et de lui faire ma cour et de lui marquer mon profond respect" (Malassis, 228, 230).

6. *Journal inédit du duc de Croÿ, 1718–1784*, ed. Vicomte de Grouchy and Paul Cottin (Paris, 1906), 1:71, 88, 92, 93.

7. "Je suis très-fâchée, mon cher père, que vous desiriez Vincennes pour M. de Malvoisin. Comment peut-il vous venir dans l'esprit de vouloir placer un homme de vingt-cinq ans (quelque sage qu'il soit), qui n'a servi que six ans? . . . Ce qu'il y a de sûr, c'est que je ne puis demander une chose aussi injuste" (Malassis, 16).

8. "J'espère que vous penserez comme moi, et que vous ne vous croirez pas plus grand pour des honneurs passagers que l'on rend à la place et non à la personne" (ibid., 48).

9. Denys Sutton characterizes Pompadour as one of the leading amateur engravers of her time, in *François Boucher*, exhib. cat., Tokyo and Kumamoto, 1982, 238, no. 51. Donald Posner, "Mme. de Pompadour as a Patron of the Visual Arts," *Art Bulletin* 72 (1990): 100–102, however, evaluates Pompadour's engraving as unoriginal and rudimentary.

10. "J'espère, Madame, que l'amitié que vous avez pour moi, et plus encore la connoissance de mon caractère, vous seront garans de ce que je vous mande" (Malassis, 229).

11. "Je suis beaucoup moins riche que je n'étois à Paris; ce que j'ai m'a été donné sans que je l'aie demandé; les dépenses faites pour mes maisons m'ont beaucoup fâchée; ça été l'amusement du maître, il n'y a rien à dire, mais j'avois désiré des richesses, toutes les dépenses faites m'auroient produit un revenu considérable. Je n'en ai jamais rien désiré" (ibid., 19–20).

12. "Mon revenu de cette année ne m'est pas encore rentré, je l'emploirai en entier pour payer les quinzaines des journaliers. J'ignore si je trouverai mes sûretés pour le paiement, mais je sais très-bien que je risquerai, avec grande satisfaction, cent mille livres pour le bonheur de ces pauvres enfans" (ibid., 130–31).

13. *Memoirs and Letters of Cardinal de Bernis*, 1:276; 2:36.

14. Ibid., 1:276–77.

15. "J'aurois préféré la grande niche, et je suis fâchée d'être obligée de me contenter de la petite; elle ne convient pas du tout à mon humeur" (Malassis, 137).

16. "Elle avait l'âme haute, sensible et généreuse" (*Mémoires du cardinal de Bernis*, 87).

17. "Elle me regarda de la tête aux pieds avec une hauteur qui me restera toute ma vie gravée dans l'esprit, la tête sur l'épaule, sans faire de révérence, et me mesurant de la façon du monde la plus imposante. . . . J'avoue que je fus émerveillé de la facilité de l'élocution, de la justesse des termes . . . et que je la considérai avec autant de plaisir que d'attention en l'entendant parler si bien" (Malassis, 181, 194).

18. "Je suis comme Cicéron qui n'avoit pas besoin des autres pour être loué" (ibid., 115).

19. "Et excepté le bonheur d'être aimé de ce qu'on aime . . . une vie solitaire et peu brillante est bien à préférer" (ibid., 47).

20. On these roles, see Kathleen Nicholson, "The Ideology of Feminine 'Virtue': The Vestal Virgin in French Eighteenth-Century Allegorical Portraiture," in *Portraiture: Facing the Subject*, ed. Joanna Woodall (Manchester and New York, 1997), 67.

21. From Donald Posner, "People on File: Picturing the King and Others in Eighteenth-Century France" (unpublished paper read at the meeting of the Northeast American Society for Eighteenth-Century Studies, New York, Metropolitan Museum of Art, 1994), n.p. Also see Olga Raggio, "Two Great Portraits by Lemoyne and Pigalle," *Metropolitan Museum of Art Bulletin* 25, no. 6 (1967): 219–29.

22. See Marie-Catherine Sahut, *Carle Vanloo: Premier peintre du roi (Nice, 1705–Paris, 1765)*, exhib. cat., Nice, Clermont-Ferrand, and Nancy, 1977, 68, no. 119. Also see the following articles by Thierry Bajou: "Madame de Pompadour, Circa 1760," in *Versalles: Retrats d'una Societat (Sègles XVII–XIX)*, exhib. cat., Barcelona, 1993–94, 210; and "Le Portrait de la Marquise de Pompadour (vers 1760), un nouveau Carle Van Loo à Versailles," *Revue du Louvre* 45, no. 1 (1995): 36–45.

23. Posner, "People on File." Also see Pierre de Nolhac, *J.-M. Nattier: Peintre de la cour de Louis XV* (Paris, 1905), 2:149. The primary version of this portrait is in the Musée de l'Hôtel Sandelin, Saint-Omer (1748).

24. See Sylvie Béguin, *L'Ecole de Fontainebleau: Le Manièrisme à la cour de France* (Paris, 1960), 70–73, for Diane de Poitiers; and Myra Nan Rosenfeld, *Largillierre and the Eighteenth-Century Portrait*, exhib. cat., Montreal, 1981, 72–75, no. 6, for Mme de Montespan.

25. For this portrait, see Alexandre Ananoff and Daniel Wildenstein, *François Boucher* (Lausanne and Paris, 1976), 2:192, no. 520; and Alastair Laing et al., *François Boucher, 1703–1770*, exhib. cat., New York, Detroit, and Paris, 1986–87, 253–54, no. 59.

26. See Ananoff and Wildenstein, *François Boucher*, 2:172, no. 497; and Elise Goodman-Soellner, "Boucher's *Madame de Pompadour at Her Toilette*," *Simiolus* 17 (1987): 41–58, for a comprehensive analysis of the Fogg portrait.

27. Perrin Stein, "Madame de Pompadour and the Harem Imagery at Bellevue," *Gazette des Beaux-Arts* 123 (1994): 29–44. Also see Sahut, *Carle Vanloo*, 76, no. 148.

28. See Katherine K. Gordon, "Madame de Pompadour, Pigalle, and the Iconography of Friendship," *Art Bulletin* 50 (1968): 249–62, for Pompadour's public announcement of her platonic friendship with

Louis XV and the works that proclaimed it; and Ananoff and Wildenstein, *François Boucher,* 2:193, no. 522, for the Wallace Collection portrait.

29. Nicholson, "Ideology of Feminine 'Virtue,'" 67, discusses this idea in reference to allegorical portraits of women.

30. See the *Recueil Clairambault-Maurepas: Chansonnier historique du XVIII*[e] *siècle,* ed. Emile Raunié (Paris, 1879), 1:lxv; (Paris, 1882), 7:50–53, 62, 114, 119, 135–39, 146–47, 149–51, 287–89, 291–92, 298, 316–20; (Paris, 1883), 8:1, 24–26. Jean Frédéric Phélypeau, comte de Maurepas, was Louis XV's Minister of State from 1738 to 1749, when he was dismissed after quarreling with Mme de Pompadour.

31. "La contenance éventée, / La peau jaune et truitée, / Et chaque dent tachetée, / Les yeux fades, le col long, / Sans esprit, sans caractère, / L'âme vide et mercenaire, / . . . La gorge vilaine, . . . / La folle indécence de son opéra, . . . Son chant fredonné, / Sa voix chevrotante, / Son jeu forcené, / . . . Elle veut qu'on prône / Ses petits talents" (ibid., 7 [Paris, 1882]: 135–39).

32. For the domestic court portrait, see George T. M. Shackelford and Mary Tavener Holmes, *A Magic Mirror: The Portrait in France, 1700–1900,* exhib. cat., Houston, 1986, 10–11, 13–14; and for the intellectual portrait: Philip Conisbee, *Painting in Eighteenth-Century France* (Ithaca, N.Y., 1981), 133–34; and Alden Gordon, *Masterpieces from Versailles,* 25.

33. See Malassis, 50, 55. For Pompadour and Boucher, see Georges Brunel, *Boucher,* trans. Simon Rees et al. (London, 1986), 247–53.

34. Laing et al., *François Boucher,* 252–55, no. 59; and Sahut, *Carle Vanloo,* 106, no. 299.

35. Posner, "People on File."

36. Malassis, 55. For the epistolary exchange between Marigny and La Tour about the delayed portrait: Albert Besnard and Georges Wildenstein, *La Tour: La vie et l'oeuvre de l'artiste* (Paris, 1928), 50–51. Also see Besnard and Wildenstein, 160, nos. 385, 387–89; and Christine Debrie, *Maurice-Quentin de La Tour: "Peintre de portraits au pastel" 1704–1788 au Musée Antoine Lécuyer de Saint-Quentin* (Thonon-les-Bains, 1991), for the pastel and its three *préparations* (studies of the head) made from life. Only the head was made from life; it was drawn on a separate sheet of paper, then impaled onto the larger sheet depicting the remainder of the portrait. For the portrait in general, see Geneviève Monnier, *Musée du Louvre, Cabinet des Dessins: Pastels XVIIème et XVIIIème siècles* (Paris, 1972), no. 74; and Laing et al., *François Boucher,* 254, no. 59.

37. For La Tour's professional and cultural history, see Alfred Leroy, *Maurice Quentin de La Tour et la société française du XVIII*[e] *siècle* (Paris, 1953), 41, 63–65, 69–73, 75–76, 81–82, 84–85, 145, 152, 158, 173, 269–70; and Debrie, *Maurice-Quentin de La Tour,* 61, 160.

38. On these elements of genius in Fragonard's *Portraits de Fantaisie,* see Mary D. Sheriff, *Fragonard: Art and Eroticism* (Chicago and London, 1990), 167, 181.

39. For the definition of an eighteenth-century philosophe, that is, a member of a coalition of cultivated and learned critics who were united on an ambitious program of spreading the ideas of the Enlightenment, and a person with an elevated, enlightened mind, see chapter 5.

40. See Ananoff and Wildenstein, *François Boucher,* 2:148, no. 475; and Laing et al., *François Boucher,*

267–71, no. 64. For Gabriel de Saint-Aubin's drawing of the portrait in the Salon of 1757: Emile Dacier, *Gabriel de Saint-Aubin: Peintre, dessinateur et graveur (1724–1780)* (Paris and Brussels, 1931), 2:163, no. 891; and Anthony Blunt, "Drawings at Waddesdon Manor," *Master Drawings* 11 (1973): 363, no. 5.

41. See Conisbee, *Painting in Eighteenth-Century France,* 126–27; Brunel, *Boucher,* 244–46; and Posner, "Mme. de Pompadour," 99, for stylistic analyses of the portrait.

42. Laing et al., *François Boucher,* 269.

43. On *honnêteté* and noble leisure: René Démoris, "Les Fêtes galantes chez Watteau et dans le roman contemporain," *Dix-Huitième Siècle* 3 (1971): 337–57; Thomas E. Crow, *Painters and Public Life in Eighteenth-Century Paris* (New Haven, Conn., and London, 1991), 66–67, 69, 72–73; and Elise Goodman, *Rubens: The Garden of Love as Conversatie à la mode* (Amsterdam and Philadelphia, 1992), 33–34, 36–37. For repose, the basis of happiness in eighteenth-century letters, see Robert Mauzi, *L'Idée du bonheur dans la littérature et la pensée françaises au XVIII*[e] *siècle,* 2d ed. (Paris, 1965), 125–27, 129, 330, 334, 338, 350, 362–63, 374, 377, 378–79; and for the philosophes who embraced repose: Peter Gay, *The Enlightenment: An Interpretation,* vol. 1, *The Rise of Modern Paganism* (New York and London, 1966), 26, 135.

44. I am most grateful to Orest and Patricia Ranum for generously sharing with me their observations on the nature of the clock and its time in two personal communications of February 4 and February 22, 1998. Orest Ranum also observes that the sweep hands of eighteenth-century clocks could indicate seconds and days of the year. Boucher's left sweep hand is between the "X" and the "XI," and his right sweep hand is between the "XII" and the "I." I am also indebted to George Basalla, who informs me that antique clocks were frequently set at 8:20 or thereabouts for purposes of display. See Gillian Wilson, *European Clocks in the J. Paul Getty Museum* (Los Angeles, 1996), 70–71, no. X, and 114, no. XVI, for eighteenth-century French clocks set at this time. Further, Boucher's *Design for a Clock* (reproduced in Sutton, *François Boucher,* 138, no. 115) shows the time of 8:13, and my twentieth-century reproduction of a Dresden porcelain rococo clock is set at exactly 8:20. Professor Basalla states that eighteenth-century clocks could have an hour hand, a minute hand, a second hand, a barometer hand, and hands indicating the month of the year and the mean and solar times, depending on the complexity of their configuration. For Pompadour's schedule on February 8, 1756, see Gallet, *Madame de Pompadour, ou le pouvoir féminin,* 1985, 212; and for the court schedule in general: Jean-François Solnon, *La Cour de France* [Paris], 1987, 322–27, 361. For Croÿ's observation, see *Journal inédit du duc de Croÿ,* 1:336: "elle fut extrêmement parée, ce jour-la, et elle fit son séjour chez la Reine, avec un air tranquille, comme si elle n'avait jamais fait autre chose." Also see Orest Ranum, "Intimacy in French Eighteenth-Century Family Portraits," *Word & Image* 6 (1990): 364, for François-Hubert Drouais's *Family Group* (National Gallery of Art, Washington), in which the hands of the clock are placed to indicate the date of the portrait, 1756.

45. For Pompadour's letters written "au soir," see Malassis, 137, 147.

46. Cesare Ripa, *Baroque and Rococo Pictorial Imagery: The 1758–60 Hertel Edition of Ripa's "Iconologia"* (New York, 1971), nos. 183, 192. Rococo clocks were sometimes fashioned in the shape of lyres; see Wilson, *European Clocks,* 10, no. II, and 12, for one owned by Jean Pâris de Montmartel, Pompadour's godfather.

47. See *Suite d'Estampes gravées par Madame la Marquise de Pompadour, d'après les Pierres gravées de Guay, Graveur du Roy* (Paris, 1782), nos. 17, 19, 40, 63.

48. For Boucher's *Poetry*, see *Paintings from the Frick Collection*, intro. Charles Ryskamp; text by Bernice Davidson, Edgar Munhall, and Nadia Tscherny (New York, 1990), n.p.

49. See *Catalogue des livres de la bibliothèque de feue Madame La Marquise de Pompadour, Dame du Palais de la Reine* (Paris, 1765), (henceforth cited as *Catalogue des livres*), 52–184, nos. 523–1459; and 381–98, nos. 1–235, for her collections of poetry and music.

50. See Ananoff and Wildenstein, *François Boucher*, 2:78–80, no. 376; and Laing et al., *François Boucher*, 255–58, no. 60.

51. Quoted from Orest Ranum's personal communication of February 22, 1998.

52. Laing et al., *François Boucher*, 257; and Goodman-Soellner, "Boucher's *Madame de Pompadour at her Toilette*," 44–45.

53. For the portrait, see C. M. Kaufmann, *Victoria and Albert Museum: Catalogue of Foreign Paintings* (London, 1973), 1:40, no. 38; and Ananoff and Wildenstein, *François Boucher*, 2:170. I am grateful to Alastair Laing for his personal communication of May 4, 1993, describing Pompadour's books in the portrait.

54. "Vers à Madame la Marquise de P***": "Mais je l'ai vu dans le bois solitaire / Où va rêver la jeune POMPADOUR," *Oeuvres complettes de M. Le C. de B*** de l'Académie Françoise* (London, 1778), 1:129–30. "Nous l'avons vue, elle a rêvé sous ces ormeaux. / C'était là que sa voix attirait les oiseaux" (quoted in Sylvain Menant, *La Chute d'Icare: La Crise de la poésie française, 1700–1750* [Geneva, 1981], 137).

55. See Laing et al., *François Boucher*, 64–72, for Boucher's literary friends and pastorals; and Alastair Laing, "Boucher et la pastorale peint," *Revue de l'Art* 73 (1986): 55–64.

56. "La vie que je mène est terrible, à peine ais-je une minute à moi: répétitions et représentations, et deux fois la semaine voyages continuels tant au Petit château qu'à La Muette, etc. Devoirs considérables et indispensables" (Malassis, 103); "Plus j'avance en âge, mon cher frère, et plus mes réflexions sont philosophiques. . . . Excepté le bonheur d'être avec le Roy, et qui assurément me console du tout, le reste n'est qu'un tissu de méchancetés, de platitudes, enfin de toutes les misères dont les pauvres humaines sont capables. Belle matière à réflexions, surtout pour quelqu'un né aussi réfléchissante que je le suis" (Malassis, 54); "Il faut bien se donner le temps de penser" (Malassis, 111). See *Mémoires et lettres de François-Joachim de Pierre, cardinal de Bernis (1715–1758)*, ed. Frédéric Masson (Paris, 1903), 1:207–8, for Pompadour's letters to the king in 1755; "J'y passe la moitié de ma vie avec grande satisfaction" (Malassis, 57).

57. *The National Gallery Director's Report, July 1975–December 1977* (London, 1978), 41, no. 6440; and for the portrait, see Michael Wilson, *The National Gallery Schools of Painting: French Paintings before 1800* (London, 1985), 112. I am grateful to Humphrey Wine, curator of French Seventeenth- and Eighteenth-Century Paintings, The National Gallery, for providing me with a copy of the director's report containing this information. The "mature woman" is treated in Pierre Fauchery, *La Destinée féminine dans le roman européen du dix-huitième siècle, 1713–1807: Essai de gynécomythie romanesque* (Paris, 1972), 496–507.

58. "Elle reçut des ambassadeurs à son métier de tapisserie. Ainsi, on passa de la toilette au métier de tapisserie . . . et qu'elle égalerait ou surpasserait Mme de Maintenon, qu'elle imitait, depuis longtemps, soigneusement" (*Journal inédit du duc de Croÿ*, 1:335–36). See chapter 3 for Pompadour's assiduous emulation of Maintenon.

59. See Conisbee, *Painting in Eighteenth-Century France,* 125.

60. "Je m'en allai rempli d'étonnement et d'admiration," "Conversations de la Marquise de Pompadour et du Président de Meinières" (Malassis, 207).

61. "Je remarquai que la Marquise était, à l'ordinaire, auprès du Roi, fort parée . . ." (*Journal inédit du duc de Croÿ*, 344).

62. Laing et al., *François Boucher,* 254. Thus the portraits, celebrated as they are today, did not significantly influence eighteenth-century portraits of women and were not eagerly sought after by subsequent patrons, female or male. Their provenance is vague at best: the Louvre sketch can be traced only to 1914 (Laing et al., *François Boucher,* 252, no. 59); the Munich portrait to the post-Revolutionary period (Laing et al., *François Boucher,* 267, 271, no. 64); the Victoria and Albert likeness to 1882 (Kaufmann, *Victoria and Albert Museum,* 1:41, no. 38); La Tour's pastel to 1792 (Monnier, *Musée du Louvre, Cabinet des Dessins,* no. 74); and the Drouais to the nineteenth century (C. Gabillot, "Les Trois Drouais," *Gazette des Beaux-Arts* 35 [1906]: 156 n. 1).

63. For the placement of the portraits in the salon, see "Portrait de Madame Henriette (1727–1752) jouant de la basse viole," in *Louis XV: Un moment de perfection de l'art français,* exhib. cat., Paris, 1974, 140–41, no. 116. In a personal communication of July 30, 1997, Carrie Hamilton kindly informed me that Jean-Baptiste Portail arranged the display of the 1755 Salon. Also see Andrew McClellan, *Inventing the Louvre: Art, Politics, and the Origins of the Modern Museum in Eighteenth-Century Paris* (Cambridge, England, and New York, 1994), 31, 47, who maintains that, from 1750, pictures at the Luxembourg Gallery were hung (under the aegis of Lenormant de Tournehem, Pompadour's relative and then superintendent of royal buildings) in order to evoke comparative viewing. Also see Colin B. Bailey, "Conventions of the Eighteenth-Century *Cabinet de tableaux*: Blondel d'Azincourt's *La première idée de la curiosité,*" *Art Bulletin* 69 (1987): 433–34, for a discussion of eighteenth-century writers who encouraged the matching of subjects in private picture cabinets.

64. ". . . C'est un ouvrage qui fait naître pour son Auteur, des sentimens d'admiration & de reconnoissance; on est enchanté de voir les Arts faire de si grands efforts pour quelqu'un qui les protege avec tant de générosité, de discernement & de grandeur. . . ." The reviewer continues, criticizing the glass that covered La Tour's portrait, since it prevented the viewer from seeing the pastel adequately. *Lettre sur Le Salon de 1755, Adressée à ceux qui la liront,* Bibliothèque Nationale, Département des Estampes. *Collection de pièces sur les beaux-arts (1673–1808): Dite Collection Deloynes* 6 (1755): 21–22 (henceforth cited as Collection Deloynes). I am grateful to Vivian Cameron for providing me with a copy of her unpublished paper "The Agreeable, the Graceful, the Pleasurable: The Rococo Reconsidered," presented at the meeting of the American Society for Eighteenth-Century Studies, Pittsburgh 1991, whose feminist interpretations of the 1755 and 1757 Salon critiques of La Tour's pastel and Boucher's Munich portrait are similar to mine.

65. "N'allez vous pas maintenant ajouteront mes respectables Censeurs sçavoir gré à M. de la Tour de l'esprit & des graces que toute la France admire dans le portrait en pied de la belle Laure qui par la délicatesse de son goût inspire nos Pétrarques Modernes. . . . Interrogés chaque Artiste en particulier & il vous dira que cette noblesse respectable qu'on applaudit, que cette douceur enchanteresse qui subjugue les coeurs ne sont que de très foibles expressions de ce que la reconnoissance a gravé dans le coeur de tous les Peintres" ([Baron Louis-Guillaume Baillet de Saint-Julien], *Lettre A Un Partisan Du Bon Goût. Sur l'Exposition des Tableaux faite dans le grand Sallon du Louvre le 28 Août 1755*, Collection Deloynes 6 [1755]: 7).

66. ". . . Personne ne reconnoit *Laure* sous cette grande & belle glace. Vous diriez que Mr. de la Tour étoit de mauvaise humeur quand il fit ce portrait. Il a enlevé à l'original toutes ses beautés. Loin d'avoir péché en prêtant des graces à la nature, . . . tout le monde vous dira qu'il a fait le contraire. . . . Si vous aviez approfondi les objets qui ont frappé vos yeux au salon, & sur-tout le profil d'une tête qui se trouve dans un dessus de porte de Bellevûë par Mr. Vanloo, vous auriez aisément reconnu que la Sultane qui va prendre son Caffé, ressemble mieux à *la belle Laure*. . . . Il nous a peint *Laure* amante des Arts qui la cherissent" (*Réponse A une Lettre adressée à un Partisan du bon goût, sur l'exposition des Tableaux faite dans le grand Salon du Louvre, le 28. Août 1755*, ibid., 9–10).

67. ". . . Si la Sultane est ressemblante, le pastel ne l'est pas. Il est vrai que ce pastel n'a pas été posé par le Peintre d'une façon avantageuse. On n'apperçoit que les trois quarts de la tête & il auroit fallu la voir en face. Les regards sont perdus & cela donne un air de distraction qui ne va pas avec les graces. La coëffure n'est pas mieux imaginée. Elle est en cheveux relevés par derriere & sans poudre. Quoique la plûpart des femmes se coëffent de cette maniere, il auroit fallu donner à la tête un ornement plus pictoresque. On diroit que M. de la Tour s'est proposé de faire le portrait d'un Philosophe. Ne sçait-il pas que la distraction & la négligence des ajustemens doivent être évités, lorsqu'on veut représenter une belle femme? Ce Peintre habile a eu trop de confiance en son art. Il a crû mal-à-propos qu'il pourroit rendre la nature sous l'aspect le moins favorable, sans lui faire perdre ses agrémens les plus précieux. Afin que son hardi projet n'échapât pas aux Spectateurs, il a eu le soin de placer sur une table qui est dans ce tableau, des livres très-serieux. De pareils voisins ne sympathisent pas avec l'agréable, leur proximité est contagieuse. En présence de l'Encyclopédie, on est forcé de prendre un maintien grave & sévere . . ." ([Baron Louis-Guillaume Baillet de Saint-Julien], *Seconde Lettre à un partisan du bon goût. Sur l'Exposition des peintures, gravures & sculptures, faite par Messieurs de l'Académie Royale, dans le grand Salon du Louvre le 28 Août 1755*, Collection Deloynes, 5–6).

68. "Grace, Graces, Gracieux," in Antoine Furetière, *Dictionnaire universel, contenant généralement tous les mots françois, tant vieux que modernes, & les termes des sciences & des arts*, 4th ed. (Paris, 1727; reprint, Hildesheim and New York, 1972), 2:n.p.

69. ". . . Une belle personne n'aura point de *graces* dans le visage, si la bouche est fermée sans sourire, si les yeux sont sans douceur. Le sérieux n'est jamais gracieux; il n'attire point; il approche trop du severe qui rebute" (*Encyclopédie, ou Dictionnaire raisonné des sciences, des arts et des métiers, par une société de gens de lettres. Mis en ordre & publié par M. Diderot . . . & quant à la partie mathématique, par M. d'Alembert . . .* [Paris, 1757], 7:805). Also see, for a discussion of "grace," Candace Clements, "The

Academy and the Other: *Les Grâces* and *Le Genre Galant*," *Eighteenth-Century Studies* 25, no. 4 (1992): 469–94.

70. ". . . monsieur Delatour n'a travaillé au contraire que pour les gens de l'art. c'est une position de tete Savante" (*Lettre d'un particulier a un de ses parens peintre en province sur le Salon. 19. 7bre 1755*, Collection Deloynes 47, Supplément, 635).

71. ". . . je ne crois pas que monsieur de la tour eu soit blamé de personne ce choix de Simple et de Serieux ajoute a la noblesse. une tete agreable fera toujours son effet partout" (*Du salon, Supplement du Samedi 20. Septembre*, Collection Deloynes 47, Supplément, 647).

72. "M. Boucher a exposé le portrait de Mme la marquise de Pompadour. Le même portrait fait par M. de La Tour, et exposé il y a deux ans, fut beaucoup critiqué. Celui-ci me paraît bien autrement mauvais; détestable pour la couleur, il est si surchargé d'ornements, de pompons et de toutes sortes de fanfreluches, qu'il doit faire mal aux yeux à tous les gens du goût" (*Correspondance littéraire, philosophique et critique par Grimm, Diderot, Raynal, Meister, etc.*, ed. Maurice Tourneux [Paris, 1878], 3:432–33).

73. "Le portrait de Madame la Marquise de Pompadour, par M. Boucher, est bien digne de son pinceau. Que de graces! que de richesses! que d'ornemens! Des livres, des desseins & autres accessoires indiquent le goût de Madame la Marquise de Pompadour pour les sciences & pour les arts qu'elle aime, qu'elle cultive avec succès, & à l'étude desquels elle sçait consacrer des moments utiles. Le Peintre des Graces n'a fait que rendre la nature, sans être peiné du soin d'embellir ou de flatter son modele" (*Mercure de France, dédié au Roi*, Octobre 1757, 2:159).

74. "Graces," in Furetière, *Dictionnaire universel*, 2:n.p.

75. "Que n'aurois-je point à vous dire, Monsieur, si j'entreprenois de vous détailler le portrait de Madame *de Pompadour* par Monsieur *Boucher!* Attitude noble, simple & agréable, parure élégante & riche sans confusion, graces & finesses d'une belle tête, . . . du même Artiste, que *Vénus* & sa Cour ont choisi pour leur Peintre" (*L'Année Littéraire. Année M.DCC.LVII., par M. Fréron . . .* [Amsterdam, 1757], 339).

76. "M. Drouais le fils, peintre de l'Académie, vient d'exposer, dans une salle du palais des Tuileries, le portrait de Mme de Pompadour, de grandeur naturelle, travaillant au métier dans un cabinet où l'on voit . . . des livres, des instruments de peinture et de musique, etc. . . . [Pompadour] a suspendu son travail et . . . paraît méditer. Ce tableau, qui est un chef-d'oeuvre, a été achevé depuis la morte de cette femme célèbre. . . . C'est le seul homme qui sache peindre les femmes, parce qu'il sait les faire ressembler sans nuire à cette délicatesse et à cette grâce qui font le charme de leur physionomie" (*Correspondance littéraire, philosophique et critique par Grimm* [Paris, 1878], 6:50–51). Also see *The National Gallery Report*, 41, no. 6440, for the *amateur* Louis Petit de Bachaumont, who in 1764 noted the striking resemblance of Drouais's image of the late Pompadour.

77. For these descriptions, see Jean-Nicolas Dufort de Cheverny, *Mémoires*, ed. Jean-Pierre Guicciardi (Paris, 1990), 97; and Charles-George Leroy's encomium, quoted in Malassis, xxv–xxvi.

78. See *Journal et mémoires du marquis d'Argenson*, ed. E. J. B. Rathery (Paris, 1863), 5:214; 1864, 6:25,

for Argenson's disparaging remarks about Pompadour's appearance, which cannot merely have been fabricated by an archenemy, since we know that the marquise suffered from ill health and infirmity. Also see Goodman-Soellner, "Boucher's *Madame de Pompadour at Her Toilette,*" 41–42.

79. Goodman-Soellner, "Boucher's *Madame de Pompadour at Her Toilette,*" 49–50.

80. See Nolhac, *J.-M. Nattier,* 1:50, who quotes the poet Jean-Baptiste Louis Gresset.

81. For the Petrarchan tradition and eighteenth-century society poetry, as well as Pompadour's acquaintance with these poets, see Goodman-Soellner, "Boucher's *Madame de Pompadour at Her Toilette,*" 50–51. This tradition resonates in other rococo pictures that privilege the themes of love and beauty; for these, see Elise Goodman-Soellner, "Nicolas Lancret's *Le Miroir ardent:* An Emblematic Image of Love," *Simiolus* 13 (1983): 218–24; and Goodman-Soellner, "L'Oiseau pris au piège: Nicolas Lancret's *Le Printemps* and the *prisonnier volontaire,*" *Gazette des Beaux-Arts* 107 (1986): 127–30. Also see, for Boucher's cultural milieu, Laing et al., *François Boucher,* 65–68; and for La Tour's: Leroy, *Maurice Quentin de La Tour.*

82. On *ut pictura poesis* and the sister arts: Elise Goodman, "'Les Jeux innocents': French Rococo Birding and Fishing Scenes," *Simiolus* 23 (1995): 252; and for the volumes by Batteux, Estève, and Du Bos in Pompadour's library treating the interrelation of the sister arts: *Catalogue des livres,* 46, nos. 465–68; 52, no. 529.

83. See Fauchery, *La Destinée féminine,* 184, 189; and Philippe Perrot, *Le Travail des apparences, ou les transformations du corps féminin XVIIIe–XIXe siècle* (Paris, 1984), 64, 67, 69.

84. See *Mémoires du chevalier Christian de Mannlich,* ed. Joseph Delage (Paris, 1948), 265; and Laing et al., *François Boucher,* 272, nos. 65–67. Also see, for Boucher's drawings of heads of generalized, lovely women, which embody his notions of ideal feminine beauty, Regina Shoolman Slatkin, *François Boucher in North American Collections: 100 Drawings,* exhib. cat., Washington, D.C., and Chicago, 1974, 125–27, nos. 96–97; and *François Boucher: His Circle and Influence,* exhib. cat., New York, Stair Sainty Matthiesen, 1987, 74, no. 45.

85. See Aileen Ribeiro, *Dress in Eighteenth-Century Europe, 1715–1789* (New York, 1985), 98, 103, 105, 111; and Ribeiro, *The Art of Dress: Fashion in England and France, 1750 to 1820* (New Haven, Conn., and London, 1995), 6, 53, 59, 163. I am most grateful to Professor Ribeiro for generously providing me with specific information about Pompadour's fashions in her personal communications of July 16 and September 16, 1996. According to her, the costumes Pompadour wears in Boucher's Louvre sketch and the Victoria and Albert portrait are generalized versions of haute couture, while in La Tour's pastel, Boucher's Munich portrait, and Drouais's canvas, she wears real dress of the period.

86. For the literary paragons of beauty, see *Poésies de M. l'abbé de Lattaignant* (London and Paris, 1756), 2:237, 281–83, 318 (all four volumes of which were in Pompadour's library: *Catalogue des livres,* 69, no. 751); *Poésies diverses et pièces inédits de Lattaignant* (Paris, 1881), 59–62; *Éloge du Beau Sexe. Publié par M.C***.* (Paris, 1773), 6–8, 12–14; Fauchery, *La Destinée féminine,* 184–86; and Perrot, *Le Travail des apparences,* 69–70.

CHAPTER 2

1. On the education of boys: Georges Snyders, *La Pédagogie en France au XVIIe et XVIIIe siècles* (Paris, 1965), 36, 61, 65–66, 85, 99, 130–31, 357–59, 362–67, 374–85; and Emile Durkheim, *The Evolution of Educational Thought: Lectures on the Formation and Development of Secondary Education in France*, trans. Peter Collins (London, 1977), 244, 249, 268, 279, 280, 298, 301.

2. For Pompadour's educational experience at Poissy, see Danielle Gallet, *Madame de Pompadour, ou le pouvoir féminin* (Paris, 1985), 11–15. Also see, for the education of eighteenth-century girls in general, Léon Abensour, *La Femme et le féminisme avant La Révolution* (Paris [1923]; reprint, Geneva, 1977), 36–79; Anne Bertout, *Les Ursulines de Paris sous l'Ancien Régime* (Paris, 1936), 13, 93–94, 100, 104; Mère Marie de Chantal Gueudré, *Histoire de l'Ordre des Ursulines en France* (Paris, 1960), 2:237, 243, 255, 269, 561, 564, 566–69; Martine Sonnet, *L'Education des filles au temps des Lumières* (Paris, 1987), 90, 200–202, 212, 233, 251–55, 258, 260, 264, 286–87; and Samia I. Spencer, "Women and Education," in *French Women and the Age of Enlightenment*, ed. Samia I. Spencer (Bloomington, Ind., 1984), 83–96.

3. See, for Maintenon and Saint-Cyr, Jacques Prévot, *La Première Institutrice de France: Madame de Maintenon* (Paris, 1981), 8–10, 23, 25, 29, 31, 46, 48–49, 54, 56.

4. See Donald Posner, "Mme. de Pompadour as a Patron of the Visual Arts," *Art Bulletin* 72 (1990): 100.

5. "Après le plaisir de m'entretenir avec vous et mes autres amis, je n'en connais pas de plus grand que la lecture" (quoted in Albert de la Fizelière, "L'Art et les femmes en France: Madame de Pompadour," *Gazette des Beaux-Arts* 3 [1859]: 313).

6. *Catalogue des livres,* 287–332, nos. 2610–3059.

7. See Jean Cordey, *Inventaire des biens de Madame de Pompadour, rédigé après son décès* (Paris, 1939), 55, no. 588; 130, no. 1699; 141, no. 1819, for the three fine harpsichords that Pompadour owned at Versailles, Fontainebleau, and the Hôtel de Pompadour in Paris. I am grateful to Suzanne Ferguson for her analysis of the nature of the musical score that Pompadour holds.

8. On women and music in the eighteenth century, see *Women in Music: An Anthology of Source Readings from the Middle Ages to the Present*, ed. Carol Neuls-Bates (New York, 1982), xiii, 73; Ursula M. Rempel, "Women and Music: Ornament of the Profession?" in *French Women and the Age of Enlightenment,* 170–80; Julie Anne Sadie, "*Musiciennes* of the Ancien Régime," in *Women Making Music: The Western Art Tradition, 1150–1950*, ed. Jane Bowers and Judith Tick (Urbana, Ill., 1986), 196–207; *Women and Music: A History*, ed. Karin Pendle (Bloomington, Ind., 1991), 56–58, 72; and Richard Leppert, *Music and Image: Domesticity, Ideology and Socio-Cultural Formation in Eighteenth-Century England* (Cambridge, Eng., 1993), 147, 149, 154, 158, 171.

9. I am grateful to Aileen Ribeiro for a personal communication of July 16, 1996, in which she described the generalized costume, based on high fashion, in Boucher's oil sketch.

10. See Sadie, "*Musiciennes* of the Ancien Régime," 195; and Wendy Gibson, *Women in Seventeenth-Century France* (New York, 1989), 171–72, for this lineage.

11. Gallet, *Madame de Pompadour, ou le pouvoir féminin,* 16–17; Danielle Gallet et al., *Madame de Pompadour et la floraison des arts*, exhib. cat., Montreal, 1988, 82–85; and *Catalogue des livres.*

12. "Cette dame d'Étiolles . . . a eu toute l'éducation possible . . . , une éducation recherchée" (*Journal historique et anecdotique du règne de Louis XV par E. J. F. Barbier*, ed. A. de la Villegille [Paris, 1849], 2:448–49). ". . . Elle a plus lu à son âge qu'aucune vieille dame du pays où elle va régner, et où il est bien a désirer qu'elle règne. Elle avait lu presque tous les bons livres, hors le vôtre; elle craignait d'être obligée de l'apprendre par coeur" (*Voltaire's Correspondence*, ed. Theodore Besterman [Geneva, 1956], 14:216).

13. For women's intelligence, ambition, and tenacity, see Elisabeth Badinter, *Emilie, Emilie: L'Ambition féminine au XVIIIe siècle* (Paris, 1983).

14. "Mais de toutes les études, la plus nécessaire & la plus naturelle aux femmes, est l'étude des hommes," *Le Nouvel Ami des femmes, ou la philosophie du beau sexe. Par M. Boudier de Villemert* (Amsterdam and Paris, 1779), 50. Also see David Williams, "The Fate of French Feminism: Boudier de Villemert's *Ami des Femmes*," *Eighteenth-Century Studies* 14, no. 1 (1980): 37–55, for Boudier's popular tract, which was first published in 1758 and reappeared in at least five subsequent editions.

15. See Spencer, "Women and Education," 83.

16. The literature on the Women's Quarrel is immense. The most important studies of the debate in the seventeenth century are: Gustave Reynier, *La Femme au XVIIe siècle: Ses Ennemis et ses défenseurs* (Paris, 1929), 1–12, 30–63, 64–74, 166–86; Ian Maclean, *Woman Triumphant: Feminism in French Literature, 1610–1652* (Oxford, 1977), 25–63; and Linda Timmermans's exhaustive *L'Accès des femmes à la culture (1598–1715): Un Débat d'idées de Saint-François de Sales à la marquise de Lambert* (Paris, 1993), 239–80, 319–86, with comprehensive notes and bibliography. For the eighteenth century, which is less studied, see Abensour, *La Femme et le féminisme,* 379–431; Katherine B. Clinton, "Femme et Philosophe: Enlightenment Origins of Feminism," *Eighteenth-Century Studies* 8 (1975): 283–99; Maïté Albistur and Daniel Armogathe, *Histoire du féminisme français du moyen âge à nos jours* [Paris, 1977], 184–93; Marc Angenot, *Les Champions des femmes: Examen du discours sur la supériorité des femmes 1400–1800* (Montreal, 1977), 71–94.

17. See De La Forge, *Le Cercle des femmes sçavantes*, 1663 (103, no. 1009); Jacques Olivier, *Alphabet de l'imperfection & malice des femmes*, 1655 (249, no. 2210); Pierre Le Moyne, *La Gallerie des femmes fortes,* 1647 (374, no. 3478); [Graillard de Graville], *L'Ami des filles* (Paris, 1761), 239, no. 2094, in *Catalogue des livres*. The philosophes' participation in the Women's Quarrel will be discussed presently.

18. For Bernis's friendship with Pompadour, see Gallet, *Madame de Pompadour, ou le pouvoir féminin,* 39–40, 42–43, 62, 87.

19. "J'ai souvent entendu agiter la question de la supériorité des hommes sur les femmes. Quand on y a bien réfléchi, j'imagine qu'on doit penser que la supériorité des hommes n'est fondée que sur la force des organes et une meilleure éducation. . . . La force du corps a dû donner aux hommes la supériorité réelle, qui est celle de la domination. Ils ont été les maîtres, ils ont du l'être: le fort soumet toujours le faible. . . . Si à cet avantage physique on joint celui d'une éducation plus éclairée et plus étendue, on concevra sans peine que les hommes, supérieurs en forces, doivent l'être aussi en connaissances" (*Mémoires du cardinal de Bernis*, ed. Jean-Marie Rouart and Philippe Bonnet [Paris, 1980], 81).

20. On the philosophes and women: Abensour, *La Femme et le féminisme,* 366–71; Clinton, "Femme et Philosophe," 283–99; Elizabeth J. Gardner, "The *Philosophes* and Women: Sensationalism and Sen-

timent," in *Woman and Society in Eighteenth-Century France: Essays in Honour of John Stephenson Spink*, ed. Eva Jacobs, W. H. Barber, Jean H. Bloch, F. W. Leakey, and Eileen Le Breton (London, 1979), 19–27; and articles by Sara Ellen Procious Malueg, Pauline Kra, Gloria M. Russo, Blandine L. McLaughlin, and Gita May under the rubric "The *Philosophes*: Feminism and/or Antifeminism?" in *French Women and the Age of Enlightenment*, 259–317.

21. "L'esclavage et l'espèce d'avilissement où nous avons mis les femmes; les entraves que nous donnons à leur esprit et à leur âme; . . . enfin, l'éducation funeste, je dirais presque meurtrière, que nous leur prescrivons, sans leur permettre d'en avoir d'autre" (*Oeuvres complètes d'Alembert* [Paris, 1822], 4:450). For the ambivalent attitudes toward women in the *Encyclopédie*, see Peter Gay, *The Enlightenment: An Interpretation*, vol. 2, *The Science of Freedom* (New York and London, 1969), 34; and Sara Ellen Procious Malueg, "Women and the *Encyclopédie*," in *French Women and the Age of Enlightenment*, 259–71.

22. Quoted in Clinton, "Femme et Philosophe," 290. Also see *Historical and Literary Memoirs and Anecdotes Selected from the Correspondence of Baron de Grimm and Diderot* . . . , 2d ed. (London, 1815), 1:192.

23. For Helvétius and women's education, see Eva Jacobs, "Diderot and the Education of Girls," in *Woman and Society in Eighteenth-Century France*, 92; and on Helvétius and education in general: Gay, *The Enlightenment*, 2:56, 168, 170, 512, 513–16.

24. Montesquieu, *Persian Letters*, trans. C. J. Betts (Harmondsworth, 1973), 92–93. Also see Pauline Kra, "Montesquieu and Women," in *French Women and the Age of Enlightenment*, 272–84.

25. *The Equality of the Two Sexes by François Poullain de La Barre*, ed. and trans. A. Daniel Frankforter and Paul J. Morman (Lewiston, N.Y., and Queenston, Ont., 1989), a bilingual edition. See especially 6–7, 34–35, 50–51, 84–86, 201–31, 160–61.

26. [François Poullain de La Barre], *De L'Education des dames pour la conduite de l'esprit. Dans les sciences et dans les moeurs. Entretiens* (Paris, 1674). I have consulted the 1679 edition.

27. *Les Femmes Sçavantes ou bibliothèque des dames qui traite des sciences qui conviennent aux dames, de la conduite de leurs études, des livres qu'elles peuvent lire, et l'histoire de celles qui ont excellé dans les sciences. Par Monsieur N.C.* (Amsterdam, 1718), 100–102.

28. "Ainsi une Dame studieuse, doit avoir un cabinet le plus solitaire qu'elle pourra trouver . . . accompagné d'une plus grande refléxion. . . . Il est necessaire de joindre la méditation à la lecture" (ibid., 104, 110). For books in the femme savante's library in the tract: 180–252.

29. Malassis, 54.

30. For the theory of the humors, see Maclean, *Woman Triumphant*, 46–50; and Ian Maclean, *The Renaissance Notion of Woman: A Study in the Fortunes of Scholasticism and Medical Science in European Intellectual Life* (Cambridge, Eng., 1980), 30, 41–42.

31. "Elle est le propre de la mémoire, & c'est dans la mémoire que s'impriment & se conservent toutes nos connoissances: il est donc vray de dire, que les gens humides ont plus de disposition aux sciences. . . . Secondement les femmes sont plus disposées aux sciences que les hommes, parce qu'elles sont plus délicates qu'eux. . . . Il faut conclure de tous cela, que les femmes ont l'esprit plus vif que les hommes,

parce qu'elles sont plus promptes, plus brillant, parce qu'elles sont plus délicates, & plus solides, parce qu'elles sont plus humides . . . l'esprit, le jugement & la raison n'ont point de sexe; ils sont autant dans les femmes, que dans les hommes & même avec plus de perfection, puisqu'elles sont plus dégagées de la matiere, qui est bien plus délicate & plus affinée dans le beau Sexe, que dans l'autre" (C. M. D. Noël, *Le Triomphe des femmes, ou il est montré par plusieurs & puissantes raisons, que le Sexe feminin, est plus noble & plus parfait, que le masculin* [Antwerp, 1698], 81–84, 100–101).

32. "Pour la défense & la justification de mon Sexe. . . . L'Envie & la médisance des Hommes, envers les Femmes, ont souvent porté ceux-là, d'entreprendre d'usurper à notre Sexe, les plus belles qualitez qui lui appartiennent; parmi lesquelles sont celles du jugement, de la pénétration, de bien parler, & d'écrire délicatement; même avec solidité. . . . Ce n'est bien seurement pas la lecture des bons Livres, ni l'aplication aux sciences, qui font les Coquettes . . . dans tous les tems, il y a eû des Femmes sçavantes, d'un esprit superieur, & que notre Sexe a toutes les qualitez requises, pour pouvoir marcher d'un pas égal, à tout le moins, avec les Hommes de mérite, dans la carriere de l'étude des belles Lettres. . . . Tout bien consideré, il est surprenant qu'on puisse trouver une seule Fille ou Femme sçavante" (*Le Triomphe du beau-sexe sur les hommes. Ou l'on fait voir les avantages & les prérogatives que rendent les Femmes superieures aux Hommes, par des preuves incontestables* [Hamburg, 1719], 2, 90–91, 96, 102).

33. Mlle Archambault, *Dissertation sur la question, lequel de l'homme ou de la femme est plus capable de constance? Ou la cause des dames* (Paris, 1750).

34. *La Femme n'est pas inférieure à l'homme. Traduit de l'Anglois* (London, 1750).

35. "Une egalité parfaite entre les deux Sexes. . . . Combien n'a-t'on pas vû de Dames, combien n'y en a-t-il pas encore qui méritent d'avoir place entre les Sçavans, & qui sont plus capables d'enseigner les Sciences, que ceux qui remplissent a présent la plûpart des Chaires des Universités? Le siécle, où nous vivons, en a produit autant qu'aucun autre jusqu'à présent, quoique leur modestie les empêche d'en faire parade publiquement" (*Le Triomphe des dames. Traduit de l'Anglois de Miledi P***** [London, 1751], 19, 87–88).

36. See Madeleine Alcover, "The Indecency of Knowledge," *Rice University Studies* 64 (1978): 25–39.

37. "Il n'y a rien, à mon avis, deplus pernicieux qu'une fausse humilité. . . . Observez tout, regardez tout & écoutez tout sans scrupule. Examinez tout, jugez de tout, raisonnez sur tout. . . . Vous avez une Raison; servez-vous en, & ne la sacrifiez aveuglément à personne" (Poullin de La Barre, *De l'Education des dames*, 147, 311).

38. "Votre sexe a naturellement l'esprit plus fin, plus vif, plus pénétrant, j'oserois même dire plus refléchi que le nôtre. . . . Il n'en est aucune, de celles qui se sont adonnées aux Arts, ou aux Sciences, qui à trente ans, n'eût donné des leçons à des barbes grises. . . . J'oserois même dire qu'une beauté parfaite est un être de raison. . . . Jeunes beautés, il ne tient qu'à vous d'unir les attraits des Graces aux charmes des Muses" ([Barthélemy-Claude Graillard de Graville], *L'Ami des filles,* 8–9, 16, 18).

39. "Je ne finirois pas, s'il falloit parler de toutes les femmes, qui se sont distinguées dans l'étude de la philosophie, & qui s'y distinguent encore tous les jours, depuis qu'on trouvé le secret de l'habiller à la françoise, & de lui donner un air de liberté et d'aisance, qu'elle n'avoit jamais eu" ([Dom Caffiaux],

Défenses du beau sexe, ou mémoires historiques, philosophiques et critiques, pour servir d'apologie aux femmes [Amsterdam, 1753], 2:133).

40. Aileen Ribeiro, *The Art of Dress: Fashion in England and France, 1750 to 1820* (New Haven, Conn., and London, 1995), 53.

CHAPTER 3

1. For the relation of Boucher's portrait to prints depicting the woman at her toilette, see Elise Goodman-Soellner, "Boucher's *Madame de Pompadour at Her Toilette,*" *Simiolus* 17 (1987): 47–53.

2. See Roger-Armand Weigert, *Bibliothèque Nationale, Département des Estampes. Inventaire du fonds français: Graveurs du XVIIe siècle* (Paris, 1939), 1:68, no. 159.

3. For the Women's Quarrel, see chapter 2; and for salon culture, see chapter 5.

4. Weigert, *Bibliothèque Nationale* (1968), 5:521, no. 6; and *Catalogue des livres,* 367, no. 3404.

5. Weigert, *Bibliothèque Nationale,* 1:358, no. 59.

6. Bibliothèque Nationale, Département des Estampes, Oa 52, petit folio (henceforth cited as B.N. Estampes). For Jean Mariette, see Maxime Préaud, Pierre Casselle, Marianne Grivel, and Corinne Le Bitouzé, *Dictionnaire des éditeurs d'estampes à Paris sous l'Ancien Régime* [Paris], 1987, 229–30, henceforth referred to as Préaud et al.

7. Weigert, *Bibliothèque Nationale,* 1:463, no. 329.

8. B.N. Estampes, Oa 50, petit folio (1695); Oa 77, petit folio (1705).

9. For the move to the new quarters and Pompadour's conscious emulation of Montespan and Maintenon, see Danielle Gallet, "Madame de Pompadour et l'appartement d'en bas au château de Versailles," *Gazette des Beaux-Arts* 117 (1991): 129–38.

10. "Nous avons été avant-hier à Saint-Cyr. Je ne peux vous dire combien j'ai été attendrie de cet établissement, ainsi que tout ce qui étoit" (Malassis, 124).

11. *Catalogue des livres,* 259, nos. 2330–32; 318, no. 2903. On Pompadour's political ascent, see Danielle Gallet, *Madame de Pompadour, ou le pouvoir féminin* (Paris, 1985), 173, 211–17; and Alastair Laing et al., *François Boucher, 1703–1770,* exhib. cat., New York, Detroit, and Paris, 1986–87, 267–69, no. 64.

12. For Maintenon's pedagogical program at Saint-Cyr, see chapter 2.

13. See Marcel Roux, *Bibliothèque Nationale, Département des Estampes. Inventaire du fonds français: Graveurs du XVIIIe siècle* (Paris, 1951), 7:215–16, no. 384.

14. "Grand air de reforme," quoted in Gallet, *Madame de Pompadour, ou le pouvoir féminin,* 214. "J'ai vu Louis XV encore avec un air de grandeur de Louis XIV, et madame de Pompadour avec celui de madame de Montespan," *Mémoires du prince de Ligne,* ed. Albert Lacroix (Brussels and Leipzig, 1860), 122.

15. On Montespan: Maurice Rat, *La Royale Montespan* (Paris, 1959), 26, 28, 83–94, 199; and Jean-Christian Petitfils, *Madame de Montespan* (Paris, 1988), 21, 24, 32–34, 98–101, 127–28, 156, 158, 159, 289–90. On Pompadour's theatrical and architectural activities, see Gallet, *Madame de Pompadour, ou le pou-*

voir féminin, 57–63, 109–38; and Danielle Gallet et al., *Madame de Pompadour et la floraison des arts,* exhib. cat., Montreal, 1988, 65–71, 73–77, 87–105.

16. B.N. Estampes, N2 folio.

17. I am grateful to Uta Neidhardt, Curator of Dutch Painting, Gemäldegalerie Alte Meister, Staatliche Kunstsammlungen Dresden, for a personal communication of February 20, 1995, describing and dating these portraits, which are neither exhibited in the Gemäldegalerie nor listed in the catalogue.

18. On Maintenon in general: C. C. Dyson, *Madame de Maintenon: Her Life and Times, 1635–1719* (London and New York, 1910), 48, 50, 51, 57, 58, 60, 78, 92–93, 159, 243; Saint-René Taillander, *Madame de Maintenon,* trans. Lady Mary Lloyd (London, 1922), 38, 40, 83, 102, 111; and Jacques Prévot, *La Première Institutrice de France: Madame de Maintenon* (Paris, 1981), 16, 57. For "la machine" and "le premier ministre," see, respectively, Taillander, *Madame de Maintenon* (Paris, 1920), 117; and *Journal et mémoires du marquis d'Argenson,* ed. E. J. B. Rathery (Paris, 1865), 7:74, 409.

19. Pierrette Jean-Richard, *Musée du Louvre, Cabinet des Dessins, Collection Edmond de Rothschild: Inventaire général des gravures. Ecole française,* vol. 1: *L'Oeuvre gravé de François Boucher dans la collection Edmond de Rothschild* (Paris, 1978), 128; 136, no. 449.

20. Jean Baptiste Poquelin de Molière, *The Learned Ladies, Comedy in Five Acts, 1672,* trans. Richard Wilbur (New York and London, 1978), 51. For the original French: Molière, *Les Femmes savantes,* ed. H. Gaston Hall (London, 1974), 108.

21. *Catalogue des livres,* 98, no. 964; 138, no. 1266.

22. On the *Recueil*: Roux, *Bibliothèque Nationale,* 7:134–266, nos. 14–625, corresponding to the engravings in the Département des Estampes's volumes Ed 89 folio and N2 folio. For Desrochers as engraver and editor, see Préaud et al., 106–7. Also see Peter Gay, *The Enlightenment: An Interpretation,* vol. 2, *The Science of Freedom* (New York and London, 1969), 3–12, 48, 50, 51, 54, for "the recovery of nerve" at the period. Further, Desmond Shawe-Taylor, *Genial Company: The Theme of Genius in Eighteenth-Century British Portraiture,* exhib. cat., London, 1987, 6, 25, 53, 55–56; and Marcia Pointon, *Hanging the Head: Portraiture and Social Formation in Eighteenth-Century England* (New Haven, Conn., and London, 1993), 54–55, 62, 65, discuss the widespread British tradition of engravings of illustrious personages, which contemporaneously parallels Desrochers's. On the tradition in France, see Marianne Grivel, *Le Commerce de l'estampe à Paris au XVIIe siècle* (Geneva, 1986), 141–44; and Roger Portalis and Henri Béraldi, *Les Graveurs du dix-huitième siècle* (Paris, 1880), 1:751–54.

23. *Catalogue de differens portraits, gravés par feu E. Desrochers, Graveur du Roy, & qui se vendent à present chez G. E. Petit, Graveur, demeurant à Paris, ruë Saint Jacques à la Couronne d'Epine, près les Mathurins* [1754], 8.

24. Linda Timmermans, *L'Accès des femmes à la culture (1598–1715): Un Débat d'idées de Saint-François de Sales à la marquise de Lambert* (Paris, 1993), 272–80, discusses the *éloge de savantes* in the seventeenth but not the eighteenth century.

25. For Marguérite de Valois's *Mémoires* in Pompadour's library, see *Catalogue des livres,* 210, no. 1744; 301, no. 2741; and for Marguérite's engraved portrait, see B.N. Estampes, N2 folio.

26. ". . . étoit aussi tres-habile & une des plus sçavantes & des plus grandes politiques de son temps. Cette Princesse aimoit si fort les sciences, que sa table estoit tousiours environnée d'hommes les plus doctes" (Marguérite Buffet, *Nouvelles Observations sur la langue françoise, . . . avec les éloges des illustres sçavantes, tant anciennes que modernes* [Paris, 1668], 301).

27. "Elle avoit une merveilleuse facilité de composer en prose & en vers, ce qu'on peut juger par les Poësies & les Mémoires qui nous restent d'elle" (*Almanach des Dames sçavantes françoises. Pour l'An de Grace 1732. Contenant un ordre alphabetique des Dames qui se sont renduës recommandables par leur Sçavoir, depuis le commencement de la Monarchie, jusqu'à present. Avec l'Abregé de leurs vies, & le catalogue de leurs ouvrages* [Paris, 1732], 45–46).

28. B.N. Estampes, N2 folio.

29. See Gustave Reynier, *La Femme au XVIIe siècle: Ses Ennemis et ses défenseurs* (Paris, 1929), 107–13; and Timmermans, *L'Accès des femmes à la culture,* 303–8, for Schurman's accomplishments.

30. Roux, *Bibliothèque Nationale,* 7:202–3, no. 321. I reproduce the engraving published by Jean-François Daumont, which is identical to the two states by Desrochers. For La Suze's biography, see Buffet, *Nouvelles Observations sur la langue françoise,* 262–64; *Almanach des Dames sçavantes,* 14–18; and P.-A. Alletz, *L'Esprit des femmes célèbres du siècle de Louis XIV, et de celui de Louis XV, jusqu'à présent* (Paris, 1768), 1:68–77. For La Suze's *Recueil* in Pompadour's library: *Catalogue des livres,* 64, no. 677.

31. Roux, *Bibliothèque Nationale,* 7:199, no. 306; *Catalogue des livres,* 209, nos. 1734–37; 316, nos. 2887–88.

32. See Roux, *Bibliothèque Nationale,* 7:167–68, nos. 161, 162. I reproduce the most elaborate state of the engraving by Pierre van Schuppen after the portrait by Elisabeth Sophie Chéron. Desrochers engraved and published other states. See the *Almanach des Dames sçavantes,* 34–35; Alletz, *L'Esprit des femmes célèbres,* 1:177–216, esp. 183: "Ses ouvrages sont regardés comme un modèle de la Poésie naturelle et tendre: On y admire la beauté du sens, les graces de l'expression, l'harmonie & la belle disposition des rimes." On the *Parnasse François,* see Judith Colton, *The Parnasse François: Titon du Tillet and the Origins of the Monument to Genius* (New Haven, Conn., and London, 1979), 21, 57, 97. Also see *Catalogue des livres,* 65, no. 682, for Titon in Pompadour's library.

33. For *Les Illustres Français,* which was begun well before the Revolution but completed only in 1816, see B.N. Estampes, Na 34 petit folio, no. 10; and Portalis and Béraldi, *Les Graveurs du dix-huitième siècle* 3 (1882): 329–30, 338–39.

34. B.N. Estampes, N2 folio; and *Catalogue des livres,* 101, no. 998; 206, no. 1699; 246, no. 2174. See Buffet, *Nouvelles Observations sur la langue françoise,* 274–75; *Almanach des Dames sçavantes,* 37–39; Alletz, *L'Esprit des femmes célèbres,* 1:78–81, esp. 79–80: "On pourroit dire qu'elle avoit consacré son esprit & sa plume à ce Dieu, & qu'elle s'étoit faite un plan de célébrer son pouvoir sur le coeur humain. . . . En un mot, c'étoit sa manie d'employer tous ses talents à parler le langage des passions." Also see Katherine Ann Jenson, "Marie-Catherine Desjardins de Villedieu (1640?–1683)," in *French Women Writers: A Bio-Bibliographical Source Book,* ed. Eva Martin Sartori and Dorothy Wynne Zimmerman (New York, Westport, Conn., and London, 1991), 503–12.

35. See Roux, *Bibliothèque Nationale,* 7:250, no. 540; and *Catalogue des livres,* 205, nos. 1675–79, for Scudéry's *Clélie, Almahide, Mathilde d'Aguilar,* and *Artemène, ou le Grand Cyrus.* For the exceptional accomplishments of Scudéry, see Iacquette Guillaume, *Les Dames illustres ou par bonnes & fortes raisons, il se prouve que le sexe féminin surpasse en toute sorte de genres le sexe masculin* (Paris, 1665), 293–94; Buffet, *Nouvelles Observations sur la langue françoise,* 244–48; *Almanach des Dames sçavantes,* 56–58; Mme de Galien, *Apologie des dames appuyée sur l'histoire* (Paris, 1718); and Alletz, *L'Esprit des femmes célèbres,* 1:332–52.

36. B.N. Estampes, N2 folio. Also see *Almanach des Dames sçavantes,* 12–14; Alletz, *L'Esprit des femmes célèbres,* 1:386–98; René Démoris, ed., *Hommage à Elizabeth Sophie Chéron: Texte et peintre à l'âge classique* (Paris, 1992); and Dominique Brême, "Elisabeth-Sophie Chéron," in *The Dictionary of Art,* ed. Jane Turner (New York and London, 1996), 6:553–54, for the many talents and accomplishments of Chéron.

37. For the engraving, see Roux, *Bibliothèque Nationale* 7:166, no. 154. Shawe-Taylor, *Genial Company,* 53, 55, discusses the signification of fictive medallions in British prints. For Dacier's translations in Pompadour's library: *Catalogue des livres,* 51, no. 515; 53, nos. 534, 539, 540; 54, no. 547; 55, nos. 558, 564.

38. "Personne n'a parlé avec plus de justesse de l'art Poëtique, & n'a mieux connu le Théatre des Anciens. . . . On trouve dans tous ses Ecrits une grande érudition, beaucoup de solidité & de force d'esprit, avec une noble éloquence" (*Almanach des Dames sçavantes,* 24, 26).

39. B.N. Estampes, Na 34 petit folio.

CHAPTER 4

1. See chapter 1, note 32.

2. See Georges Wildenstein, *Le Peintre Aved: Sa Vie et son oeuvre, 1702–1766,* 2 vols. (Paris, 1922), for Aved's life and career.

3. Ibid., 1:121; 2:106, no. 82.

4. Ibid., 1:53; 2:136, no. 104. Also see Philip Conisbee, *Chardin* (Lewisburg, Pa., 1985), 168–69, who identifies the print after Raphael's *Galatea.*

5. Wildenstein, *Le Peintre Aved,* 1:65; 2:90, no. 67.

6. Albert Besnard and Georges Wildenstein, *La Tour: La Vie et l'oeuvre de l'artiste* (Paris, 1928), 163, no. 427.

7. Ibid., 141, no. 133.

8. See Anthony Blunt, *Art and Architecture in France 1500 to 1700* (Baltimore, 1953), 241.

9. For a discussion of the Largillierre and related portraits, see Myra Nan Rosenfeld, *Largillierre and the Eighteenth-Century Portrait,* exhib. cat., Montreal, 1981, 182–86, no. 32.

10. For this portrait: *Louis XV: Un moment de perfection de l'art français,* exhib. cat., Paris, 1974, 149–50, no. 123; and Pierre Rosenberg, *The Age of Louis XV: French Painting, 1710–1774,* exhib. cat., Toledo, Chicago, and Ottawa, 1975, 75–76, no. 104.

11. Besnard and Wildenstein, *La Tour,* 164, no. 436; 177.

12. Quoted in Edmond de Goncourt and Jules de Goncourt, *French Eighteenth-Century Painters*, trans. Robin Ironside (Ithaca, N.Y., 1981), 191; and George T. M. Shackelford and Mary Tavener Holmes, *A Magic Mirror: The Portrait in France, 1700–1900*, exhib. cat., Houston, 1986, 12.

13. Besnard and Wildenstein, *La Tour,* 145, no. 182. Also see Christine Debrie, *Maurice-Quentin de La Tour: "Peintre de portraits au pastel" 1704–1788 au musée Antoine Lécuyer de Saint-Quentin* (Thonon-les-Bains, 1991), 123–27, for the version at Saint-Quentin contemporaneous with this portrait.

14. See Wildenstein, *Le Peintre Aved,* 1:33; 2:139, no. 106; and Georges Wildenstein, "Premier supplément à la biographie et au catalogue de J. A. J. Aved (1922–1935)," *Gazette des Beaux-Arts* 13 (1935): 166, 168, no. 106.

15. For example, see Arthur K. Wheelock, Jr., *Jan Vermeer* (New York, 1981), pl. 7, 21, 42. Also, for the theme of absorption, which permeates this and other eighteenth-century French paintings, see Michael Fried, *Absorption and Theatricality: Painting and Beholder in the Age of Diderot* (Berkeley, 1980).

16. Bibliothèque Nationale, Département des Estampes, Collection Deloynes 47 (1738): 119; and Wildenstein, *Le Peintre Aved,* 1:29–44; 2:112–13, no. 86.

17. See Pierre de Nolhac, *J.-M. Nattier: Peintre de la cour de Louis XV* (Paris, 1905), 2:78–82. Also see Michael Levey, *Painting and Sculpture in France, 1700–1789* (New Haven, Conn., and London, 1993), pl. 194, for a convenient illustration.

18. Pierre de Nolhac, *Nattier: Peintre de la cour de Louis XV* (Paris, 1925), 99–100; and *The Toledo Museum of Art, European Paintings* (Toledo, Ohio., 1976), 117–18, pl. 200.

19. I am most grateful to Orest Ranum for informing me about the nature of Nattier's painted book in a personal communication of February 12, 1996.

20. Nattier's fictive volume has specific-looking texts: on page 268, we barely make out the words "non juifs," and on page 270, we assume that the beginning lines read "LES GRECS ET LES ROMAINS A VOIENT pour ses coutumes . . . ," but upon closer examination we realize that they read, erroneously, "LES GRECS ET LES ROCIMINS A VOINT pour . . . coutumes. . . ." Thus we are forced to conclude that Nattier gives us not a literal rendering of a text but the feel of one. While Jews, Greeks, and Romans abound in the universal histories that the Princesse de Rohan is likely to have known, none of them corresponds either in title, pagination, orthography, or most signally text, to her fictive tome. Jacques-Bénigne Bossuet's influential *Discours sur l'histoire universelle* (1681, 1682, 1700) may very well have been in Marie-Sophie de Courcillon's library, for she was the granddaughter of the famous writer Dangeau, who was persuaded to take orders by Bossuet, and the wife of Hercule-Mériadec, prince de Soubise and duc de Rohan-Rohan, one of the most steadfast allies of Louis XIV, under whom Bossuet wrote his *Discours.* Their similar quarto formats notwithstanding, Nattier did not copy it. Neither did he mimic Claude de L'Isle's chronologically plausible *Abrégé de l'histoire universelle* (ca. 1731, 7 vols.), or Dom Augustin Calmet's enticingly contemporaneous *Histoire universelle, sacrée et profane, depuis le commencement du monde jusqu'à nos jours* (1735–47, 8 vols.), published in Strasbourg, a Rohan seat of power, dedicated not to the princess but to the duc de Lorraine. And Nattier's putative volume bears no relation at all to the exactly contemporaneous *Histoire universelle, depuis le commencement du monde jusqu'à présent; traduite de l'Anglois d'une Société de Gens de Lettres* (12 vols.), first printed in 1742, the year after Nat-

tier's princess would have approved it for publication. Thus Nattier's fictitious tome was not buttressed by reality; the twelve volumes of the *Histoire universelle* were dedicated to important patrons of the period but not to the Princesse de Rohan.

21. ". . . une des plus belles femmes de la cour . . . dont l'âme était aussi noble que la figure," in *Mémoires et lettres de François-Joachim de Pierre, cardinal de Bernis (1715–1758)*, ed. Frédéric Masson (Paris, 1903), 1:107.

22. *Catalogue des livres,* 269–71, nos. 2430–54.

23. Ed[ouard] Humbert and Alphonse Revilliod, *La Vie et les oeuvres de Jean Etienne Liotard (1702–1789): Étude biographique et iconographique* (Amsterdam, 1897), 24–26, 119, no. 45; François Fosca, *La Vie, les voyages et les oeuvres de Jean-Etienne Liotard, citoyen de Genève, dit le peintre turc* (Lausanne and Paris, 1956), 84; and Renée Loche and Marcel Roethlisberger, *L'Opera completa di Liotard* (Milan, 1978), 110, no. 233.

24. "Je remerci à deux genoux la philosophe qui met son doigt sur son menton, et qui a un petit air penché que lui a fait Liotard; son âme est aussi belle que ses yeux" (*Voltaire's Correspondence*, ed. Theodore Besterman [Geneva, 1958], 41:104); and Anne de Herdt, *Dessins de Liotard, suivi du catalogue de l'oeuvre dessiné*, exhib. cat., Geneva, 1992, 18. I am grateful to Mme de Herdt for supplying me with photographs of the portrait.

25. "Je ne suis point jolie; je ne suis cependant pas laide. Je suis petite, maigre, très bien faite. J'ai l'air jeune, sans fraîcheur, noble, doux, vif, spirituel et intéressant" (quoted in Fosca, *Jean-Etienne Liotard,* 86).

26. For Epinay's biography, see Elisabeth Badinter, *Emilie, Emilie: L'Ambition féminine au XVIIIe siècle* (Paris, 1983); and for Epinay's literary career: Ruth Plaut Weinreb, *Eagle in a Gauze Cage: Louise d'Epinay, Femme de Lettres* (New York, 1993). See pages 25–27 for her early writings.

27. Weinreb, *Eagle in a Gauze Cage,* 23, 31, 33, 46–47, 111–12, 117.

28. Ibid., 163.

29. See Peter Gay, *The Enlightenment: An Interpretation,* vol. 2, *The Science of Freedom* (New York and London, 1969), 126–87, for the Enlightenment and science.

30. On women and science, see Gustave Reynier, *La Femme au XVIIe siècle: Ses Ennemis et ses défenseurs* (Paris, 1929), 141, 154–55, 162–64, 172–80; Linda Gardiner, "Women in Science," in *French Women and the Age of Enlightenment*, ed. Samia I. Spencer (Bloomington, Ind., 1984), 181–93; Londa Schiebinger, *The Mind Has No Sex? Women in the Origins of Modern Science* (Cambridge, Mass., and London, 1989); Jeanne Peiffer, "L'Engouement des femmes pour les sciences au XVIIIe siècle," in *Femmes et pouvoirs sous l'Ancien Régime*, ed. Danielle Haase-Dubosc and Elaine Viennot (Paris and Marseille, 1991), 196–222; and Erica Harth, *Cartesian Women: Versions and Subversions of Rational Discourse in the Old Regime* (Ithaca, N.Y., and London, 1992).

31. My discussion is based on those of Penelope Hunter-Stiebel, *Chez Elle, Chez Lui: At Home in 18th Century France*, exhib. cat., New York, 1987, 8–10, no. 1; and Georges Poisson, "La Leçon d'astronomie de la duchesse du Maine par François de Troy," *La Revue du Louvre et des Musées de France* 4 (1989): 239–44.

32. Among the many studies of du Châtelet's life and work are: Badinter, *Emilie, Emilie;* Esther Ehrman, *Mme du Châtelet* (Leamington Spa, England, 1986); and Schiebinger, *The Mind Has No Sex?,* 29, 60, 62–64, 127. For Pompadour and du Châtelet: Danielle Gallet, *Madame de Pompadour, ou le pouvoir féminin* (Paris, 1985), 53, 62, 255.

33. Pierre de Nolhac, *J.-M. Nattier: Court Painter under Louis XV* (Paris and New York, 1905), 139, 156; and Theodore Dell, "French Art History and the Eighteenth Century," *Connoisseur* 167 (1968): 30–32.

34. *Peintures du dix-huitième siècle au Musée des Beaux-Arts de Bordeaux*, exhib. cat., Paris, Bordeaux, 1969–70, 45, no. 18; and Ann Sutherland Harris and Linda Nochlin, *Women Artists: 1550–1950*, exhib. cat., New York, 1976, 167–68, no. 44.

35. "Je sens tout le poids du/preiugé qui nous exclud si universellement des sciences, et cest une des contradictions de ce monde, qui m'a touiours le plus etonnée, car il y a de grands pays, dont la loy nous permit de regler la destinée, mais, il ny en a point ou nous soyions elevées a penser. . . . Pourquoy ces creatures dont l'entendement paroit en tout si semblable a celuy des hommes, semblent pourtant arrestées par une force invincible en deça de la bariere, et qu'on m'en donne la raison, si l'on peut . . . a ce quils l'ayent trouvée, les femmes seront en droit de reclamer contre leur education. Pour moy i'avoüe que si i'etois roy, . . . je reformerois un abus qui retranche, pour ainsi dire la moitié du genre humain. Je ferois participer les femme a tous les droits de l'humanité, et sur tout a ceux de l'esprit. Il semble quelles soient nées pour tromper, et on ne laisse gueres que cet exercise a leur ame. Cette education nouvelle, feroit en tout un grand bien a l'espece humaine. Les femmes en vaudroient mieux et les hommes y gagnereoientun nouveau suiet d'emulation. . . . Je suis persuadée que bien des femme ou ignorent leurs talents, par le vice de leur education, ou les enfoüissent par preiugé, et faute de courage dans l'esprit. Ce que i'ay eprouvé en moy, me confirme dans cette opinion. Le hazard me fit connoitre de gens de lettres, qui prirent de l'amitié pour moy. . . . Je commencai a croire alors que i'etois une creature pensant" (Ira O. Wade, *Studies on Voltaire with Some Unpublished Papers of Mme du Châtelet* [Princeton, N.J., 1947], 135–36; translated by Ehrman, *Mme du Châtelet,* 61).

36. "C'est ainsi que la Verité / Pour mieux établir sa puissance, / A pris les traits de la bauté [*sic*] / Et les graces de l'Eloquence" (Edmond Pognon and Yves Bruand, *Bibliothèque Nationale, Département des Estampes, Inventaire du fonds français: Graveurs du XVIIIe siècle* [Paris, 1962], 9:111, no. 1255).

37. "A côté de Neuton, l'immortelle Emilie / S'éleve dans les Airs: / Et parcourant des Cieux la Carriere infinie. / Mesure l'univers. / Ornement de son sexe, et du siècle où nous sommes / Le but de ses travaux est d'éclairer les Hommes" (B.N. Estampes, N2).

38. "A Madame la marquise Du Châtelet": "Lecteur, ouvrez ce docte écrit; / La physique, pour nous, a quitté son air sauvage, / Et vous devinerez à son charmant langage / Que c'est Vénus qui nous instruit. / Qui, Vénus-Uranie, elle en a le corsage, / Et de l'autre elle a tout l'ésprit./ Le vrai philosophe la lit; / Qui la voit, je le sais, est bien loin d'être sage" (*Oeuvres complètes de Voltaire*, nouvelle édition, ed. Louis Moland [Paris, 1880], 36:19).

39. See Nolhac, *J.-M. Nattier,* 1905 (French edition), 2:105; and Andrew McClellan, "Watteau's Dealer:

Gersaint and the Marketing of Art in Eighteenth-Century Paris," *Art Bulletin* 78 (1996): 447. Bonnier's *Histoire naturelle* is not Buffon's famous work, which first appeared in 1751.

40. See Gay, *The Enlightenment,* 2:125–50; and *The Complete Works of Voltaire*, ed. Robert L. Walters and W. H. Barber (Oxford, 1992), 15:29, 40, 44–46, 53.

41. Besnard and Wildenstein, *La Tour,* 142, no. 145; *Meisterwerke des 18. Jahrhunderts. Sammlung der Bayerischen Hypotheken-und Weschel-Bank in der Alten Pinakothek München*, ed. Wolf-Dieter Dube, cat. Hermann Bauer, Munich, 1966, 36–37.

42. *Elémens de la philosophie de Neuton, mis à la portée de tout le monde. Par Mr de Voltaire* (Amsterdam, 1738), 10.

43. Theodore Besterman, *Voltaire* (New York, 1969), 192–95; A. Owen Aldridge, *Voltaire and the Century of Light* (Princeton, N.J., 1975), 108–9; and *The Complete Works of Voltaire,* 15:29, 40, 44–46, 53, 59, 95, 98, 119, 127, 129–30, 135–36, 192.

44. *Catalogue des livres,* 27, no. 286; 255, no. 2282.

45. The principal study of les Pouplinière is Georges Cucuël, *La Pouplinière et la musique de chambre au XVIIIe siècle* (Paris, 1913).

46. Besnard and Wildenstein, *La Tour,* 147, no. 208; and Debrie, *Maurice-Quentin de La Tour,* 129–32.

47. "Cette heureuse facilité de mémoire et d'intelligence . . . cette verve d'éloquence qui tenait de l'inspiration . . . cette accord de l'ésprit et du goût" (quoted in Cucuël, *La Pouplinière,* 101).

48. "Mon coeur, mon sang est encore d'une agitation la plus vive. Je suis d'une sensibilité et d'une vivacité à me jeter par la fenêtre. . . . Mon imagination est toujours en mouvement" (ibid., 102).

49. Perhaps corresponding to Besnard and Wildenstein, *La Tour,* 147, nos. 209, 210, or 211, which are listed but not described.

50. Cucuël, *La Pouplinière,* 94–95, 99–100; Michaela Maria Keane, "The Theoretical Writings of Jean-Philippe Rameau" (Ph.D. diss., Catholic University of America, 1961), 142, 144; and Bibliothèque Nationale, *Jean-Philippe Rameau 1683–1764*, exhib. cat., Paris, 1964, 32, no. 159.

51. See Roberte Machard, *Jean-Joseph Cassanéa de Mondonville: Virtuose, compositeur et chef d'orchestre* (Béziers, 1980), 62–63; and Gallet, *Madame de Pompadour, ou le pouvoir féminin,* 67.

52. Besnard and Wildenstein, *La Tour,* 157, nos. 344, 347. Also see Thelma R. Stockho, "French Paintings of the Seventeenth and Eighteenth Centuries," *Saint Louis Art Museum Bulletin* 16 (1981): 18–19; and Debrie, *Maurice-Quentin de La Tour,* 144, 146.

53. On this aspect of *honnêteté,* see "honnête and "honneste" in Antoine Furetière, *Dictionnaire universel, contenant généralement tous les mots françois, tant vieux que modernes, & les termes des sciences & des arts,* 4th ed. (Paris, 1727; reprint, Hildesheim and New York, 1972), 2:n.p. Also see Elise Goodman, *Rubens: The Garden of Love as Conversatie à la mode* (Amsterdam and Philadelphia, 1992), 33–34.

54. Cuthbert Girdlestone, *Jean-Philippe Rameau: His Life and Work* (New York, 1969), 48–49, 600; and *The New Grove Dictionary of Music and Musicians*, ed. Stanley Sadie (London, 1980), 15:562.

55. Besnard and Wildenstein, *La Tour,* 56; Machard, *Jean-Joseph Cassanéa de Mondonville,* 62. La Tour's

portrait of Mme de Mondonville was number seventy-six in the Salon of 1753, described as "Madame de Mondonville Leaning on a Harpsichord" (*Exposition des peintures, sculptures, et autres ouvrages de messieurs de l'Academie royalle,* Paris, 1753, 19–20). An anonymous critic of the Salon noted that "Madame de Mondonville will appear to again delight by her lovely works for the harpsichord" (*Le Salon,* n.p., n.d., 28), while another reviewer of the Salon was struck by the stunning likeness of her in La Tour's pastel (*Lettres à un ami, sur l'exposition des tableaux faites dans le grand salon du Louvre,* n.p., August 1753, 15). Unfortunately, none of Mme de Mondonville's compositions survives.

56. Nolhac, *J.-M. Nattier* (French edition), 92–96, 97–99; and A. P. de Mirimonde, "Musiciens isolés et portraits de l'école française du XVIIIe siècle dans les collections nationales," *La Revue du Louvre et des Musées de France* 16 (1966): 147–52, the definitive study of the portraits of Mesdames, on which my discussion is based.

57. Simone Poignant, *Les Filles de Louis XV: L'Aile des princes* (n.p., 1970), 212, 215, 221–28, 257, 273–79, 286–88.

58. See Julie Anne Sadie, "*Musiciennes* of the Ancien Régime," in *Women Making Music: The Western Art Tradition, 1150–1950,* ed. Jane Bowers and Judith Tick (Urbana, Ill., 1986), 205.

59. Mirimonde, "Musiciens isolés et portraits," 151–52; Poignant, *Les Filles de Louis XV,* 274–75.

60. For Mme Favart's biography, see Auguste Font, *L'Opéra-Comique et la comédie-vaudeville aux XVIIe et XVIIIe siècles* (Paris, 1894; reprint Geneva, 1970), 126–27, 144–47; Arthur Pougin, *Madame Favart: Étude théâtrale, 1727–1772* (Paris, 1912); and *The New Grove Dictionary of Music and Musicians,* 6:439–40.

61. Charles Sterling, *The Metropolitan Museum of Art: A Catalogue of French Paintings, XV–XVIII Centuries* (Cambridge, Mass., 1955), 146–47; *Stiftung Oskar Reinhart Winterthur* (Zurich, 1977), 1:219–20, no. 101; and Loche and Roethlisberger, *L'Opera completa di Liotard,* 108, no. 213.

62. For a convenient illustration, see Shackelford and Holmes, *Magic Mirror,* 58–59, no. 13.

63. "Une âme sensible, un fond de gaîté inaltérable, une philosophie douce constituoient son caractère" (anonymous author in the almanac *Les Spectacles de Paris* [1772], quoted in Pougin, *Madame Favart,* 55).

64. "Chantant gaîment une chanson / Et portant lestement sur sa tête une gerbe" (ibid., 45).

65. See Loche and Roethlisberger, *L'Opera completa di Liotard,* 108, no. 212; and *Stiftung Oskar Reinhart,* 219. I thank Marcel Roethlisberger for providing me with an illustration of this portrait.

66. The most famous portrait of this type is David's *Portrait of Monsieur and Madame Lavoisier,* 1788, Metropolitan Museum of Art (conveniently illustrated in Philip Conisbee, *Painting in Eighteenth-Century France* [Ithaca, N.Y., 1981], 136, fig. 110).

CHAPTER 5

1. "Ces femmes . . . forment une espèce de république dont les membres toujours actifs se secourent et se servent mutuellement: c'est comme un nouvel État dans l'État; et celui qui est à la Cour, à Paris, dans les provinces, qui voit agir des ministres, des magistrats, des prélats, s'il ne connaît les femmes qui les gouvernent, est comme un homme qui voit bien une machine qui joue, mais qui n'en connaît

point les ressorts" (Charles-Louis de Secondat, baron de La Brède et de Montesquieu, *Lettres persanes* [Paris, 1975], 224 [Lettre CVII]).

2. See Peter Gay, *The Party of Humanity: Essays in the French Enlightenment* (New York, 1964); Peter Gay, *The Enlightenment: An Interpretation,* vol. 1, *The Rise of Modern Paganism* (New York and London, 1966), 3, 14, 26; and R. G. Saisselin, "*philosophes,*" in *The Blackwell Companion to the Enlightenment,* ed. John W. Yolton et al. (Oxford, 1991), 395–97.

3. See Roger Picard, *Les Salons littéraires et la société française, 1610–1789* (New York, 1943), 155; Katherine B. Clinton, "Femme et Philosophe: Enlightenment Origins of Feminism," *Eighteenth-Century Studies* 8 (1975): 285–86; and Evelyn Gordon Bodek, "Salonnières and Bluestockings: Educated Obsolescence and Germinating Feminism," *Feminist Studies* 3–4 (1976): 186.

4. See Bodek, "Salonnières and Bluestockings," 185–86; and the following works by Dena Goodman: "Seriousness of Purpose: Salonnières, Philosophes, and the Shaping of the Eighteenth-Century Salon," *Proceedings of the Annual Meeting of the Western Society for French History* 15 (1988): 111, 115; "Enlightenment Salons: The Convergence of Female and Philosophic Ambitions," *Eighteenth-Century Studies* 22 (1989): 333, 334; and *The Republic of Letters: A Cultural History of the French Enlightenment* (Ithaca, N.Y., and London, 1994), 76.

5. See Goodman, "Seriousness of Purpose," 111; Goodman, *Republic of Letters,* 5, 53, 74, 76, 131.

6. On Mme de Lambert's coterie: Amelia Gere Mason, *The Women of the French Salons* (New York, 1891), 136–44; Lucien Brunel, "Les Salons, la société, l'Académie," in *Histoire de la langue et de la littérature française, des origines à 1900,* ed. L. Petit de Julleville (Paris, 1925): 6:396–98; and Picard, *Les Salons littéraires,* 182–86. Also see Léon Abensour, *La Femme et le féminisme avant La Révolution* (Paris [1923]; reprint, Geneva, 1977), 382, 415; and Virginia E. Swain, "Hidden from View: French Women Authors and the Language of Rights, 1727–1792," in *Intimate Encounters: Love and Domesticity in Eighteenth-Century France,* exhib. cat., Princeton, N.J., 1997, 23–25, for Lambert's *Avis d'une mère à sa fille* and *Réflexions nouvelles sur les femmes,* in which, respectively, she prescribed a classical education for her daughter and argued, in the tradition of the Women's Quarrel, that women should be allowed to study the sciences and fine arts. For the *Oeuvres de Mme la Marquise de Lambert* (Paris, 1748, 2 vols.) in Pompadour's library, see *Catalogue des livres,* 254, no. 2275.

7. "Des plus rares esprits sans cesse environnée, / Et de mille vertus ornées: / Le Ciel qui la chérit et elle nous fait voir / Vne autre Athenais par son profond sçavoir" (B.N. Estampes, N2 folio).

8. Danielle Gallet, *Madame de Pompadour, ou le pouvoir féminin* (Paris, 1985), 245.

9. For Deffand's salon, see Mason, *Women of the French Salons,* 199–209; and Benedetta Craveri, *Madame du Deffand et son monde,* trans. Sibylle Zavriew (Paris, 1987), 41, 47–50, 64–91.

10. See Lionel Duisit, *Madame du Deffand épistolière* (Geneva, 1963).

11. See *Correspondance de Mme de Pompadour avec son père, M. Poisson, et son frère, M. de Vandières,* ed. M. A. P. Malassis (Paris, 1878); *Memoirs and Letters of Cardinal de Bernis,* trans. Katharine Prescott Wormeley (New York, 1901), 1:197; and Jacques Levron, *Pompadour,* trans. Claire Eliane Engel (Lon-

don, 1963), 242–43, for the marquise's especially eloquent letters to Chancellor Kaunitz and Maria-Theresa.

12. See Picard, *Les Salons littéraires,* 148; Carolyn C. Lougee, *Le Paradis des Femmes: Women, Salons, and Social Stratification in Seventeenth-Century France* (Princeton, N.J., 1976), 41, 50, 52–53, 158, 170; and Goodman, "Enlightenment Salons," 330–31.

13. "Cette femme extraordinaire. . . . Ah! que de finesse d'esprit, de souplesse et d'activité" (*Mémoires de Marmontel,* ed. Maurice Tourneux [Paris, 1891; reprint, Geneva, 1967], 1:271).

14. For Tencin's salon, frequented by Fontenelle, the dramatist Marivaux, the poet Piron, and the historian Duclos, among others, see Mason, *Women of the French Salons,* 156–69; Pierre-Maurice Masson, *Une Vie de femme au XVIIIe siècle: Madame de Tencin (1682–1749)* (Paris, 1909; reprint, Geneva, 1970); and Picard, *Les Salons littéraires,* 187–95. See also, for Tencin as novelist, Eva Martin Sartori, "Claudine-Alexandrine Guérin de Tencin (1682–1749)," in *French Women Writers: A Bio-Bibliographical Source Book,* ed. Eva Martin Sartori and Dorothy Wynne Zimmerman (New York, Westport, Conn., and London, 1991), 473–83.

15. Pierre de Nolhac, *Louis XV et Madame de Pompadour* (Paris, 1902), 45; and Gallet, *Madame de Pompadour, ou le pouvoir féminin,* 21, 24, 29, 42, 51, 219.

16. On Geoffrin's "Mondays," which were also frequented by the painters Carle Van Loo, Hubert Robert, and later Vien, as well as the sculptors Bouchardon, Falconet, and Lemoine; and her "Wednesdays," attended by the mathematician Maupertuis; Diderot and d'Alembert, whose *Encyclopédie* Geoffrin sponsored; the critic Grimm; the versifiers Gentil-Bernard and Bernis; and the regulars from Tencin's salon, see Marquis de Ségur, *Le Royaume de la rue de Saint-Honoré: Madame Geoffrin et sa fille* (Paris [1897]); Masson, *Madame de Tencin,* 172–83; and Picard, *Les Salons littéraires,* 199–220.

17. "Jolie, bien faite, naturelle, parfaitement bonne, chantant à merveille, douée de tous les talents pour séduire, elle plut beaucoup aux vieux philosophes des réunions du mercredi," quoted in Ségur, *Le Royaume de la rue de Saint-Honoré,* 159.

18. Albert de La Fizelière, "L'Art et les femmes en France: Madame de Pompadour," *Gazette des Beaux-Arts* 3 (1859): 132; and Gallet, *Madame de Pompadour, ou le pouvoir féminin,* 24.

19. ". . . elle sait la musique parfaitement, elle chante avec toute la gaieté et tout le goût possible, sait cent chansons, joue la comédie à Étiolles sur un théâtre aussi beau que celui de l'Opéra . . ." (*Correspondance complète de la marquise du Deffand avec ses amis le président Hénault, Montesquieu, d'Alembert, Voltaire, Horace Walpole,* ed. M. de Lescure [Paris, 1865; reprint, Geneva, 1971], 1:70).

20. Nolhac, *Louis XV et Madame de Pompadour,* 49; E. de Goncourt, *The Confidantes of a King,* trans. Ernest Dowson (New York, 1909), 1:140; and Jean Nicolle, *Madame de Pompadour et la société de son temps* (Paris, 1980), 172–73.

21. "Je lui conseillai de protéger les gens de lettres: ce furent eux qui donnèrent le nom de Grand à Louis XIV" (*Mémoires du cardinal de Bernis,* ed. Jean-Marie Rouart and Philippe Bonnet [Paris, 1980], 89).

22. "Je suis fort aise d'avoir contribué à la satisfaction de Messieurs de la société des Sciences de Toulouse,

et de leur avoir donné une preuve de l'estime et du cas que je fais des sciences et des beaux-arts" (Malassis, 169–70).

23. Ibid., 70; Nolhac, *Louis XV et Madame de Pompadour,* 114; and Gallet, *Madame de Pompadour, ou le pouvoir féminin,* 181.

24. "J'aime les talents et les lettres, et ce sera toujours pour moi un grand plaisir que de contribuer au bonheur de ceux qui les cultivent" (quoted in Gallet, *Madame de Pompadour, ou le pouvoir féminin,* 181).

25. Ibid., 57, 176, 179.

26. The physiocrats were a group of scientific economists who believed that political administration should be founded on scientific principles; they advocated currency reform, elimination of tariff barriers to trade and industry, and particularly the rational planning of agricultural production. See, for this definition, Robert Wokler, "physiocracy," in *The Blackwell Companion to the Enlightenment*, ed. John W. Yolton et al. (Oxford, 1991), 402.

27. *Mémoires de Marmontel*, 2:22–27.

28. "Avez-vous regretté madame de Pompadour? Oui, sans doute, car dans le fond de son coeur elle était des nôtres; elle protégeait les lettres autant qu'elle le pouvait: voilà un beau rêve de fini" (*The Complete Works of Voltaire: Correspondence and Related Documents*, ed. Theodore Besterman [Banbury, England, 1973], 27:364).

29. See, for an analysis of these definitions, Ann Thomson, "Le Philosophe et la société," Transactions of the Fifth International Congress on the Enlightenment, *Studies on Voltaire and the Eighteenth Century* 190 (1980): 276, 277.

30. Georges Duplessis, *Catalogue de l'oeuvre de Abraham Bosse* (Paris, 1859), 17–18, no. 46.

31. Bibliothèque Nationale, *Au Temps des Précieuses: Les Salons littéraires au XVIIe siècle,* exhib. cat., Paris, 1968, 17, no. 66.

32. See Erica Harth, *Cartesian Women: Versions and Subversions of Rational Discourse in the Old Regime* (Ithaca, N.Y., and London, 1992), 33; and Goodman, *Republic of Letters,* 6.

33. Nicole Hubert and Alain Pougetoux, *Châteaux de Malmaison et de Bois-Préau, catalogue sommaire illustré des peintures et dessins* (Paris, 1989), 35, no. I. 49.

34. *Traité des Pierres Gravées par P.-J. Mariette* (Paris, 1750), plate between 208 and 209; and *Catalogue des livres*, 362, no. 3373.

35. For the history of the *Suite*, see J.-F. Leturcq, *Notice sur Jacques Guay, graveur sur pierres fines du Roi Louis XV* (Paris, 1873), 13–17; and for the engravings in the portrait, see Alastair Laing et al., *François Boucher: 1703–1770*, exhib. cat., New York, Detroit, and Paris, 1986–87, 270, no. 64. See also Donald Posner, "Mme. de Pompadour as a Patron of the Visual Arts," *Art Bulletin* 72 (1990): 100–102.

36. *Catalogue des livres*, 263–65, nos. 2379–402.

37. For Vaugondy's globes, see Gallet, *Madame de Pompadour, ou le pouvoir féminin,* 129; and Danielle Gallet et al., *Madame de Pompadour et la floraison des arts*, exhib. cat., Montreal, 1988, 88–89; and for Cassini: Nicolle, *Madame de Pompadour,* 176.

38. I am most grateful to Alden R. Gordon for a personal communication of March 28, 1995, imparting this information.

39. *Catalogue des livres,* 179, nos. 1407, 1408 (Italian); 179, nos. 1409–12 (French).

40. Jules Marsan, *La Pastorale dramatique en France à la fin du XVIe siècle et du commencement du XVIIe siècle* (Paris, 1905; reprint, Geneva, 1969), 50–53; and Walter F. Staton, Jr., and William E. Simeone, *A Critical Edition of Sir Richard Fanshaw's 1647 Translation of Giovanni Battista Guarini's Il Pastor Fido* (Oxford, 1964), xv.

41. Gallet, *Madame de Pompadour, ou le pouvoir féminin,* 58.

42. E. Kegel-Brinkgreve, *The Echoing Woods: Bucolic and Pastoral from Theocritus to Wordsworth* (Amsterdam, 1990), 354, 358.

43. Vauvenargues: "le plus grand ouvrage de ce siècle"; Marais: "la gloire de nôtre nation," quoted in Voltaire, *La Henriade,* ed. O. R. Taylor, *Studies on Voltaire and the Eighteenth Century,* ed. Theodore Besterman (Geneva, 1965), 38:52, 188.

44. *Catalogue des livres,* 67, nos. 721–23 (*La Henriade*); 304–7, nos. 2770–96 (histories of the reign of Henri IV).

45. Voltaire, *La Henriade,* 346–47, 349, 353–54.

46. "Discours au roi": "HENRI IV était, de l'aveu de toutes les nations, le meilleur prince, le maître le plus doux, le plus intrépide capitaine, le plus sage politique de son siècle" (Voltaire, *La Henriade,* ed. O. R. Taylor, *Studies on Voltaire and the Eighteenth Century,* ed. Theodore Besterman [Geneva, 1965]: 39:249). The dedication was suppressed on the advice of the young king's tutor and adviser, Fleury.

47. "Disce, puer, virtutem ex me, verumque laborem" (from Vergil's *Aeneid,* Book 12, verse 435), *Oeuvres complètes de Voltaire,* nouvelle édition, ed. Louis Moland (Paris, 1877), 8:371. Voltaire was called the French Vergil by enthusiastic readers of *La Henriade,* the new (and better) *Aeneid.*

48. "Il sait aimer, il sait combattre; / Il envoie en ce beau séjour / Un brevet digne d'Henri Quatre, / Signé LOUIS, Mars, et l'Amour" (ibid., 516); "Un roi . . . plus aimé qu'Henri" (quoted in Nolhac, *Louis XV et Madame de Pompadour,* 90); "Mon *Henri IV* et ma Zaïre / Et mon Américaine *Alzire*" (ibid., 4:272).

49. "A chaque heure, la réputation du roi se raccommode dans le public, et bientôt elle éclatera comme celle d'Henri IV, tant l'opinion du roi chemine vite!" (*Journal et mémoires du marquis d'Argenson,* ed. E. J. B. Rathery [Paris, 1862], 4:50). See Michel Antoine, *Louis XV* (Paris, 1989), 601, for a discussion of this historical moment. Antoine's biography revises the traditional assessment of Louis XV as an indolent, mediocre monarch, recasting him as intelligent, cultivated, and well informed.

50. "Je vois bien que je mourrai comme Henri IV" (quoted in Gallet, *Madame de Pompadour, ou le pouvoir féminin,* 98).

51. See Josèphe Jacquiot, "Les Camées et les intailles," in *Louis XV: Un moment de perfection de l'art français,* exhib. cat., Paris, 1974, 633, nos. 941, 942.

52. See chapter 1, and also Elise Goodman-Soellner, "Boucher's *Madame de Pompadour at Her Toilette*," *Simiolus* 17 (1987): 42–44.

53. *Catalogue des livres*, 21, nos. 220, 221.

54. *The Spirit of the Laws by Baron de Montesquieu*, trans. Thomas Nugent (New York and London, 1949), 292–315. For the original French, see Montesquieu, *De l'Esprit des loix*, ed. Jean Brèthe de La Gressaye (Paris, 1958), 3:5–39. Also see, for an excellent critical analysis of *l'esprit général*, J. Robert Loy, *Montesquieu* (New York, 1968), 81, 115, 161, 163.

55. *The Spirit of the Laws*, 294–95, 300. My reading is based on that of Pauline Kra, "Montesquieu and Women," in *French Women and the Age of Enlightenment*, ed. Samia I. Spencer (Bloomington, Ind., 1984), 282–84.

56. See Frank A. Kafker, "Encyclopédie," in *The Blackwell Companion to the Enlightenment*, 145–50.

57. *Encyclopédie, ou Dictionnaire raisonné des sciences, des arts et des métiers, par une société de gens de lettres. Mis en ordre & publié par M. Diderot . . . & quant à la partie mathématique, par M. d'Alembert . . .* (Paris, 1754), 4:1, 23, 30.

SELECTED BIBLIOGRAPHY

Abensour, Léon. *La Femme et le féminisme avant La Révolution.* Paris [1923]. Reprint, Geneva, 1977.

Alletz, P.-A. [Pons-Augustin]. *L'Esprit des femmes célèbres du siècle de Louis XIV, et de celui de Louis XV, jusqu'à présent.* 2 vols. Paris, 1768.

Almanach des Dames sçavantes françoises. Pour l'An de Grace 1732. Contenant un ordre alphabetique des Dames qui se sont renduës recommandables par leur Sçavoir, depuis le commencement de la Monarchie, jusqu'à present. Avec l'Abregé de leurs vies, & le catalogue de leurs ouvrages. Paris, 1732.

Ananoff, Alexandre, and Daniel Wildenstein. *François Boucher.* 2 vols. Lausanne and Paris, 1976.

Argenson, René-Louis de Voyer, marquis d'. *Journal et mémoires du marquis d'Argenson.* Ed. E. J. B. Rathery. 9 vols. Paris, 1859–67.

Badinter, Elisabeth. *Emilie, Emilie: L'Ambition féminine au XVIIIe siècle.* Paris, 1983.

Bajou, Thierry. "Le Portrait de la Marquise de Pompadour (vers 1760), un nouveau Carle Van Loo à Versailles." *La Revue du Louvre et des Musées de France* 45, no. 1 (1995): 36–45.

Barbier, E. J. F. *Journal historique et anecdotique du règne de Louis XV par E. J. F. Barbier.* Ed. A. de la Villegille. 4 vols. Paris, 1847–56.

Bernis, François-Joachim de Pierre, cardinal de. *Mémoires du cardinal de Bernis.* Ed. Jean-Marie Rouart and Philippe Bonnet. Paris, 1980.

———. *Mémoires et Letters de François-Joachim de Pierre, cardinal de Bernis (1715–1758).* Ed. Frédéric Masson. 2 vols. Paris, 1903.

———. *Memoirs and Letters of Cardinal de Bernis.* Trans. Katharine Prescott Wormeley. 2 vols. New York, 1901.

Besnard, Albert, and Georges Wildenstein. *La Tour: La Vie et l'oeuvre de l'artiste.* Paris, 1928.

Bibliothèque Nationale, Département des Estampes. *Collection de pièces sur les beaux-arts (1673–1808): Dite Collection Deloynes.* 63 vols. Paris, 1673–1808.

The Blackwell Companion to the Enlightenment. Ed. John W. Yolton et al. Oxford, 1991.

Bodek, Evelyn Gordon. "Salonnières and Bluestockings: Educated Obsolescence and Germinating Feminism." *Feminist Studies* 3–4 (1976): 185–99.

Brilliant, Richard. *Portraiture*. London, 1991.

Brunel, Georges. *Boucher*. Trans. Simon Rees et al. London, 1986.

Buffet, Marguérite. *Nouvelles Observations sur la langue françoise, . . . avec les éloges des illustres sçavantes, tant anciennes que modernes*. Paris, 1668.

[Caffiaux, Dom Philippe-Joseph]. *Défenses du beau sexe, ou mémoires historiques, philosophiques et critiques, pour servir d'apologie aux femmes*. 2 vols. Amsterdam, 1753.

Catalogue des livres de la bibliothèque de feue Madame La Marquise de Pompadour, Dame du Palais de la Reine. Paris, 1765.

Clinton, Katherine B. "Femme et Philosophe: Enlightenment Origins of Feminism." *Eighteenth-Century Studies* 8 (1975): 283–99.

Colton, Judith. *The Parnasse François: Titon du Tillet and the Origins of the Monument to Genius*. New Haven, Conn., and London, 1979.

Conisbee, Philip. *Painting in Eighteenth-Century France*. Ithaca, N.Y., 1981.

Croÿ, Emmanuel, duc de. *Journal inédit du duc de Croÿ, 1718–1784*. Ed. Vicomte de Grouchy and Paul Cottin. 4 vols. Paris, 1906–7.

Cucuël, Georges. *La Pouplinière et la musique de chambre au XVIIIe siècle*. Paris, 1913.

Debrie, Christine. *Maurice-Quentin de La Tour: "Peintre de portraits au pastel" 1704–1788 au Musée Antoine Lécuyer de Saint-Quentin*. Thonon-les-Bains, 1991.

Desrochers, Etienne Jahandier, and Gilles Edme Petit. *Recueil de Portraits des personnes qui se sont distinguées tant dans les Armes que dans les belles Lettre[s] et les Arts*. Paris, 1726–54.

Ehrman, Esther. *Mme du Châtelet*. Leamington Spa, England, 1986.

Encyclopédie, ou Dictionnaire raisonné des sciences, des arts et des métiers, par une société de gens de lettres. Mis en ordre & publié par M. Diderot . . . & quant à la partie mathématique, par M. d'Alembert . . . 17 vols. Paris, 1751–65.

Fauchery, Pierre. *La Destinée féminine dans le roman européen du dix-huitième siècle, 1713–1807: Essai de gynécomythie romanesque*. Paris, 1972.

Les Femmes Sçavantes ou bibliothèque des dames qui traite des sciences qui conviennent aux dames, de la conduite de leurs études, des livres qu'elles peuvent lire, et l'histoire de celles qui ont excellé dans les sciences. Par Monsieur N.C. Amsterdam, 1718.

Fosca, François. *La Vie, les voyages et les oeuvres de Jean-Etienne Liotard, citoyen de Genève, dit le peintre turc*. Lausanne and Paris, 1956.

French Women and the Age of Enlightenment. Ed. Samia I. Spencer. Bloomington, Ind., 1984.

French Women Writers: A Bio-Bibliographical Source Book. Ed. Eva Martin Sartori and Dorothy Wynne Zimmerman. New York, Westport, Conn., and London, 1991.

Furetière, Antoine. *Dictionnaire universel, contenant généralement tous les mots françois, tant vieux que modernes, & les termes des sciences & des arts*, 4th ed. 4 vols. Paris, 1727. Reprint, Hildesheim and New York, 1972.

Gallet, Danielle. *Madame de Pompadour, ou le pouvoir féminin*. Paris, 1985.

Gallet, Danielle, et al. *Madame de Pompadour et la floraison des arts*. Exhib. cat. Montreal, 1988.

Gay, Peter. *The Enlightenment: An Interpretation*. Vol. 1, *The Rise of Modern Paganism*. New York and London, 1966.

———. *The Enlightenment: An Interpretation*. Vol. 2, *The Science of Freedom*. New York and London, 1969.

Gétreau, Florence, and Denis Harlin. "Portraits de clavecins et de clavecinistes français (II)," *Musique, Images, Instruments,* no. 3 (1997): 64–88.

Goodman, Dena. "Enlightenment Salons: The Convergence of Female and Philosophic Ambitions." *Eighteenth-Century Studies* 22 (1989): 329–50.

———. *The Republic of Letters: A Cultural History of the French Enlightenment.* Ithaca, N.Y., and London, 1994.

———. "Seriousness of Purpose: Salonnières, Philosophes, and the Shaping of the Eighteenth-Century Salon." *Proceedings of the Annual Meeting of the Western Society for French History* 15 (1988): 111–18.

Goodman, Elise. "'Les Jeux innocents': French Rococo Birding and Fishing Scenes." *Simiolus* 23 (1995): 251–67.

———. *Rubens: The Garden of Love as Conversatie à la mode.* Amsterdam and Philadelphia, 1992.

Goodman-Soellner, Elise. "Boucher's *Madame de Pompadour at Her Toilette.*" *Simiolus* 17 (1987): 41–58.

Gordon, Alden R. *Masterpieces from Versailles: Three Centuries of French Portraiture.* Exhib. cat. Washington, D.C., 1983.

Gordon, Katherine K. "Madame de Pompadour, Pigalle, and the Iconography of Friendship." *Art Bulletin* 50 (1968): 249–62.

[Graillard de Graville, Barthélemy-Claude]. *L'Ami des filles.* Paris, 1761.

Grimm, Melchior, baron de. *Correspondance littéraire, philosophique et critique par Grimm, Diderot, Raynal, Meister, etc.* Ed. Maurice Tourneux. 16 vols. Paris, 1877–82.

Harth, Erica. *Cartesian Women: Versions and Subversions of Rational Discourse in the Old Regime.* Ithaca, N.Y., and London, 1992.

Hohenzollern, Johann Georg Prinz von. "Die Porträts der Marquise de Baglion und der Marquise de Pompadour." *Pantheon* 4 (1972): 300–311.

Jean-Richard, Pierrette. *Musée du Louvre, Cabinet des Dessins, Collection Edmond de Rothschild: Inventaire général des gravures. Ecole française.* Vol. 1, *L'Oeuvre gravé de François Boucher dans la collection Edmond de Rothschild.* Paris, 1978.

Koerner, Joseph Leo. *The Moment of Self-Portraiture in German Renaissance Art.* Chicago and London, 1993.

Laing, Alastair, et al. *François Boucher: 1703–1770.* Exhib. cat. New York, Detroit, and Paris, 1986–87.

Leroy, Alfred. *Maurice Quentin de La Tour et la société française du XVIIIe siècle*, Paris, 1953.

———. "The Portraits of Madame de Pompadour." *Connoisseur* 103 (1939): 301–6.

Leturcq, J.-F. *Notice sur Jacques Guay, graveur sur pierres fines du Roi Louis XV.* Paris, 1873.

Levron, Jacques. *Pompadour.* Trans. Claire Eliane Engel. London, 1963.

Loche, Renée, and Marcel Roethlisberger. *L'Opera completa di Liotard.* Milan, 1978.

Louis XV: Un moment de perfection de l'art français. Exhib. cat. Paris, 1974.

Maclean, Ian. *Woman Triumphant: Feminism in French Literature, 1610–1652.* Oxford, 1977.

Marmontel, Jean-François. *Mémoires de Marmontel.* Ed. Maurice Tourneux. 3 vols. Paris, 1891. Reprint, Geneva, 1967.

Mason, Amelia Gere. *The Women of the French Salons.* New York, 1891.

Masson, Pierre-Maurice. *Une Vie de femme au XVIIIe siècle: Madame de Tencin (1682–1749).* Paris, 1909. Reprint, Geneva, 1970.
Mauzi, Robert. *L'Idée du bonheur dans la littérature et la pensée françaises au XVIIIe siècle.* 2d ed. Paris, 1965.
Mirimonde, A. P. de. "Musiciens isolés et portraits de l'école française du XVIIIe *siècle* dans les collections nationales." *La Revue du Louvre et des Musées de France* 16 (1966): 147–52.
Montesquieu, Charles-Louis de Secondat, baron de La Brède et de. *Lettres persanes.* Paris, 1975.
———. *The Spirit of the Laws by Baron de Montesquieu.* Trans. Thomas Nugent. New York and London, 1949.
The New Grove Dictionary of Music and Musicians. Ed. Stanley Sadie. 20 vols. London, 1980.
Nicholson, Kathleen. "The Ideology of Feminine 'Virtue': The Vestal Virgin in French Eighteenth-Century Allegorical Portraiture." In *Portraiture: Facing the Subject,* edited by Joanna Woodall, 52–72. Manchester and New York, 1997.
Nicolle, Jean. *Madame de Pompadour et la société de son temps.* Paris, 1980.
Noël, C. M. D. *Le Triomphe des femmes, ou il est montré par plusieurs & puissantes raisons, que le Sexe feminin, est plus noble & plus parfait, que le masculin.* Antwerp, 1698.
Nolhac, Pierre de. "François Boucher: Portraitiste de Mme de Pompadour." *La Revue de l'Art Ancien et Moderne* 41 (1922): 193–202.
———. *J.-M. Nattier: Court Painter under Louis XV.* Paris and New York, 1905.
———. *J.-M. Nattier: Peintre de la cour de Louis XV.* Paris, 1905.
———. *Louis XV et Madame de Pompadour.* Paris, 1902.
———. *Nattier: Peintre de la cour de Louis XV.* Paris, 1925.
Perrot, Philippe. *Le Travail des apparences, ou les transformations du corps féminin XVIIIe–XIXe siècle.* Paris, 1984.
Picard, Roger. *Les Salons littéraires et la société française, 1610–1789.* New York, 1943.
Poignant, Simone. *Les Filles de Louis XV: L'Aile des princes.* N.p., 1970.
Pointon, Marcia. *Hanging the Head: Portraiture and Social Formation in Eighteenth-Century England.* New Haven, Conn., and London, 1993.
Pompadour, Jeanne-Antoinette Poisson, marquise de. *Catalogue des livres de la bibliothèque de feue Madame La Marquise de Pompadour, Dame du Palais de la Reine.* Paris, 1765.
———. *Correspondance de Mme de Pompadour avec son père, M. Poisson, et son frère, M. de Vandières.* Ed. M. A. P. Malassis. Paris, 1878.
———. *Suite d'Estampes gravées par Madame la Marquise de Pompadour, d'après les Pierres gravées de Guay, Graveur du Roy.* Paris, 1782.
Posner, Donald. "Mme. de Pompadour as a Patron of the Visual Arts." *Art Bulletin* 72 (1990): 74–105.
———. "People on File: Picturing the King and Others in Eighteenth-Century France." Unpublished paper read at the meeting of the Northeast American Society for Eighteenth-Century Studies, Metropolitan Museum of Art, New York, 1994.
Pougin, Arthur. *Madame Favart: Étude théâtrale, 1727–1772.* Paris, 1912.
Poullain de La Barre, François. *The Equality of the Two Sexes by François Poullain de La Barre.* Ed. and trans. A. Daniel Frankforter and Paul J. Morman. Lewiston, N.Y., and Queenston, Ont., 1989.

[Poullain de La Barre, François]. *De l'Education des dames pour la conduite de l'esprit. Dans les sciences et dans les moeurs. Entretiens.* Paris, 1679 (first published Paris, 1674).
Préaud, Maxime, Pierre Casselle, Marianne Grivel, and Corinne Le Bitouzé. *Dictionnaire des éditeurs d'estampes à Paris sous l'Ancien Régime.* [Paris], 1987.
Pressly, William L. "Genius Unveiled: The Self-Portraits of Johan Zoffany." *Art Bulletin* 69 (1987): 88–101.
———. *The Life and Art of James Barry.* New Haven, Conn., and London, 1981.
Prévot, Jacques. *La Première Institutrice de France: Madame de Maintenon.* Paris, 1981.
[Puisieux, Madeleine d'Arsant, Mme de]. *Le Triomphe des dames. Traduit de l'Anglois de Miledi P****.* London, 1751.
Recueil Clairambault-Maurepas: Chansonnier historique du XVIIIe siècle. Ed. Emile Raunié. 10 vols. Paris, 1879–84.
Reynier, Gustave. *La Femme au XVIIe siècle: Ses Ennemis et ses défenseurs.* Paris, 1929.
Ribeiro, Aileen. *The Art of Dress: Fashion in England and France, 1750 to 1820.* New Haven, Conn., and London, 1995.
———. *Dress in Eighteenth-Century Europe, 1715–1789.* New York, 1985.
Rosenberg, Pierre. *The Age of Louis XV: French Painting, 1710–1774.* Exhib. cat. Toledo, Chicago, and Ottawa, 1975.
Rosenfeld, Myra Nan. *Largillierre and the Eighteenth-Century Portrait.* Exhib. cat. Montreal, 1981.
Roux, Marcel, Edmond Pognon, and Yves Bruand. *Bibliothèque Nationale, Département des Estampes. Inventaire du fonds français: Graveurs du XVIIIe siècle.* 14 vols. Paris, 1930–77.
Rupprecht, Bernhard. "Bouchers Pompadour-Porträt von 1756." In *Festschrift für Hermann Bauer zum 60. Geburtstag,* edited by Karl Möseneder and Andreas Prater, 274–83. Hildesheim, 1991.
Sadie, Julie Anne. "*Musiciennes* of the Ancien Régime." In *Women Making Music: The Western Art Tradition, 1150–1950,* edited by Jane Bowers and Judith Tick, 191–223. Urbana, Ill., 1986.
Sahut, Marie-Catherine. *Carle Vanloo: Premier peintre du roi (Nice, 1705–Paris, 1765).* Exhib. cat. Nice, Clermont-Ferrand, and Nancy, 1977.
Schiebinger, Londa. *The Mind Has No Sex? Women in the Origins of Modern Science.* Cambridge, Mass., and London, 1989.
Ségur, Marquis de. *Le Royaume de la rue de Saint-Honoré: Madame Geoffrin et sa fille.* Paris, [1897].
Shackelford, George T. M., and Mary Tavener Holmes. *A Magic Mirror: The Portrait in France, 1700–1900.* Exhib. cat. Houston, 1986.
Shawe-Taylor, Desmond. *Genial Company: The Theme of Genius in Eighteenth-Century British Portraiture.* Exhib. cat. London, 1987.
Sheriff, Mary D. *Fragonard: Art and Eroticism.* Chicago and London, 1990.
Smith, David R. *Masks of Wedlock: Seventeenth-Century Dutch Marriage Portraiture.* Ann Arbor, Mich., 1982.
Solnon, Jean-François. *La Cour de France.* [Paris], 1987.
Sonnet, Martine. *L'Education des filles au temps des Lumières.* Paris, 1987.

Stein, Perrin. "Madame de Pompadour and the Harem Imagery at Bellevue." *Gazette des Beaux-Arts* 123 (1994): 29–44.

Stiftung Oskar Reinhart Winterthur. 3 vols. Zurich, 1977–84.

Sutton, Denys. *François Boucher*. Exhib. cat. Tokyo and Kumamoto, 1982.

Timmermans, Linda. *L'Accès des femmes à la culture (1598–1715): Un Débat d'idées de Saint-François de Sales à la marquise de Lambert*. Paris, 1993.

Le Triomphe du beau-sexe sur les hommes: Ou l'on fait voir les avantages & les prérogatives que rendent les Femmes superieures aux Hommes, par des preuves incontestables. Hamburg, 1719.

Villemert, Pierre-Joseph Boudier de. *Le Nouvel Ami des femmes, ou la philosophie du beau sexe. Par M. Boudier de Villemert*. Amsterdam and Paris, 1779.

Voltaire [François-Marie Arouet]. *The Complete Works of Voltaire*. Ed. Theodore Besterman et al. 78 vols. to date. Geneva and Toronto, 1968–.

———. *Oeuvres complètes de Voltaire*. Nouvelle édition. Ed. Louis Moland. 52 vols. Paris, 1877–85.

Weigert, Roger-Armand, and Maxime Préaud. *Bibliothèque Nationale, Département des Estampes. Inventaire du fonds français: Graveurs du XVIIe siècle*. 12 vols. to date. Paris, 1939–.

Weinreb, Ruth Plaut. *Eagle in a Gauze Cage: Louise d'Epinay, Femme de Lettres*. New York, 1993.

Wildenstein, Georges. *Le Peintre Aved: Sa Vie et son oeuvre, 1702–1766*. 2 vols. Paris, 1922.

Wilson, Gillian. *European Clocks in the J. Paul Getty Museum*. Los Angeles, 1996.

Woman and Society in Eighteenth-Century France: Essays in Honour of John Stephenson Spink. Ed. Eva Jacobs, W. H. Barber, Jean H. Bloch, F. W. Leakey, and Eileen Le Breton. London, 1979.

INDEX

Page numbers in italic refer to illustrations.

Text: 11/13 Adobe Garamond
Display: Adobe Garamond and Centaur
Composition: Integrated Composition Systems, Inc.
Printing and binding: Malloy Lithographing, Inc.